COLLECTABLES
JAMES·MACKAY

COLLECTABLES

JAMES·MACKAY

MACDONALD
&JANE'S

FOR BRENDA AND ADRIAN

First published in Great Britain in 1979 by
Macdonald and Jane's Publishers Limited,
Paulton House, 8 Shepherdess Walk, London N.1

Copyright © James Mackay, 1979

ISBN 0 354 04371 4

Filmset in 'Monophoto' Sabon by
Servis Filmsetting Limited, Manchester
Made and printed in Great Britain by
Purnell & Sons Limited, Paulton, Bristol

INTRODUCTION

Here are over 250 collectables, ranging alphabetically from *Advertisements* to *Zwischengoldgläser*, enough to satisfy the appetite of the most avid magpie and hopelessly addicted junk rummager. These objects are diverse in material, craftsmanship and quality but they have several common factors. They are, for the most part, fairly small and therefore ideally suited to the collector with limited house-room. The vast majority of them are still available at no great cost and thus are within the price range of the collector on a small budget. A few of them have been around for many years and collected for almost as long, but most of them are 'new collectables' which have only begun to attract the attention of collectors in very recent years. They offer considerable scope to the beginner who often bemoans the fact that he or she was not collecting ten or twenty or thirty years ago when (so the story goes) Old Masters and Louis Quinze furniture could still be picked up for a song.

Ten years ago I could write glibly about all those neglected objects of yesteryear, the unconsidered trifles, bygones and Victoriana cluttering up the junk shops, lumber rooms and country cottages. Now there are no junk shops any more, only antique shops, the attics and lumber rooms were long since cleared and converted into bed-sitters, and the country cottages have become the rich man's tax loss or second home. The erstwhile contents, far from being neglected, are now preserved in museums and have formed the subject of several notable exhibitions in recent years.

Undoubtedly there is a dearth of original, good quality antiques, but though the traditional areas of collecting have all but dried up there has been no diminution in collecting. I would estimate that the number of collectors of one kind or another has increased five-fold in the past decade alone. This is a period which has witnessed the rapid rise of two phenomena – the antique super-market or hypermarket, and the antiques fair. The latter

has now developed to such a point that there are many fair circuits supported by dealers (both full- and part-time) whose trading is almost entirely conducted through this medium.

Few of these fairs cling to the rigid tenets of such organizations as the British Antique Dealers' Association whose traditional criterion for an antique was that it was manufactured before 1830. This date-line has been severely dented in recent years, certain classes of objects being now considered antique providing they were made before 1870. The Customs in both Britain and the United States apply the much more flexible and practical hundred years' rule. Some dealers operate a date-line of 1930, which thus encompasses the flower of late-Victorian, Edwardian and Art Deco collectables, while others frankly extend the date-line to cover whatever they happen to have in stock at that moment in time!

Glancing down the list of entries you may think that many of them have little to commend them to the would-be collector, but herein lies their promise to the collector looking for something that the other fellow hasn't thought of. But ideas about what is collectable are changing very quickly and what at first glance may sound ridiculous often turns out to be fascinating and absorbing and offering enormous scope for collectable variety. In compiling this book I have applied only one major criterion, that everything discussed here is currently being collected seriously. In the course of my perambulations round the antique markets and fairs I see many objects which intrigue me and set me wondering about their potential as collectables. But 'one swallow does not make a summer' and a solitary example of an article on a dealer's stall does not automatically make it collectable.

In every instance I have played safe and concentrated on objects which crop up time and time again. Moreover, I have scoured the advertisements in newspapers and magazines. In particular, I have found that the collectors' wants and sales columns in *Exchange and Mart* and similar periodicals are a useful and accurate barometer of trends in modern collecting.

If any trends can be detected in the collecting pattern of the present day they are that people are tending to collect on a regional basis – i.e. taking anything and everything relating to one particular town, county, district or region. Another approach which is increasingly evident is the thematic one – seeking objects whose common denominator is a trade or profession (like dentistry, pharmacy, plumbing), or perhaps an extension of other leisure interests like sports, games, music, motion pictures and the theatre. Other major collecting fields are railwayana and militaria and it is highly significant that these fields appeal particularly to a generation which has had little direct contact with either. Thus the number of rail enthusiasts rises as the mileage operated by British Rail or Amtrak diminishes. Militaria is immensely popular in Britain with a generation which never knew National Service, far less the horrors of World War Two. Significantly this subject is proportionately less fascinating to American collectors for whom the grim realities of Vietnam are too recent a memory, but if modern militaria has relatively little appeal there the interest in both World Wars and the Civil War of 1861–5 is very strong.

Nostalgia plays a very important part in current collecting trends. We seem to have moved forward rapidly from the Art Deco and Art Moderne of the Jazz Age to the war years and now the Austerity period of the late 1940s and early 1950s, the era of the Festival of Britain, the Korean War and the Truman-Eisenhower administrations. The trend is also towards smaller and more compact collectables, reflecting the less spacious accommodation of modern homes.

Fully half the entries here have never appeared in print before, so it is high time that some guidance was given to the people who collect them. Of those entries which may already be found in other antique encyclopaedias I have concentrated here on their down-market aspects.

If you take note of the new collectables and discern the patterns and common factors you may even be able to foretell what the next round of collectables are likely to be. There must be many quite utilitarian objects of the present day which, thanks to built-in obsolescence, will be the collectables of the future. Of course there are numerous collectors' pieces of the present day, limited editions of modern silver, pewter, ceramics and glassware which may turn out to be a good investment in years to come. I have a sneaking feeling, however, that despite their undeniably high aesthetic qualities and superb craftsmanship, many of these collectables have an air of artificiality about them and rely not so much on their innate collector appeal as the efficiency with which they have been promoted in the media. The things to keep an eye on are those everyday objects which no one in their right mind would dream of collecting but which, through the caprice of fashion or advancing technology, become outmoded tomorrow. After a decent interval (of, say, a year or two) they tend to re-emerge as fully-fledged collectables. Don't say I didn't warn you!

James A. Mackay
Dumfries, October 1978

A

ADVERTISEMENTS

Modern advertising began in the 1860s with the development of the cheap wood-pulp paper known as newsprint, the perfection of monotype machinery and, above all, the emergence of women as the most important element in the consumer society. Women as well as slaves were emancipated by the American Civil War and it was at this time that women took over from their menfolk the responsibility for family budgetting. The producers of household commodities and other consumer goods were quick to spot the change in spending habits and devised eye-catching advertisements accordingly. Within a decade this trend had spread to Europe, and newspaper and magazine advertisements from 1875 onwards are far more attractive and pictorial than they were before.

Old newspaper cuttings may not be very collectable, but there are plenty of other early forms of advertising that are. Up to about 1920 colour could only be achieved by using chromolithography to print the advertisements on separate sheets which were then tipped into magazines and periodicals. These chromo inserts are now highly desirable. They

An advertisement for Coca-Cola of 1904 (Coca-Cola).

developed alongside the rise of branded goods in the late nineteenth century and the soap manufacturers are probably the best-known users of this advertising medium. The makers of Pears Soap even put forward a plan to the Post Office, envisaging advertisements on the backs of postage stamps. Though the scheme was turned down a few sheets of stamps were thus printed and specimens are now much prized by philatelists. New Zealand had a wide range of advertisements on the backs of its stamps in the 1890s and both France and Germany permitted commercial advertising on the sheet margins of stamps.

Apart from the magazine inserts, there are many TRADE CARDS available still at no great cost, though examples before 1850 are now elusive and becoming expensive. The earliest

Two advertisement cards issued by Smith's of Glasgow

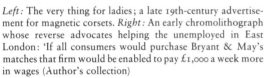

Left: The very thing for ladies; a late 19th-century advertisement for magnetic corsets. *Right:* An early chromolithograph whose reverse advocates helping the unemployed in East London: 'If all consumers would purchase Bryant & May's matches that firm would be enabled to pay £1,000 a week more in wages (Author's collection)

ones were small and almost square and range from the tastefully engraved, with handsome pictorial vignettes, to the quaint jumbles of typography using many different founts in artless confusion – which accounts for much of their appeal today. Posters, hand-bills, flyers and price-lists are among the assorted ephemera of advertising and they are produced down to the present time, though the more appealing examples date before 1920 when advertising became more of an exact science combining the latest ideas in graphic design with psychology and market research.

Advertisements in three dimensions include pin-back badges, pens and pencils and even bars of soap with trademarks, slogans and brand names of all manner of consumer goods.

Even the PACKAGING of goods could be used to advertise a company's products. Allied to advertisements are the premium offers and giveaways which induced the customer to buy a certain product, perhaps for a period of time, or were exchanged for so many tops, labels or vouchers. The premium offers of the present day are rather prosaic, but a century ago they took the form of ornaments and other decorative items, many of which were treasured by the original recipients and have been preserved for the delectation of modern collectors. Old mail-order catalogues are a form of advertisement which has been around now for over a century and they provide a goldmine of information on many of the objects which have now become collectable.

AERONAUTICA

Most people have the impression that this is something that started with two men in cloth caps at Kitty Hawk in 1903, but in fact aeronautics is a science which dates back to the sixteenth century when Leonardo da Vinci devised the ornithopter. Books, pamphlets and manuscripts on flying abound from the seventeenth century onwards and working models of balloons, helicopters and box-kites from the mid-eighteenth century. Steam-powered aero engines date from the 1840s but were only practicable with balloons and even then enjoyed only limited success.

From the collector's viewpoint, aeronautica begins with the ballooning craze of the 1780s when the Montgolfier Brothers and Vincent

Left: A 1915 series of cigarette cards issued by W.D. & H.O. Wills commemorated the first parachute descent (from a hydrogen balloon at 2,000 feet) by Garnerin. *Below:* An album page from *Aircraft of the Royal Air Force,* issued in 1938 by John Player & Sons (Ian Fleming)

Lunardi enjoyed the kind of popularity today reserved for pop-singers. Balloons and balloonists were depicted in all manner of objects, from chair-backs to snuff-boxes, from watch-cases to fan-leaves. Ballooning as a sport has waxed and waned over the past two centuries, but there is considerable scope in the mementoes of the international balloon races of the 1920s. The more serious aspects of lighter-than-air machines are represented by the letters and flimsy newspapers flown by *ballon monté* during the Siege of Paris (1870–71) and the memorabilia of the epic flights of the *Graf Zeppelin* and the *Hindenburg* between the two World Wars.

Other aspects of aeronautica deal with the UNIFORMS, insignia and equipment of the world's air forces dating from the Italo-Turkish War of 1911 and the Mexican civil wars of 1912–16, as well as the two World Wars and a host of minor campaigns. Psychological warfare is now an important branch of aeronautica in its own right and covers all forms of propaganda by aerial bombardment, from the poems dropped by the quixotic Gabriele d'Annunzio over Vienna in 1918 to the packets of instant coffee dropped on Warsaw by the USAAF during the Second World War.

The more peaceful aspects of aeronautica, however, include POSTCARDS, programmes and other souvenirs of the pioneer aviation meetings, the TICKETS and TIMETABLES of the airlines, especially in their formative years, and the commemorative items which have honoured such pioneer aviators as Alcock and Brown, Lindbergh, Amy Johnson and Amelia Earhart.

ALPHABET PLATES AND MUGS

We know from archaeological evidence that the Greeks used feeding bowls with rather salty motifs as a not very subtle way of teaching children the facts of life at a very tender age. Since the Roman Empire declined and fell this didactic element in children's crockery has been absent and I suppose the modern counterpart would be these attractive little pictures of characters from familiar nursery rhymes, fairy stories and TV serials which distract the infant from the serious business of eating and drinking.

It was left to the Victorians, of course, to raise both the moral and educative tone of plates and mugs by covering them with letters of the alphabet. The idea seems to have started in the English potteries about 1835 and reached its zenith in the 1890s. Alphabet plates were exported to America after the Civil War but were manufactured locally from about 1875 onwards and were immensely popular (with the fond parents at least) till the mid 1920s.

Both upper and lower case letters were featured, often accompanied by small pictures. Less common are those plates which also depict numerals, while a comparatively rare type depict Biblical characters and texts. Plates and bowls are the articles most frequently found, but beakers, mugs and cups were also given the alphabet treatment. The most sought after are complete suites of children's crockery with matching alphabet motifs. The same idea may be encountered in enamelled metal plates and glassware at the turn of the century.

ALUMINIUM

Or aluminum as they say in America. Though alum salts were known to mankind as long ago as the fifth century BC and widely used as an astringent, it was not suspected that they had a metallic base till Sir Humphrey Davy looked into the matter in 1809. It proved to be extremely difficult to isolate and it was not till 1855 that aluminium made its debut at the Paris Exposition. Its silvery appearance, lightness and sheer novelty made it an instant success and countless figurines and plaques were produced at considerable expense. It was not until 1886, when the technique of electrolysis was first applied, that aluminium became commercially viable. By that time the novelty had worn off, the public preferred bronze or even ZINC for their ornaments and surprisingly little use was subsequently made of this alloy, though the statue of Eros at Piccadilly Circus in London is a witness to the durable properties of aluminium as a sculptural medium.

If nineteenth-century aluminium statuettes and plaques are now decidedly rare, there is a

A selection of aluminium articles – a water bottle as recommended by the War Office, a hot water bottle, a teapot, jelly mould and lemon squeezer – offered in the 1939–40 Army and Navy Stores catalogue.

superabundance of decorative articles in this material from the early 1920s onwards. Aluminium leant itself admirably to the spirit of the Jazz Age and may be found with Art Deco motifs in ASHTRAYS, COCKTAIL EQUIP-MENT and all the collectables associated with cigarettes. It was first used for coins in 1907 but was widely employed in the manufacture of cheap medals from the Diamond Jubilee of Queen Victoria onwards.

ANDIRONS

An earlier form is *anderne* though the ultimate derivation seems to have been from end-irons which succinctly describes the purpose for which they were intended. Though strictly speaking this term should only be applied to the outermost pair of fireplace stands it is convenient usually to apply it to the lot. The widest and best-appointed hearths had a set of six iron stands in three pairs. The andirons stood at the extreme left and right; next came the fire-dogs and lastly a pair of creepers in the middle. They were all constructed on the same lines, with an iron bar extending back from a frontal upright. They merely varied in height, the andirons being the largest and the creepers the smallest. Huge logs of wood were supported on the iron horizontal bars dipping towards the centre of the fire.

The upright guard was frequently decorated, first with Renaissance or Gothic ornament and latterly with ormolu gilding and intricate filigree work. From the late seventeenth century onwards, as fireplaces gradually became smaller, andirons took on a more ornamental role. With the advent of coal-buring grates they disappeared entirely for a time, but were resurrected as part of the Gothic Revival of the early nineteenth century and have enjoyed periodic bouts of popularity ever since. The plain kind with ratcheted uprights were called spit-dogs and are a hangover from the days when cooking was done over open fires. The most desirable examples of andirons have cast ornament on feet and finials, sometimes resembling the heads and feet of animals, birds and humans. In the more modern specimens steel replaced wrought iron, but is just as collectable if the decorative features are particularly fine and interesting.

ANTIMACASSARS

That symbol of Victorian suburban gentility, the anti-macassar, has had a somewhat chequered career. It originated in the mid-nineteenth century when men turned from powdering their hair to smothering it in pomade. Most of the unguents applied to the hair were derived from animal grease and it is difficult at this remove in time to understand why the vegetable oils of the Macassar Islands in the then Dutch East Indies should get all the blame for leaving nasty greasy stains on cushions and chair-backs.

The earliest antimacassars were crocheted in a very stiff white material, often incorporating beadwork; but by the late nineteenth century soft, coloured materials were used, embroidered in wools or silks. By that time the antimacassar had come to be regarded by the upper classes as *outré*, but it survived in the front parlours of the lower middle and upper working classes and even took on a new lease of life in the 1920s when elaborate lace patterns became fashionable. Regardless of the social conventions the railway companies continued to use antimacassars at the turn of the century and examples with the crest or initials of these companies are worth looking for.

APPRENTICE PIECES

There is something particularly enchanting about these miniature pieces of furniture, correct in every detail, with the dovetailing of joints flawlessly accomplished. Perhaps they conjure up the idyllic picture of the jolly apprentices as depicted in the prints of Hogarth or the theatres of Southwark, or the ballads and rhymes about the apprentice who married his master's daughter, or the roistering apprentice mobs of London in the days of the Civil War. Probably apprenticeship was never anything like that. Seven years' indentured slavery before a lad could set up as a journeyman and practise his trade could have left little time for roistering and revelry. Similarly many of these delightful pieces of miniature furniture, traditionally regarded as the apprentice's masterpiece or practical examination by which he demonstrated the skills of his calling, were probably made by expert craftsmen of long standing as a labour of love. Significantly, they seem to belong predominantly to the eighteenth and early nineteenth centuries, a period when miniaturised furniture was fashionable purely as collector's pieces. Such items represented many hours of skilled work and were expensive to produce, but here and there you may come across splendid examples of country cabinet-making on a tiny scale.

They should not be confused with working models and small-scale versions of products used by manufacturing industries from about 1850 onwards as sales aids. Though often machine-made, these models and samples are of considerable interest and have a certain charm of their own. A more recent counterpart is the miniaturised object used as a display piece for shop windows. Engineering models in particular are much sought after.

ASHTRAYS

Here is one of those subjects which readily commends itself to the collector of limited means and house room, for its variety is infinite and it takes up so little space. Ashtrays for pipe-smokers existed from the early nineteenth century and were relatively large and cumbersome affairs with a characteristically deep rim so that pipes could rest without fear of being knocked over. The smaller and shallower ashtray was evolved in the mid nineteenth century, as cigarette smoking became more fashionable and even acceptable among the fair sex. When the smoking habit was taken up by women, ashtrays became more and more elegant and decorative. As a result they may be found in every conceivable material from glass and ceramics to inlaid wood, bone and metalwork, with fine enamelling and even ZELLENMOSAIK.

Interest has switched in recent years to the ashtrays produced by breweries and tobacco

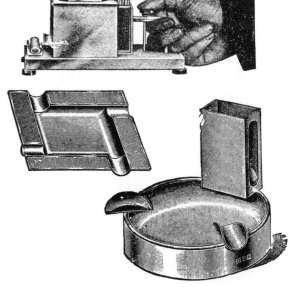

Two hall-marked silver ashtrays, one with attached match holder, and an automatic cigarette box with attached ashtrays (Army & Navy Stores Ltd)

companies to advertise their wares. The ashtray, in fact, has become a three-dimensional ADVERTISEMENT, and may often be found with well-known brand names, trademarks, logotypes and symbolism associated with famous products of many kinds. The ashtray was also an ideal medium for the manufacturer of novelties and souvenirs and appealed to the lower end of the tourist market from the 1920s onwards. Ashtrays seem to have been more prone to high camp and low humour than any other small object and tend to epitomise KITSCH at its best (or worst). The decoration of ashtrays ranges from the exotic to the erotic, from the whimsical to the bizarre, from the faintly risqué to the downright saucy. The Anglo-Saxon race having no monopoly in lavatorial humour, ashtrays in the form of CHAMBER POTS may be found with witty slogans in many different languages.

AUTOGRAPHS

I cannot recall now whether autograph-hunting was one of those perennial pursuits, like kite-flying and conkers, or whether it was a passing fad of longer duration, like yo-yos and hula hoops, but I do remember that it infected my school to epidemic proportions one year and every minor actress, footballer and circus clown that came within a ten-mile radius of the town was badgered by boys brandishing grubby albums, demanding that celebrity's signature. This kind of craze seems to have gone in cycles since the early nineteenth century, judging by the albums that have survived. The majority contain few signatures of note and are worth very little. At the other end of the scale are the late-medieval *album amicorum* maintained by those who moved in the high society of their day and got the famous and the influential to record their thoughts and aphorisms, their doodles and lightning sketches, as well as their distinguished signatures for posterity. These are rarities which even now tend to cause a considerable stir when they pass infrequently through the more august London salerooms.

Between these two extremes are the many albums which were formed in the mid nineteenth century by young ladies as a pastime for rainy Sunday afternoons. Before the advent of Uniform Penny Postage members of parliament and peers of the realm were privileged to 'frank' their mail, i.e. to send it free through

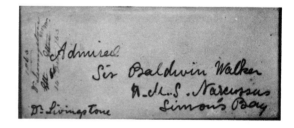

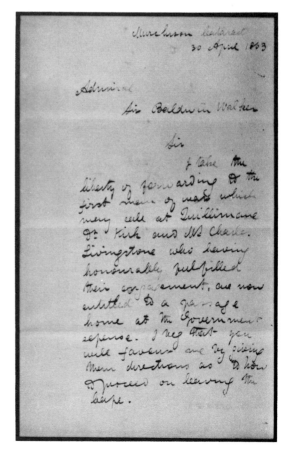

A letter written by Dr Livingstone (Stanley Gibbons)

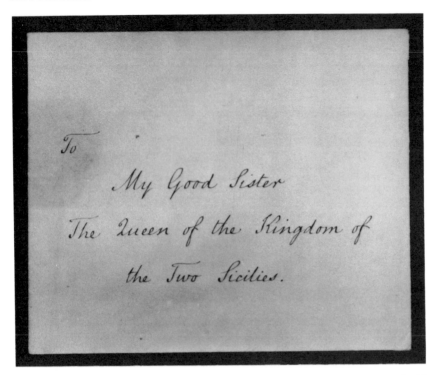

To

My Good Sister

The Queen of the Kingdom of

the Two Sicilies.

A letter addressed by Queen
Victoria (Stanley Gibbons)

the post provided they placed their signatures in the bottom left hand corner. The fronts of such parliamentary franks were avidly collected and pasted in albums, a refinement being to place alongside cuttings from directories and biographical dictionaries. For many years there was virtually no interest in these albums – until postal historians woke up to the fact that they contained examples of the 'Free' and other postmarks of the period.

Today autograph collecting is no longer confined to signatures. Collectors distinguished between Autographed Letters signed (A.L.s.), Letters signed (L.s.), Autograph Document signed (A. Doc.s.), Documents signed (Doc.s.) and Typewritten Letters signed (T.L.s.), the abbreviations given in parentheses being widely used in sales catalogues and dealers' lists. Autographed Letters are those in which the handwriting is entirely that of the person concerned, whereas Letters signed are those in the handwriting of a clerk or secretary, with no more than the signature in the hand of the sender. Copies of books autographed by the author are generally worth a premium – unless they happen to be written by certain politicians, in which case *unsigned* copies are probably rarer!

B

BABY RATTLES AND TEETHERS

Like the man who invented the wheel, the genius who discovered the power of the rattle to pacify the fretful infant must have been living a very long time ago, since examples of his (or her) handiwork have been recovered from archaeological sites from pre-Dynastic Egypt onwards. The earliest examples were of wood, bone or horn with small round pieces of bone or metal imprisoned within. The Greeks and Romans favoured baby rattles of terracotta or bronze, and the Romans added the refinement of tiny bronze bells.

My old grannie, who belonged to the 'no-nonsense' school of child-rearing, found that a button inside a candy tin was just as effective a pacifier, even though there was an enormous range of commercially-produced rattles available by the turn of the century. Eighteenth- and early nineteenth-century examples in gold or silver come rather expensive nowadays, but

A silver and pearl rattle offered to varying sizes of babies – small 9/-, medium 13/-, large 14/- (Army & Navy Stores Ltd)

from 1850 onwards electroplate was widely used and rattles were produced in every conceivable shape, animal heads being especially popular. In the early years of this century novelty shapes extended to include characters from fairy tales and nursery rhymes. The most interesting examples, technically speaking, are those which incorporate bells, whistles and a teether, a strip of coral, bone or latterly plastic, which enables the baby to cut his teeth.

BADGES

There is nothing new under the sun, it seems. The present craze for badges as male jewelry originated in America in the mid-1970s, but thirty years ago I can recall that there was a fashion for decorating leather belts with old military badges. The broader the belt the better, enabling you to cram as many badges on as possible, until the result resembled the penitential iron belt worn by King James IV of Scotland. The present fad favours small enamelled badges bearing the emblems, logotypes and trademarks of various organizations, institutions and companies.

The purist, of course, regards this form of collecting with distaste, not to say horror, and his specimens are carefully preserved in shallow trays or mounted on baize-covered boards. Firm favourites are the badges and

Three badges for infantry and artillery from the price list of Johnson, Simpson and Simons, Gold and Silver Lacemen (Author's collection)

The shoulder rank badge of the London Fire Brigade (Greater London Council)

insignia of military formations, particularly regiments which have long since been swallowed up in the re-organization of the Army. The best-known are the cap badges, but others to look for, in matching sets, include 'collar dogs', lapel badges, the insignia from epaulet-tes and shoulder boards, and the crests from sporrans. Military and naval insignia may also be found on BELT-BUCKLES.

These badges are usually struck in metal, silver and occasionally silver-gilt for officers, bronze, brass or white-metal for the enlisted men and NCOs. Many other badges, however, consist of woven cloth patches sewn on to the sleeves and breasts of tunics, and include formation signs, chevrons and other badges of rank, trade and specialist insignia and regimental shoulder and cuff titles. The most desirable are those woven in gold or silver wire.

In recent years collectors have begun to turn their attention to badges of non-military formations, such as police and law-enforcement agencies, the Scout movement, fire services and para-military units, but there is still tremendous scope for the beginner who decides to specialize in one of the less fashionable aspects of badges.

BAKELITE

Though not the first of the PLASTICS by any means, bakelite dominated the market for upwards of forty years and provides us with a wide range of collectables dating from 1910 to the end of the Second World War. It takes its name from the Belgian physicist, Leo Baekeland, who chanced upon this versatile phenolic compound in 1907. As is so often the case, he was actually looking for something else at the time – an artificial substitute for shellac, but he had the sense to recognize a good thing when he saw it. The Bakelite Corporation of the United States was formed three years later and bakelite and related phenolic compounds swept the electrical industry before the First World War.

It took the Jazz Age of the Twenties to find alternative and more aesthetic uses for bakelite. Appropriately it was applied at first to the handsome fretted grilles protecting the loudspeakers of early RADIO sets. The breakthrough came about 1930 when it was possible to produce bakelite in colours other

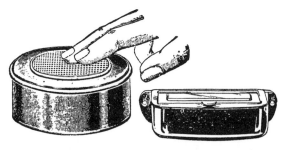

A hygienic envelope and stamp moistener, and a car ashtray, both in bakelite (Army & Navy Stores Ltd)

than sombre hues of brown and black. Contrasting blocks and strips of coloured bakelite replaced enamelling in the ornamentation of CIGARETTE CASES, COCKTAIL EQUIPMENT and VANITY CASES. Moulded bakelite was widely employed in BELT-BUCKLES, the handles of UMBRELLAS, the backs of brushes and a host of other articles, many of which are discussed in this book. Its disadvantages were its brittleness and comparatively limited range of colours, and inevitably it lost ground rapidly in the 1950s when urea and vinyl plastics were developed.

BARBED WIRE

Although some form of protective wire fencing existed in France in the first half of the nineteenth century, it was in America, where traditional fencing materials were scarce, that wire came into its own. The first protective wire was patented by W. H. Meriwether of Texas in 1853, a snake wire of black iron with a Foster curl, to use the correct technical term. Alphonso Dabb, Lucien Smith, Lyman P. Judson, Joseph Haish and Michael Kelly are among the many claimants to have invented true barbed wire, but the addition of tightly wound barbs to two- or three-strand wire was the invention of Henry Rose in 1873. Hundreds of patents for barbed wire were taken out in the 1870s alone, but eventually the market was dominated by Joseph F. Glidden of Dekalb, Illinois. Glidden Two-Point rapidly became a best-seller and to this day 'glidden' is a term used for any simple, two-ply wire. No more than five tons of barbed wire was produced in the United States in 1874; six years later annual production had risen to 40,000 tons and by the end of the century had increased five-fold again.

Barbed wire rather than the six-gun tamed the Old West. At first there was great bitterness between the farmers, who saw the rich potential of wire in areas where timber for fencing was scarce, and the cattlemen for whom the song, 'Don't Fence Me In' had a very real meaning. But eventually the ranchers themselves appreciated the benefits from controlling the cattle ranges by wire. In the rapid development of barbed wire in the late nineteenth century, many companies sprang up, each producing their own distinctive brands, differing in gauge, number of strands and the size and composition of the barbs.

A great deal of showmanship is evident in the catalogues of these companies and to this day the exotic names of their products evoke something of the spirit of the Wild West – Meriwether's Snake, Hart-McGlin Star, Dodge Rowel, Mexican Barb, Iowa Three-Point, Kittleson's Half-Hitch and Merrill's Twirl being some of the more popular brands.

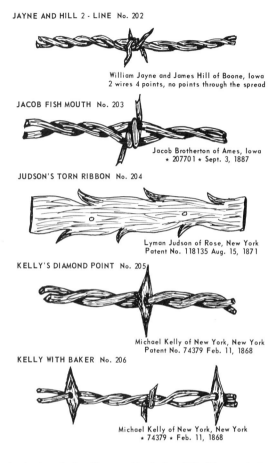

JAYNE AND HILL 2 - LINE No. 202

William Jayne and James Hill of Boone, Iowa
2 wires 4 points, no points through the spread

JACOB FISH MOUTH No. 203

Jacob Brotherton of Ames, Iowa
★ 207701 ★ Sept. 3, 1887

JUDSON'S TORN RIBBON No. 204

Lyman Judson of Rose, New York
Patent No. 118135 Aug. 15, 1871

KELLY'S DIAMOND POINT No. 205

Michael Kelly of New York, New York
Patent No. 74379 Feb. 11, 1868

KELLY WITH BAKER No. 206

Michael Kelly of New York, New York
★ 74379 ★ Feb. 11, 1868

A selection of wires illustrated in *Antique Wire Illustrated*, the magazine which shows you '315 different kinds of barbed wire that fenced the West' (Antique Wire Sales Inc., Oklahoma)

More than 1,200 different kinds of barbed wire are thought to have been produced in the past century. Modern meshed wire and electric fences have rendered barbed wire obsolete, which enhances its appeal to collectors. Today there are around 250,000 collectors in America alone and the hobby has spread to Britain, Europe and Australia. There are numerous collectors' clubs, several specialist dealers and a growing body of literature, including the periodicals *Barbarian* and *Barbed Wire Gazette*.

17

BEE SMOKERS

The injection of smoke into a bee-hive alarms the bees and makes them fill up their honey-pouches, a normal reaction in times of emergency. In this state bees are less likely to attack and thus the bee-keeper can work on the hive. In times gone by a few puffs from an old briar pipe full of thick shag did the trick, but as not all apiarists were addicted to the tobacco habit patent devices producing the same effect were manufactured. These bee-smokers consisted of a canister of brass or copper (known as the stove) with a curved chimney at the top and a bellows arrangement at the side. Smouldering decayed wood, straw, burlap sacking or rags produced the best effects. Bee-smokers are, of course, used by apiarists to this day, but the more collectable varieties are those with unusual patent devices and brass or copper parts capable of taking a bright polish. From 1850 to 1880 was the hey-day of other mechanical devices in bee-keeping and some of these, such as the Hruschka patent honey extractor, honey-pumps and bee feeding bottles, are attractive and unusual examples of apicultural bygones.

A Taylor's 'Country Life Outfit' which comprises a hive, the bees themselves, a smoker with 12 paper cartridges, a bee veil, a queen excluder, a feeder etc, and the 'Cottage' Outfit for beginners (Army & Navy Stores Ltd)

BELLEEK WARE

One of the confusions of ceramics is that this term is used to denote two quite different types of porcelain, manufactured on either side of the Atlantic. True Belleek takes its name from the town on the river Erne in Northern Ireland where a pottery was established in 1857. It manufactured some robust ironstone tablewares and a considerable quanity of painted or transfer-printed earthenware, often distinguished by gilding; but it is best known for its highly distinctive nacreous or iridescent glazes on porcelain. The mother of pearl effect was often heightened by modelling the porcelain in the form of nautilus shells, though more recently Belleek of Fermanagh have tended to concentrate on figurines in delicate shades of grey and green.

Apart from the very thin body, Irish Belleek had nothing in common with American Belleek which was manufactured by Messrs Ott and Brewer of Trenton, New Jersey, at the turn of the century. Ott and Brewer even copied the Belleek marks, but fortunately added their own initials below. American Belleek was mainly applied to highly distinctive vases, modelled and decorated in the style of Art Nouveau, with a penchant for the asymmetry of French Rococo and more than a hint of *Japonaiserie*.

BELLOWS

In medieval England this handy fireside implement had the jaw-breaking name of *blastbaelig* – literally a 'blow-bag'. This was later shortened to 'bellies' (bags) but by the sixteenth century 'bellows' was in common use. Bellows, for fanning a reluctant fire into flames, have been around for thousands of years and the primitive goatskin bellows used in some parts of Africa and Asia to this day have changed little since the times of the Pharaohs. The Chinese used cylindrical bellows, operating on the piston principle, but in Europe from the Middle Ages onwards two flat boards, either triangular or heart-shaped, were used. The sides of the boards were joined by leather and kept from collapsing by means of primitive springs or ribs made from animal bone. An inlet valve of leather was let into the lower valve and air was expelled through a narrow nozzle.

Much of the appeal of bellows as a collectable stems from the fact that the boards were usually decorated with pokerwork or chip-carving, or inlaid with strips of brass or studded with tiny nails in an ornamental pattern. Relatively scarce are bellows whose

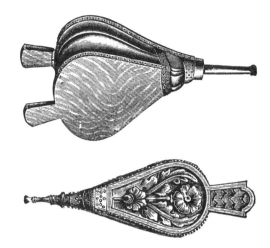

Kitchen, and carved oak, bellows (Army & Navy Stores Ltd)

boards are painted with scenery or floral motifs. Copper and brass were used for banding, reinforcements and the nozzle. Modern grates and improved flues at the turn of the century did away with the necessity for bellows, and the replacement of the open hearth by other forms of domestic heating has meant that the bellows, along with the warming-pan, has quite literally 'gone to the wall'.

BELTS AND BELT BUCKLES

Belts themselves have a fairly limited appeal to the collector, though there is considerable variety in the leather and webbing belts for the collector of MILITARIA, just as the fashion belts in those periods when women's dress has been worn close to the body appeal to the student of costume and its accessories.

The main attraction of belts lies in their fastening – the buckle – which, though in existence in Elizabethan times, is rare before the eighteenth century. Pure silver buckles are decidedly scarce from this early period, and even those in which the precious metal is confined to the rims, with a steel base and prongs or locking bar, are quite elusive, prior to 1790.

A late 18th-century papier-mâché mourning buckle (Christies, South Kensington)

Nineteenth-century silver buckles are much more plentiful and may be found in a wide range of shapes, artistic styles and sizes, often with the addition of semi-precious stones and enamelling.

Base metal buckles followed the same styles as those in silver but have extended down to the present day. From the mid nineteenth century onwards, die-stamped buckles in electroplate were commonplace and may be found in an enormous variety of styles and shapes.

Like BADGES, uniform belt-buckles are of consummate interest to the student of mili-

taria. They range in size from the gigantic belt-plates from the cross-belts worn by Highland troops to the small silver-gilt buckles on the ceremonial braided belts worn with full dress uniform. In between come the more serviceable, day-to-day buckles in brass, iron, steel or bronze decorated with regimental or national emblems. The belt-buckles worn by mail-coach guards, especially those of the Wells Fargo Company, had large rectangular plates which simply invited ornate pictorial embellishment – but, beware, many of these old-timers have been extensively reproduced in recent years.

BERLIN WOOLWORK

Other names for this female accomplishment of yesteryear were crewel-work, canvas-work and worsted-work, which give more of a clue to its form than the name now in popular use. It is loosely applied to any kind of needlework picture, using wool of bright colours on a coarse canvas backing, but strictly speaking it denotes the rather stereotyped pictures produced in Germany for export to other parts of Europe and America in the second half of the last century. Run-of-the-mill Berlin woolwork consists of floral patterns, Biblical scenes and indeterminate landscapes and examples produced by needlewomen of independent spirit who devised their own pictures are much sought after. These pictures were applied to cushion covers, upholstery and the decorative panels of furniture, as well as being preserved behind glass in the form of pole-screens and wall-hangings.

An early 19th-century woolwork picture of a leopard (Christies, South Kensington)

BETEL-NUT CUTTERS

Visitors to South-East Asia and the Philippines will often come across, in the bazaars and tourist emporia, rather fierce-looking instruments resembling a cross between small shears and pliers, with stout metal handles and

generally broad steel blades. These are used in cutting betel nut, the fruit of the Areca palm, which looks like a hen's egg. The fibrous husk is peeled off to reveal a small, very hard kernel and this is prepared by first boiling in water, slicing it with special cutters, and drying the slices in the sun. The chewing of betel is so widespread, from India and Sri Lanka to Thailand and Indonesia, that it has been estimated that a tenth of all mankind engage in the habit.

The cutters are richly ornamented as befits a highly-prized personal possession, and inlaid decoration follows the national character-istics of each region. Some have elaborately twisted shanks; others have cast animal and human figures, creatures and deities associated with Hinduism and Buddhism; or rich inlays of gold and silver. Some idea of the tremend-ous scope of betel-nut cutters is afforded by viewing the magnificent collection now as-sembled in the Victoria and Albert Museum, London.

BICYCLING MEMORABILIA

The parish church of Stoke Poges in Bucking-hamshire is best-known for Grey's *Elegy* composed in its churchyard, but it also deserv-es to be better known for a stained glass win-dow depicting a seventeenth-century figure seated on a wheeled contraption and using his feet against the ground as a means of propul-sion. This window is undoubtedly the oldest

Below: A turn-of-the-century art nouveau poster for a Chicago bicycle company (Sotheby & Co.). *Right:* A Lucas Silver King No. 300 cycle lamp (Christies, South Kensington)

piece of bicycling memorabilia on record. Similar vehicles were invented in France in the late eighteenth century, first the draisienne, then velocipede and the celeripede or hobby-horse. All of these machines relied on foot propulsion on the ground and the first true bicycle, a dandy-horse fitted with pedals, cranks and twin driving-rods, was invented in 1839 by Kirkpatrick MacMillan of Dumfries – known to his contemporaries as 'Daft Pate' since they could see no future in such an invention.

The invention of the rotary crank by Pierre Lallement of Paris in 1865 revolutionized the bicycle. Almost overnight the bicycling craze swept western Europe and Britain and soon spread to America. The 'boneshaker', the

A card from *Famous Inventions* issued by W.D. & H.O. Wills in 1915, showing the Hobby Horse (Ian Fleming)

'ordinary' or 'penny-farthing' and the rear-driven 'safety' were the precursors of the modern bicycle and subsequent refinements, such as pneumatic tyres, light-metal alloy frames, variable gears and calliper brakes have developed in the past eighty years.

Before the advent of the gas buggy or horse-less carriage in the 1890s bicycling as a craze reached epidemic proportions and most of the memorabilia now collected dates before the First World War. There were cyclists' maps, guides and touring handbooks, posters, PICTURE POSTCARDS, programmes of race meetings and club BADGES, medals and mementoes. In more recent years there have been numerous labels, stamps, pictorial postmarks and maximum cards honouring the Tour de France, the International Peace Race and the World Cycling Championship.

Bicycling has also left its mark in many of the decorative objects of the late nineteenth century, from Staffordshire figures to CHINA FAIRINGS, from fan-leaves to STEVENGRAPHS.

BIDETS

Ever since the French took their word for a little horse and bestowed it on this invention of the eighteenth century, there has been no small measure of coyness surrounding this item of hygienic hardware. In its antique form it consisted of a stool with a metal or ceramic basin set in the top. From the outset many attempts were made to disguise it when not in use and this gave rise to some pretty ingenious devices with sliding or folding covers. The more elaborate examples, dating from the early nineteenth century, had attached backs and elaborate plunger devices. Portable bidets are nothing new, since travelling versions, folding compactly into small chests, were designed for the intrepid traveller well over a century ago, when hotels left much to be desired in the matter of plumbing. Bidets may be found in every kind of ceramics, with an infinite variety of decoration, and also in pewter, brass or copper. The carving and turning of the stool follow contemporary styles in decorative cabinet-making.

Even more portable were the douches and enemas which catered to the Victorian obsession with personal hygiene and the regularity of their bodily functions. They were obviously tailored to suit every purse, ranging

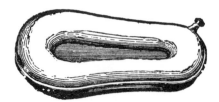

A pedestal bidet of *c.*1896 for sale from 93/- plain, 99/- embossed, 103/- printed and 107/- decorated, and (below) an inflatable bidet available in red rubber (Army & Navy Stores Ltd)

from a rather wicked-looking, all-metal syringe to the elegant set 'as patronised by the gentry', with gleaming copper and brasswork and ivory nozzle. Examples of both types are displayed in my local museum, no doubt to illustrate the terrible class distinctions of a century ago.

BILLS AND BILL HEADINGS

Of the two dozen or so meanings which this handy little four-letter word has acquired, we are concerned here only with the more specific meaning, as a statement of charges for food and drink or an itemized account of goods sold, services performed or work done. In America a synonym for this would be a check – a slightly longer word that has acquired just as many disparate meanings. Bills (or checks) are the most informative, and often one of the more decorative, forms of ephemera. They are invariably dated and thus give us useful information on the costs of goods and services at different periods, in different parts of the world. They often provide an illuminating insight into the way people lived, what they ate and drank, what they wore and how they spent their money.

The earliest bills were entirely handwritten and I have seen examples up to a metre in length – bills from members of the legal and medical professions come into this category! By the early eighteenth century printed bill-headings were coming into use; at first confined to a mixture of founts of letterpress only, but as the century wore on, becoming increasingly decorative. The most attractive specimens belong to the nineteenth century, when tasteful copperplate was combined with steel engravings, often depicting shop-fronts or the façades of hotels. Aesthetically bills deteriorated from 1890 onwards, when lithography and latterly the use of half-tone illustrations detracted from their earlier artistic

Above: The improved water closet from a plumber's bill heading of 1851. *Below:* A very early (*c.*1815) vintner's bill (both Author's collection)

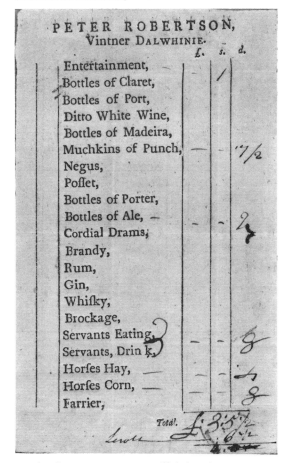

merit. One can trace parallel developments in the PICTORIAL NOTEPAPER of the nineteenth and early twentieth centuries.

BLOTTERS AND BLOTTER HOLDERS

In that seemingly prehistoric period before the advent of the ballpoint pen the blotter was an indispensable adjunct of the escritoire or desk. Blotters consisted of semi-circular pieces of wood, with sheets of blotting-paper affixed to the convex face, and a wooden handle on the flat, upper side. The blotter was rocked carefully back and forward across the still-wet ink. They range from the plain, functional variety to the highly ornate blotters with marquetry inlay or carved sides. They may be found in papier-mâché with mother of pearl inlay, in delicate porcelain or even silver. The most desirable examples have cunning little compartments set into the back for postage stamps. Blotter-holders were leather-bound folios containing larger sheets of blotting-paper, their interest lying mainly in the different methods

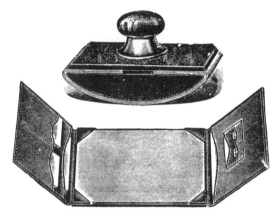

A leather and a hand blotter (Army & Navy Stores Ltd)

of embossing and pokerwork used to decorate them. The most ornate examples have enamelled or *repoussé* plaques in brass, copper, pinchbeck or silver set into their outer covers.

BOOK ENDS

As far as I can determine, these useful ornaments were developed in the late nineteenth century, at the dawn of the era of the bedsitter or bachelor apartment. When cramped quarters made a full-size bookcase impracticable any mantelpiece or broad ledge could easily be transformed into a bookshelf by means of these articles.

The earliest examples were very solid in construction, cast iron, bronze and spelter being much favoured, often with the addition of gilding or enamelling. Tin-glazed earthenware was also widely used but, being lighter in material, required relatively large and clumsy figures. At the turn of the century the cantilevered book-end was invented, whereby books rested on a metal sheet attached to the upright and held themselves in position by virtue of their own weight. This freed the book-end from its former limitations of weight and size and permitted a much wider range of designs, which were both more compact than before and also utilised many other materials.

Two sets of book ends (Army & Navy Stores Ltd)

Book-ends of this type may be found in porcelain plaques, wooden panels or embossed metal – copper and pewter with Art Nouveau motifs were especially fashionable in the early 1900s. These contrast sharply with the Art Moderne and Art Deco book-ends of the Twenties and Thirties, with their geometric BAKELITE and chromium patterns. Book-ends are still being produced, of course, but the modern ones tend to prefer a more restrained approach, with a penchant for polished woods of sombre hue.

BOOK MARKERS

A friend of mine who works in a public library tells me that he has found everything from a banknote to a slice of bacon in books returned by members of the public – evidence of the ingenuity of mankind in utilising anything that comes to hand, rather than commit the unpardonable sin of folding the corner of the page down to mark the place. The book marker was specifically designed to obviate this problem and seems to have developed in the early nineteenth-century when rising literacy went with the mass-marketing of literature.

Book markers were made of leather or some woven substance, and this was a popular and profitable sideline for the manufacturers of STEVENGRAPHS. The cheaper ones were made of card and were designed as giveaways by stationers, booksellers and publishers, often advertising other goods and titles in stock. Chromolithographed book markers, with Biblical scenes and texts, were given to children at Sunday school for attentiveness or good attendance. The GREETINGS CARD manufacturers of the late nineteenth century also turned their attention to book markers and produced many ornate examples, often using embossed and fretted card or even sheets of thin, imitation ivory. There were even PICTURE POSTCARDS in the early 1900s intended for use as book markers after they had served their postal function.

Left: A small silk woven book marker, a souvenir of the Independence of America. *Right:* A book marker postcard (Author's collection)

BOOTS AND SHOE TREES

This aspect of treen has been overlooked by collectors until lately, yet offers a great deal of scope. Trees or stretchers are known to have been in use since the Middle Ages, though most of the examples now extant date from the late eighteenth century. As they continued to be produced down to about 1920 – and are still manufactured for riding boots – they should not present much difficulty for the

A boot drier and airer which is recommended for drying fishing boots: thick stockings should be put over the drier to absorb condensation Army & Navy Stores Ltd)

beginner. They consist of finely carved pieces of wood resembling the foot and ankle, with a handle set into the top. The more interesting examples have articulated joints and various patent spring-loaded devices for facilitating insertion into even the most awkward top-boot.

They were generally made of beechwood, highly polished or varnished and further interest is imparted by the fact that they frequently bear the trademark, name and address of cobblers and shoemakers.

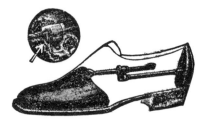

A popular and efficient shoe tree in aluminium (Army & Navy Stores Ltd)

BOSUN'S PIPES

Specially high-pitched whistles were needed for the transmission of signals to seamen that could be heard above the noise of the sea, and thus the distinctive bosun's whistle was evolved some time in the middle of the seventeenth century. The earliest examples, made of brass, latteen, copper or tinware, were lacquered, painted or silvered to prevent erosion from salt water. Pure silver pipes date from about 1750 but do not become reasonably plentiful before the era of Trafalgar. The basic shape has remained the same down to the present day, with three main parts: the keel or broad underblade, the gun or cannon (the slightly curved pipe) and the buoy or barrel-shaped finial.

Apart from size and stylistic variations, the interest in these pipes lies in their decoration. The ends of the buoy are usually decorated with naval insignia and occasionally the emblems or arms of individual ships, naval establishments and colonies overseas. The keel is often ornamented with engraving and chasing. Many examples bear inscriptions indicating that they were presented to the proud recipient for long service and good conduct.

BOTTLE OPENERS

Botopulism is not a word that seems to have found its way into any dictionary as yet, but it is already well-established among the fraternity of collectors of bottle openers. Botopulism is, in fact, the latest collecting mania to infect the United States and there have been sporadic outbreaks of the epidemic in Britain and Western Europe. The invention of the crown cork in 1905 led inevitably to an implement for removing it. The basic design of the bottle opener has not varied much in the past three quarters of a century and consists of a triangular piece of iron attached to a short handle. As with so many minor collectables, the interest lies not so much in the gadget itself but in its ornamentation. From the outset it was customary for breweries and taverns to give away crown cork bottle openers with their names, emblems and trademarks stamped on the handle. Gradually they became more and more decorative, even featuring tiny pictures, and finally they were issued with inscriptions commemorating events such as world's fairs and important anniversaries, like the American Bicentennial.

A late Victorian bottle opener

BOUGIE BOXES

The Algerian town of Bougie has left its mark in the collecting of silver and Sheffield plate from the fact that its principal export in the mid-eighteenth century was a type of bleached wax which was ideally suited to indoor lighting. The molten wax was mixed with a little turpentine and fed into a trough, through which was passed a coil of cotton. The wick became impregnated with the wax and was then wound on to a drum to form a coiled taper. These tapers came to be known as bougies and the special containers, which held the little drum and had an aperture through which the wick was drawn before lighting, were called bougie boxes. They were easily carried around the house, providing a fine light for hours on end. They resembled small drums, about three inches in diameter, with a slip-on lid. A fitted tube rising from the centre contained the tightly fitting nozzle controlling the emerging taper. Eighteenth-century examples are generally flat-topped but later a slightly conical shape was used and from 1810 to 1850 a domed top was preferred.

The taper nozzle, lid, sides and rims of the box were usually decorated with reeding, beading, gadrooning, moulded ornament or bright-cutting. Elegant vase-shaped nozzles were fashionable for a time in the early 1800s. From 1790 to about 1820 the sides of the drum were often pierced and fretted and from 1815 onwards the cover itself was frequently pierced. Other later refinements include a fretted gallery with fine air vents and a cylindrical chimney of flint glass. Cone snuffers were often attached by silver chains to the handle of the box. Improvements in the composition of candles and the design of candle-sticks in the 1840s led to the demise of the bougie and its distinctive container by 1850.

BRACKETS AND SCONCES

Metal brackets have been in existence for many centuries, ever since the Egyptians devised a form of domestic lighting that required a wall fixture. From the practical viewpoint, however, brackets only came into widespread use in the seventeenth century and were made in cast or wrought iron, bronze or brass. Though they are chiefly associated with lighting, there are many other uses to which brackets could be put. In the nineteenth century ornamental brackets were used to hold up shelves and mantels. Even the old-fashioned high-level lavatory cisterns rested on elaborate brackets often decorated with dolphins and other aquatic creatures. Wall sconces were also used as containers for lamps, but were more often designed to hold flowers and house plants – a use which has been revived within recent years. They may be encountered in various ceramic substances as well as glass and metal and the most sought

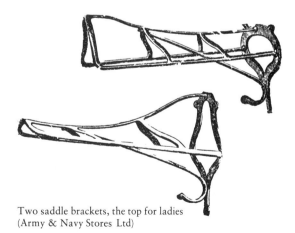

Two saddle brackets, the top for ladies
(Army & Navy Stores Ltd)

after are those from the turn of the century with delicate Art Nouveau motifs. Even the candle-brackets of fretted brass which used to decorate pianos are becoming elusive. A great deal of skill was often lavished on their decoration, as befitted an instrument which was the focal point of the front parlour.

BREADBOARDS

Now that bread is usually sold pre-sliced and pre-packed, the bread board is becoming a thing of the past, but there are still plenty of examples around at no great cost. Now is the time to look out for them at bargain prices in church bazaars and jumble sales before their true worth as collectables becomes widely recognized. The shapes are surprisingly varied, from circles and squares to chamfered rectangles, ellipses and ovals. Their interest lies, of course, in their decoration, many intricate floral or foliate patterns of carving and moulding being found round the edges. In many parts of Europe, notably France, where bread

Two wooden breadboards, one carved with the City of London Arms (Army & Navy Stores Ltd)

is still sold uncut by the metre, bread boards continue to hold their own, and it is there that some of the most unusual patterns are to be found.

BRICKS

My interest in this esoteric subject was kindled some years ago when I chanced upon a specimen bearing the name of a long-defunct colliery that I remembered from my childhood. A walk along the disused railway line near my home yielded over thirty different specimens, some of which I later identified as having originated many miles away. Many of the collieries worked fireclay deposits in their locality, which explains why a small country like Scotland seems to have had so many different brickworks all within the past century or so. Today my collection has grown to over 200 examples, all gathered locally. Brickmaking was a relatively new industry to Scotland, the first bricks having been made not ten miles away at Kirkconnell. James Maxwell of Kirkconnell, a noted Jacobite, imported the industry from France where he had been in exile after the rebellion of 1745–6.

Early bricks – and there are many examples in England dating from the Middle Ages – were uneven in size and shape and were seldom marked in any way. They were usually flat on both sides, but by the early nineteenth century a frog (the hollow depression which holds the mortar) was added to one or both

sides and this was often impressed with the maker's name and sometimes his address as well. The most elaborate specimens even include the date of manufacture. Some enterprising brickworks even produced bricks with inscriptions commemorating the Diamond Jubilee of Queen Victoria and this charming custom has continued to the present day.

I thought I was unique in my eccentricity until I learned of Henry Holt of Bacup, Lancashire. A retired builder, he began collecting old bricks some fifteen years ago and has recently acquired his thousandth specimen. He has unearthed bricks with unusual frogs, in diamond, oval and figure-eight patterns, with names and trademarks and even pictorial designs. One of his most prized specimens even has the bust of Abraham Lincoln and a brickworks in St Helens has even presented him with personalized bricks, bearing his own name. This is an aspect of industrial archaeology which has been sadly neglected, but the raw material is still plentiful, particularly in the decayed inner districts of towns and cities scheduled for redevelopment, and it is surprising how decorative a selection of local bricks can be.

CAKE STANDS

Where are all those cake stands which used to be such an indispensible feature of afternoon tea in the drawing-room? Every household boasted at least one which, when not in use, formed an attractive decoration to the room in its own right. Many beautiful examples of this small item of furniture were produced from the early eighteenth century till the Second World War and, combining fine craftsmanship in wood with the skills of the potter and glassworker, provided infinite variety in decorative features. They may be found in bentwood or bamboo, wickerwork, marquetry, papier-mâché or plain wood, with platters of turned wood, earthenware, porcelain or glass, with silver or silver-plated frames and surrounds. Their zenith seems to have been reached between 1880 and 1920 and it is to this period that the most decorative examples belong.

CALENDARS

Mention this subject and most people will immediately think of these exotic confections published by Pirelli which have been keenly sought after for some years now and change hands for considerable sums nowadays. At the upper end of the spectrum is the famous calendar of the early 1950s which depicts the late Marilyn Monroe reclining nude on red satin. And if this seems beneath your dignity I should point out that, as long ago as 1973, Sotheby's sold a fine example of the Monroe calendar for £120. I trust it has turned out to have been a good investment.

Though calendars in published form have been around for centuries, the more collectable varieties date only from the mid-nineteenth century, when bakers, grocers and other tradesmen had a six-month calendar printed on sheets of wrapping paper, decorated with seasonal vignettes and their trademark, and used them to gift-wrap the purchases of their customers at Christmas and other seasons of the year. The trade calendar, with chromolithographs of scenery and beautiful women, is a gesture of goodwill which developed in the 1890s and has continued in more sophisticated forms down to the present day.

A lithographed calendar issued in 1929 (Coca-Cola)

Calendars are known in more compact form, printed in minuscule lettering on small cards of ivorine or plastic. Many companies even struck calendar medallions in bronze, pewter or white metal and some of these were no larger than a silver crown or dollar. Calendar plates in pottery or porcelain date back to the early nineteenth century and have been revived on a large scale in recent years and the same treatment has been extended to textiles, in the guise of tea towels and printed handkerchiefs and head scarves.

Three-dimensional calendars include the perpetual variety, designed for the desk top. These have been produced in porcelain, wood, silver, glass and even ivory, with small tablets or discs changed by hand each day, or the ingenious rotary types which have the days and months of the year on revolving bands. Look out for examples with inscriptions in unusual languages and scripts.

CAMERAS

From left: A Kodak Junior No. 1 camera; a pocket Kodak, 1889 model; a pocket Kodak, 1886 model (Christie's, South Kensington)

Nicephore Niepce of France produced the first fixed photographic image as long ago as 1826 and over the ensuing three decades many experiments were conducted before satisfactory cameras, capable of production on a commercial scale, were evolved. The earliest Daguerre cameras date from 1840 and are among the major rarities in this field, but there are plenty of other types which were produced up to the 1880s which followed the same principle. They were exceedingly cumbersome affairs, with much polished hardwood and gleaming brasswork. Leather bellows were a comparatively late refinement and one should beware of damaged or repaired examples.

The original 'wet plate' cameras were superseded from 1880 onwards by the 'dry plate' cameras, pioneered by George Eastman of Kodak. Eastman's invention revolutionized cameras, making them more compact and incidentally much cheaper, so that photography was brought within the price range of everyone. The early dry plate cameras were still quite large by modern standards, but after Eastman invented roll film in 1888 they became very much smaller. Thereafter the progress of the camera can be signposted by technical innovations, such as the improved shutters (1895), the invention of the folding pocket camera (1896), the miniature cameras developed during the First World War, and the reflex camera, anastigmat lens, wide-angle lens, flash synchronization and other refinements of the 1920s and 1930s. The interwar period was the heyday of the early Leica, Contax, Rollei and Zeiss cameras and examples of these in good condition are now much sought after, particularly if they possess unusual technical features. The end-products of the camera, the PHOTOGRAPHS, are also highly collectable.

CANDLE TRIMMERS AND SNUFFERS

Prior to 1840 candles used loosely plaited wicks of Turkey cotton which tended to curl over as it burned, and dipped into the molten grease, causing a sputtering flame. A bright, steady flame could only be maintained by constantly clipping off the charred wick (known as the snuff). The gentle art of candle-sniting as it was called required long practice, and the aid of special instruments known as snuffers and trimmers. These resembled long narrow scissors with blades terminating in two tiny boxes which formed a heart shape when closed and held the charred wick. A seventeenth century variant had one box only, attached to the lower blade. Early examples in solid silver are major rarities but from 1750 onwards they were commonly manufactured in Sheffield plate. These have long been studied and collected and are quite expensive nowadays, but collectors have tended to neglect their more humble cousins, in pewter, brass, bronze, Britannia metal, japanned iron or cut steel. Associated with trimmers were the snuffer-dishes and stands, resembling either a very short, squat candlestick or an egg-cup with a handle, into which the snuffers were placed when not in use.

Another variety was the conical snuffer or douter which capped the candle to put out the flame. These were produced in every kind of metal and ceramic material and were in use till quite recently in the remoter parts of the British Isles where the benefits of electricity had not spread.

The invention of the hard stearic candle, with its closely plaited or twisted wick which lacked the disadvantages of the earlier variety, did away with the need for trimmers and by the late 1840s they had largely disappeared from use.

CAN OPENERS AND CANS

The canning industry goes back quite a long way, thanks to the invention of the tin can by the Englishman, Peter Durand, in the 1830s. His invention first received wide application in the United States in 1839 and with the development of branded foodstuffs in the late nineteenth century became the largest consumer of mild steel throughout the world. No one considered the cans themselves as collectables since the PACKAGING was completed by paper labels which have, for the most part, long since parted company from the cans. Since the Second World War the wider application of tin cans to beer and soft drinks, and the advent of direct printing on to tinplate, have combined to make the cans themselves the object of study and collecting. Specialists concentrate on particular brands – the number of different Coca Cola cans, for example, now runs into several hundreds, counting variations in background colour, can shape, pictorial decoration and instructions in many languages.

Can openers are as old as the cans themselves, though patent keys and ring-pulls in recent years are making the traditional openers obsolescent. The earliest types were stout steel

The can of baked beans which was recovered from Captain Scott's ill-fated camp in Antarctica, 1911–12 (H.J. Heinz Co. Ltd)

blades set in a plain wooden handle, but it was not long before the Victorians, with their innate love of ornament, began designing openers with decorative handles in brass, copper, nickel and enamelled metal, and

mounted cast ornament above the cutter, the heads of birds, animals and characters from history and mythology being particular favourites.

CANES AND CANE HANDLES

When I was learning the not so gentle art of soldiering, more years ago than I care now to remember, I once in all innocence asked the Regimental Sergeant-Major at the officer training school why it was that officers carried canes. He hardly paused to ponder this before answering that it was his opinion that officers needed to carry a cane to keep their hands occupied; otherwise they would probably slouch around with their hands in their pockets. NCOs and enlisted men did not have this tendency, I suppose – nor, indeed, the officers in other services or the armies of other countries. Perhaps it was really no more than a genteel hangover from the days when no self-respecting gentleman walked abroad without a cane – preferably gold-tipped – in his hand.

The custom dates from the early eighteenth century, when swords ceased to be worn in public. At various times, however, canes have been carried by both sexes, and this is evident in the wide range of ornamentation found on their handles. Gentlemen might prefer a simple gold or silver-gilt knob on the end, the only concession to ornament being a regimental crest if he was a military man, but ladies had the entire gamut of decorative materials and styles of ornamentation to choose from. Cane handles (collectable in their own right) may be found in precious metals, pinchbeck, brass, bronze, gun-metal, white metal, ivory, ebony, porcelain and glass, with filigree work, mother-of-pearl inlay, beadwork, carving, *repoussé* plaques and even novelty shapes in the form of animal or bird heads.

Canes with unusual technical features are highly prized and include those which conceal a bladed weapon or a firearm. Others have a hollow top and the handle unscrews to reveal a tiny spirit flask. There was even an illuminated cane, dating from the late eighteenth century, which held a miniature candle and reflector in the handle – very useful for nocturnal perambulation before the advent of street lighting.

Left: An American snake and fist cane carved out of whalebone with a knob of whale ivory, inlaid with silver and tortoiseshell (Charles R. Meyer, Southold, New York)

Below: A selection of cane and stick handles, mounted in gold and silver, offered by the Army & Navy Stores in their 1939 catalogue.

CAR BADGES AND MASCOTS

A Lalique glass Longchamps mascot.

The horseless carriage has been around now for the best part of a century and since Messrs Daimler and Benz first took to the road in 1885 cars have been identified by their own peculiar styles of badges and insignia. There is a timeless quality about the female figure sculpted by Charles Sykes for Rolls-Royce seventy years ago and still adorning every model of this famous marque, but if you examine the Rolls mascot carefully you will see that she epitomises the very essence of Art Nouveau in the swirling tresses and the folds of her dress. Relatively few makes of car today continue the old tradition of a mascot built into the radiator filler cap but this was a popular fashion up to 1940. Allegorical figures, demons, spirits of speed, animals, birds, sphinxes, Viking warriors and coronets are among the mascots which became virtually trademarks.

The emblems chosen by car manufacturers varied considerably, from the restrained RR monogram of Rolls to the flamboyant escutcheons favoured by Hispano-Suiza and the aristocratic Porsche. Gaily enamelled badges of car clubs and other organizations added a touch of colour to the radiator but current tastes in automobile design leave little room for such decoration. The badges of the Automobile Association alone have changed radically over the years, polished brass giving way to chrome plate, and the lettering and styling parallelling developments in the graphic arts. Car cemeteries and breakers'· yards used to be the happy hunting ground for discarded badges and mascots but most of these baubles seem to gravitate automatically to the antique shops these days. Non-standard mascots, affixed to radiator grilles or suspended above the windscreen to distract the driver, are the present-day counterpart of the talismans carried by travellers centuries ago. Many of them bordered on KITSCH and reflect the taste (or lack of it) of the Twenties.

CARNETS DE BAL

These elegant mementoes from a more gracious era are now being sought by collectors of objects of *vertu*. At their best they were very expensive, consisting of thin leaves of ivory sheathed in slim cases decorated with costly enamels and precious stones. The less expensive examples had satin, leather or shagreen cases, with 'Carnet de Bal' picked out in silver or embossed in gold on the cover. They were used by young ladies attending balls and dances and recorded the names of partners for the various dances. More ephemeral, but usually more interesting, are the carnets de bal of folded card, resembling small MENUS, with the programme of a particular ball printed therein, with spaces for the partners' names to be inserted. Examples from military balls, with regimental badges and vignettes of cavalry officers resplendent in their finery, are now keenly sought by collectors of militaria.

The front and reverse of a chromolithographed carnet for a military ball, *c*.1890 (Author's collection)

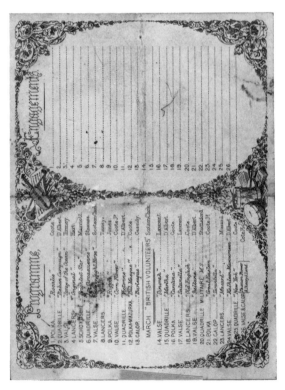

CASH REGISTERS

The earliest devices for recording transactions and storing money appeared in the early nineteenth century. They were very simple in design, with compartments for the various denominations of coins and a simple till-lock attachment. The amounts of the transactions had to be written by hand on account sheets, visible through an aperture set in the lid of the cabinet. These registers were stoutly constructed and often beautifully finished examples of the cabinet-maker's art.

Mechanization came in 1879 when James Ritty of Ohio invented the first cash register in the modern sense. The machine had twin banks of keys, rather like a typewriter, and not only recorded a transaction but calculated totals and checked the sums as well. The record was indicated on a clock-face with concentric dials reading amounts in dollars and cents respectively. A later refinement was a machine which not only recorded the amount on a dial but punched holes in a column of paper and, by mechanically adding the number of holes, computed the total. More complex machines appeared at the turn of the century, with adding counters on each key, adding wheels which recorded and classified different types of transactions, for different goods by different salespeople, and finally the modern cash register issuing a receipt and maintaining an audit strip.

Not surprisingly, these machines were never cheap, and much care was lavished on their impressive ornamentation. The sides of the register and the money compartment below were usually decorated with handsome panels of electroplate or white metal, often with bronze inlay, brass fretting, beaten copper plaques and a surfeit of gilding and japanning. In Britain, many old registers dating back to

Two National cash registers, the top c.1910, the lower, c.1917 (Geller Business Equipment Ltd)

the early 1900s came on the market in the late 1960s when decimalization was imminent. It was hardly worth converting these old-timers from £sd to £p and they were eagerly snapped up by collectors, blinded to their fiscal shortcomings by their splendid appearance.

CHAIN PULLS

A friend of mine, observing with more sagacity than cynicism that anything was collectable provided it offered sufficient scope within itself for variation, once put an advertisement in a well-known weekly periodical devoted entirely to small ads, stating that he wished to purchase the appendages from the chains of old-fashioned, high-level lavatories. He was astonished by the response which consisted of offers of duplicates from like-minded individuals, or enquiries from other hopefuls as to whether he had any spare examples for sale. Unwittingly he had stumbled on a subject which he fondly imagined no one else had thought of – only to discover that quite a few

people had already got the same bright idea.

The chain-pull has had a fairly short, if honourable, career in the history of domestic PLUMBING. When water closets became commonplace in the mid nineteenth century they were fitted with a motley assortment of valves and pans which performed their function in an unsavoury fashion. These valve closets were operated by plungers or levers at the side of the seat. Hygiene improved dramatically in the 1870s with the introduction of the washout closet, pioneered by Doulton. Closets of this type relied on a good flush of water from a 2-gallon cistern situated at least five feet above. The siphon flush was operated by pulling on a chain. Low-flush suites were in use by the 1880s and became standard in America though they did not oust the high-level cistern in Britain till the 1950s. The chain-pulls used over a period of eighty years ranged from turned wood to BAKELITE and composition rubber materials, but the most collectable varieties are those made in vitreous porcelain, decorated with the name of the manufacturer, trademarks, advertising slogans, and a wide range of floral and geometric ornament under the glaze. Tangs and hoops of copper or brass enhanced the appearance of these chain-pulls.

CHAMBER POTS

These used to be regarded with the sort of quizzical, amused raising of eyebrows now reserved for the previous subject, but have now been elevated in status to become the object of serious study and research. Inevitably, prices have risen correspondingly. At one end of the scale are the chamber pots of solid silver, often bearing the crests of royalty and the aristocracy, which appear in the more august salerooms from time to time and fetch four-figure sums. Even examples from the seventeenth and early eighteenth centuries, in pewter and tin-glazed earthenware, can be worth quite large amounts, especially if they have a proven association with historical personalities. At the other end of the scale, however, there are thousands of varieties of domestic chamber pots of the nineteenth and early twentieth centuries, in earthenware, ironstone, stoneware and porcelain, with almost infinite scope in their underglaze decoration. They were one of the stock lines manufactured by every pottery, and the willow patterns, floral motifs and scenic transfer-prints more often associated with bowls and dishes and other forms of tableware will also be found in this humble medium.

A giant chamber pot with a bust of Napoleon inside with the message 'May he perish'!

A concomitant of rising collector interest is the spate of modern chamber pots in the last few years, either reproducing nineteenth-century ADVERTISEMENTS (which would never have graced the real thing) or decorated with motifs and inscriptions commemorating contemporary events, such as the American Bicentennial or the Royal Silver Jubilee. You may well feel, as I do, that the commemoration of such occasions is better left to RACK PLATES.

CHINA FAIRINGS

Here is a subject which, a few short years ago, was totally neglected, then suddenly hit the big time with a few acknowledged rarities passing the £1,000-mark at auction in 1973. Since then prices have levelled off and many of the commoner varieties are still available for quite modest sums. Fairings seem to have been a peculiarly British form of souvenir though, paradoxically, the vast majority of them were manufactured in Germany and latterly in

An interesting late 19th-century Royal Vienna fairing (Phillips)

Japan. They were designed as cheap figure groups, sold for a few pennies or given away as prizes at fairgrounds – hence the name 'fairings'. They were made in Saxony and Thuringia from about 1860 until the outbreak of the First World War when their market was abruptly cut off. The inferior Japanese copies date from the beginning of this century and consist mainly of Welsh tea party groups.

The German fairings covered the entire range of genre situations, modelled in a naïve, artless manner which explains much of their charm today. But behind the artless simplicity of the fairings themselves lay a very shrewd piece of market research by firms such as Conta and Boehme of Possneck, since they had immense appeal to the British public and dealt the larger and more traditional Staffordshire flatback figures a blow from which they never recovered. The commoner and cheaper fairings echo the later seaside PICTURE POSTCARDS with their not too subtle attempts at low humour. Domestic situations, particularly what are known in the trade as Marriage Difficulties, comprise the bulk of them, with other everyday scenes, children and humanoid animals trailing behind. The genuine articles have a solid base, so watch out for later, and much inferior, imitations with hollow bases.

CIGAR AND CIGARETTE CASES

The habit of smoking cigars is said to have been introduced to North America by General Israel Putnam who commanded the British expeditionary force in Cuba during the Seven Years War (1756–63). Thereafter cigars were imported from Cuba and Louisiana and it was not until 1810 that cigar-making, as a cottage industry, developed in Connecticut. The earliest cigars were irregular in shape and size and packed in barrels of 100 or 500 and sold loose. By the early nineteenth century, however, shapes and sizes were becoming standardized and it became customary to pack them in the now familiar boxes of Spanish cedar. The Spanish manufacturers were quick to realize the sales potential of marketing cigars in boxes with colourful labels. These were beautifully engraved and subsequently chromolithographed and constitute the most beautiful forms of PACKAGING ever devised. Most countries operated a tobacco excise and the revenue stamps used to seal the boxes are now collected by philatelists. Though most cigar boxes were made of wood, the more costly and elaborate containers were produced in various metals as well as glass, while, at the other end of the scale, both paper and card have been used in more recent years.

Parallel with the introduction of commercial cigar boxes were slim cases, capable of holding four or five small cigars and carried in the vest pocket. These cases may be found in leather, hardwoods, shagreen or papier-mâché, often with decorative inlays. Cigar cases gradually went out of fashion at the end of the nineteenth century, as cigars became much larger and declined in popularity in face of the competition from cigarettes. These were, in effect, merely a much smaller form of cigar with a shredded filler and rice-paper wrapper and developed rapidly from 1865 onwards, spreading to Europe in the 1890s. Cigarette smoking overtook pipe and cigar smoking before the First World War, but it was during the war that sales rose dramatically, doubling in 1915–17 alone and rising fivefold between 1917 and 1938. The interwar

A selection of cigar and cigarette cases, in a variety of materials, offered by the Army & Navy Stores, one of which automatically opens and closes. On the far right is a combined cigarette case and lighter.

period, therefore, was the heyday of the cigarette case which became an indispensible item of personal jewelry for both sexes. Like the snuff-box of an earlier era, the cigarette case was produced in every conceivable material, and subjected to every form of artistic treatment imaginable, from gold and silver tastefully engraved with *guilloché* patterns to the gaudy enamels and BAKELITE cases of the Thirties. Many of the UNION CASES of an earlier generation were also converted for use as receptacles of cigarettes.

CIGAR AND TOBACCO CUTTERS

Special knives for cutting cigars and plugs of tobacco developed in the early nineteenth century and continue to be produced to this day. The pocket variety consists of a small spring-loaded blade mounted in a casing with a circular opening at one end into which the butt of the cigar is placed. By depressing the blade the incision is made cleanly. These pocket cutters often have a ring for suspension from a watch chain or fob and were often richly ornamented with precious metals and stones. Larger desk models have more substantial cases, often of semi-precious stones such as malachite and lapis lazuli, with gilding on the metal parts.

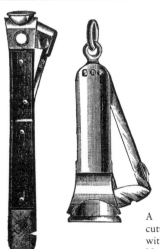

A wedge-cut pocket cigar cutter and a table cigar cutter with box opener (Army & Navy Stores Ltd)

Less common in Europe, but once a familiar sight in America are the large tobacco cutters mounted on the counters of cigar stores. The usual type has a long curved handle and resembles a small paper guillotine, but the handle and case were frequently decorated and cast figures of Indians, clowns and imps mounted on the back of the handle. Some of these devices were coin-operated, dispensing a 'chaw' of tobacco for a nickel. Among the more macabre novelty shapes are the tobacco and cigar cutters designed like miniature guillotines.

CIGARETTE CARDS

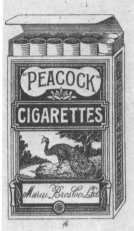

From left: a card from *Flowering Shrubs and Trees*, 1924, W.D. & H.O. Wills; a card from *Proverbs*, 1936, Ardath Tobacco Co. Ltd; the back of a cigarette card; and *below*, an early card issued by Kensitas, concerning Henry's adventures.

These little picture cards, which many collectors remember with nostalgia from their childhood days, attain the respectability of antiques in every sense of the word since it is now a century since they made their debut in the United States as stiffeners in the paper packs in which cigarettes were sold. The earliest cards carried on a much older tradition of TRADE CARDS, in that they bore the name, address and advertisements of the manufacturer. Emphasis was laid on ornate styles of lettering and the pictorial element was kept to a minimum. By the middle Eighties, however, chromolithography was being used to produce cards with a colourful picture on one side and the trade advertisement on the other as before. Gradually the trade aspect was played down and it became customary to add a piece of text relating to the picture. At first, sets of cards were open-ended but eventually standard sets of 50 or 100 with a uniform theme were evolved.

The heyday of the cigarette card is from 1885 to 1902 when the number of different manufacturers was drastically reduced and the great combines were formed.

Cigarette cards died out in the land of their birth when the giant American Tobacco Company won a virtual monopoly and no longer needed to entice customers by providing picture cards, but they flourished in Britain and many other parts of the world, until wartime shortages of paper brought about their demise in 1940. Various attempts have been made to revive them in recent years but cigarette smokers now prefer trading stamps and vouchers for 'free gifts'. Instead picture cards in the tradition of the cigarette card are now included with other consumer goods, such as tea, breakfast cereals, bubble gum and other forms of confectionary aimed at the juvenile market. This, in itself, is no new phenomenon, since picture cards were given away with beef extract and other foodstuffs of the Liebig Company and may be found with texts in various languages.

Jeannette Williams, from an unidentified set entitled *Modern Beauties* (Author's collection)

CIGARETTE LIGHTERS

Apart from lucifers, vestas and safety matches, various gadgets for lighting cigars and cigarettes were devised from the middle of the nineteenth century onwards. The earliest table lighters were of fairly basic construction, usually consisting of a container for matches and tapers, combined with some kind of ASHTRAY or ashbowl, and often a decorative feature, such as a porcelain figure with an abrasive patch used as a striker. Smaller lighters using a flint to ignite petrol, benzene or gasoline, developed at the turn of the century and afford tremendous scope in the multiplicity of the patent devices which tried to overcome the problems of leaking and controlling the flames. In the Twenties the pocket lighter rivalled the CIGARETTE CASE as an object of *vertu*, as smoking in public became more socially acceptable. The most decorative lighters belong to the period before the Second World War. Since then, though

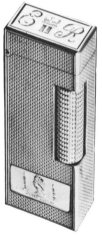

A limited edition Silver Jubilee lighter, 1977 (Alfred Dunhill) and a silver smokers' lamp (Army & Navy Stores Ltd)

there have been many technical improvements, ornament has tended to be secondary. Some extremely elegant table lighters are still being manufactured and are well on the way to becoming the antiques of the future, particularly if government legislation against the tobacco habit becomes any more draconian.

COASTERS AND DRIPMATS

Tegestology (from the Latin word *tegesta*, a tile) is another of the newer collecting interests that have become immensely popular on both sides of the Atlantic. This is only a grand way of describing the collecting of dripmats, beermats and the like. These transient counterparts of the felt and wooden coasters of earlier times developed at the end of the nineteenth century and consisted originally of thin discs of porcelain or wood mounted on a cork base. The industry was revolutionized in 1892 by Robert Smith of Dresden when he invented the wood-pulp throwaway coaster, printed with firms' ADVERTISEMENTS. The idea spread slowly from Germany to other parts of Europe but only became really popular when it was introduced to the United States about 1910. Oddly enough coasters of this type did not appear in Britain till the mid-1920s and were then confined to wines, beers, spirits and tobaccos.

Originally circular and chamfered square shapes were used but in more recent years octagons, ovals, hearts and other unusual shapes have been used. They range in size from

A modern pulp drip mat advertising the real ale of Masham, Yorkshire.

tiny drip-mats no more than an inch in diameter, up to the large tray mats over a foot square. Nowadays coasters and dripmats are used to publicize all manner of goods and services and even to commemorate important current events and historic anniversaries. Though wood-pulp is the most usual substance, they may be found in other materials, from paper, card and cork to plastic and textiles.

COAT HANGERS

We are accustomed nowadays to plain wooden, wire or plastic hangers, so it seems hard to believe that there was a time when coat hangers were much more elaborate contrivances, capable of ornamentation and therefore fitting into the criterion of collectability. The coat hangers used in the mid-nineteenth century were often beautiful objects, with floral painting, lacquer ornament and carving on their broad backs. Gilding, embossing and pokerwork decoration may also be encountered and there was a fine range of all-metal hangers with gilded bronze or electro-plated mouldings. Aside from the more obvious aesthetic considerations, there are those hangers which, from their inscriptions,

The 'Savile' valet stand, with an inbuilt trousers press, offered for 12/9d in the 1939 catalogue (Army & Navy Stores Ltd)

started life in the closets of hotels up and down the land. Mercifully the modern hotel guest is unlikely to be tempted by the anonymous and standardized hangers now widely used. There are also hangers dating from the turn of the century fitted with complicated springs and struts, designed for the retention of clothing in a secure grip or intended to impart creases to trousers. These merit attention if only for their technical interest.

COCKTAIL EQUIPMENT

Etymologists argue over the derivation of this word so evocative of the Bright Young Things and the Jazz Age. Since I cannot see the connection between a horse with a docked tail and an iced drink with diverse ingredients I am inclined to favour the more fanciful explanation that it is a corruption of Coctel, the Aztec princess who won immortality by the exotic potions she concocted. Cocktails have become almost synonymous with Prohibition and the Roaring Twenties. They originated in the United States about 1920 and swiftly spread to Europe. They inspired a completely new aspect of social life – the cocktail hour, with its own special blend of semi-formal costume. The cocktail lounge did for interior decoration what the cocktail bar did for a whole host of the decorative arts, from cabinet-making to glassware and silversmithing.

An electro-plate cocktail shaker and an English cut glass cocktail set on tray (Army & Navy Stores Ltd)

Cocktails may have had a chequered history over the past sixty years, waxing and waning in public esteem and now enjoying something of a comeback, but they have left us a rich legacy of collectables. In glassware we have distinctive cocktail glasses, decanters, shakers, lemon squeezers and sticks, often surmounted by tiny cockerels in brightly coloured glass. The cockerel was a favourite motif on the glasses and shakers themselves, in enamels, opaque glass or milk glass with contrasting bands of black and gold decoration. Cocktail cabinets, with marquetry panels in the Art Deco idiom, opened to reveal coloured glass mirrors and racks and shelves for the glassware and ingredients. There were even glass cocktail trays, ornamented with geometric motifs. Shakers were produced in silver, electroplate, stainless steel or coloured glass. The interwar period also produced a voluminous literature and many of the recipe books have brilliant cover designs and illustrations which typify the futuristic graphics of that era.

COFFEE MILLS AND GRINDERS

Although Italian warehousemen and grocers often roasted and ground coffee in enormous cast iron mills, many people from the early nineteenth century onwards preferred to grind their own coffee beans as required – a custom which, even in these days of high prices and instant coffee powders, continues to survive. The earliest coffee mills consisted of circular or square pine boxes surmounted by a metal grinder and a turned wooden handle. The coffee beans were fed into the mill and the grounds gathered in a tray at the bottom. More elaborate grinders had an all-metal construction and many varieties were produced from the mid-nineteenth century onwards, often brightly enamelled or japanned. The most sought after examples are those with a high dome and a surfeit of late-Victorian ornament, with beaten copper or pewter plaques on the sides. Some of the large grocer's mills had

Two coffee mills (Army & Navy Stores Ltd)

elegant containers resembling Grecian urns, with wrought iron stands and fly-wheels and an abundance of copper and brass imparting a handsome appearance.

COMBS

Cavemen (and women) it seems, were quite particular about their appearance, judging by the quantity of primitive combs of animal bone, horn and wood which have been excavated from archaeological sites. The Greeks, Egyptians and Romans brought comb manufacture to the level of an art, with elegant carved horn and ivory combs, often carved out of a single piece, or with teeth of porcupine quills and sharpened bones inserted separately. Most of these early combs are now in museums, but there is still a vast field left for the collector of modest means. Nineteenth-century tortoiseshell combs come in all shapes and sizes, from the simple moustache combs of military gentlemen to the elaborately carved back combs worn by ladies in Latin countries. There are even combs of silver, but more commonly met with are similar combs of electroplate with die-stamped ornament on the blocks.

A comb case in crimson velvet (Christies, South Kensington)

COMPACTS

These are one of the more modern collectables dating back no farther than the early Twenties when it became socially acceptable for women to apply their make-up in public. They are a development of the earlier and larger VANITY CASES and have been marketed under various names, such as dorine cases and flapjacks. The most widely used term is compact, either from the fact that these little cases are very compact, or because they contain compressed and compacted face powder. Generally circular, though ovals and rounded rectangles are not unknown, they contained a mirror on the inside of the lid and an inner lid which protected the mirror from the powder. They also contained a cloth disc which served as a powder puff. Compacts were contemporary with CIGARETTE CASES and were produced in the same materials, and with the same diversity of ornamental features. Indeed, it should be possible to find matched sets of compacts and cigarette cases from the period before the Second World War. They survived into the 1950s but declined as the wearing of face powder went out of fashion. Now that heavier make-up seems to be coming back again perhaps the compact is due for a revival.

Two silver flapjacks, one with enamelled colours and raised badge of the Royal Artillery (Army & Navy Stores Ltd)

COMMUNION TOKENS

In the Protestant churches of the Calvinist persuasion it was customary to precede the annual service of Holy Communion by a catechizing of the congregation – a test of religious knowledge and the doctrines of the faith. Those who were examined and found worthy of partaking at the Lord's Table were given a token which admitted them to the following Sabbath. Communion tokens are associated mainly with the various brands of Presbyterian worship in Scotland and were in use from the late sixteenth to the early twentieth centuries. Though now largely superseded by nondescript cards, they are still employed in a few of the more conservative churches, particularly in the Highlands and Islands, and there is evidence that other churches are beginning to revive them. They may be found with the names or emblems of churches in other countries too, notably the United States, England, Australia, Canada and New Zealand, and of course, were also used in the Netherlands, parts of Germany, Switzerland and South Africa by the Dutch Reformed and other Calvinist sects. Tokens were produced in lead, often struck or cast locally from

A selection of tokens from the author's collection

matrices held by the church elders. The more sophisticated examples were struck in pewter, brass, bronze or white metal and bore pictorial elements, such as the Burning Bush, emblem of Presbyterianism, the Communion plate or even views of the church building itself. Tokens have also been struck in recent years to commemorate church anniversaries and are thus more in the nature of medalets than tokens in the strict sense.

Actually, tokens play an important part in the ceremonies of other religions, and include the Pidyon shekels of Judaism and the temple tokens of Hinduism.

COOKING UTENSILS

Junkyards used to be the happy hunting ground of collectors seeking old pots and pans in non-ferrous metals; today the best bet is the country house sale where the odd lots at the end often include the dull and blackened copperware, the detritus of the great kitchens of yesteryear. Quite a few bronze skillets, with their ornate handles and three pointed feet, seem to have survived from the seventeenth and eighteenth centuries, probably because their decorative qualities were recognized even though they ceased to have a utilitarian function. Similarly the cast-iron pots with three or four stumpy feet, which were widely used in northern Europe and America until recent times for cooking over open fires, are still relatively abundant and make attractive planters when covered with a glossy coat of black paint. But the most desirable items are the brass and copper saucepans, frying-pans, skillets, fish kettles, tea kettles and the like, all of which can be brightly polished then carefully preserved with one of those clear lacquers now on the market. JELLY MOULDS are a large and diverse group, but other utensils and related cooking accessories include colanders, pancake turners, toasters, WAFFLE IRONS, rotary broilers, meat jacks, plate warmers, ladles, and mote skimmers, which occur in iron, brass, bronze or copper, often silvered or tinned. They make an impressive decoration in even the most antiseptic of modern kitchens.

A selection of collectable cooking utensils. *From top:* a 1957 toaster (Kenwood); a chip potato-cutter, an aluminium fish kettle; a combined graduated measure and milk saucepan; and an electro-plate tea urn (Army & Navy Stores Ltd)

COQUILLA NUT BOXES

If you are very lucky, you may come across small carved objects with skilfully concealed hinges and a lid that opens to reveal a hollow interior. The surfaces are intricately and totally carved and the surface has a distinctive mottled appearance. These are snuff-boxes carved from coquilla nuts, the fruit of the piassaba palm found in the coastal swamp-lands of the Caribbean and South America. Very little is known about these boxes but it is thought that they were carved by French seamen and marines serving in places like Martinique, Guadeloupe and Cayenne during the Napoleonic Wars. A common motif is a ship, sometimes with the name of a real man o' war incised. The carving of decks and bulwarks is correct to the smallest detail, and usually the decking forms the lid of the box. Forecastle, stern and superstructure were carved separately and then affixed by means of tiny dowels. Another favourite device of the craftsmen was to carve coquilla nuts in the form of whimsical human figures, portly gentlemen whose coat-tails lift to reveal the inside of the box. Other boxes retain the original shape of the coquilla nut but are covered with strange carving which owes more to the ancient Mayas, Arawaks and Aztecs than European culture. Most of the examples encountered seem to belong to the early nineteenth century, though it is not impossible that similar boxes are being produced to this day by the Indians of Colombia, Venezuela and Guyana.

CORK PICTURES

The most fascinating, three-dimensional pictures are those which have been assembled from layers of cork, intricately carved and superimposed to give an amazing amount of depth. The raw material for this art form is the outer bark of the evergreen oak (*Quercus suber*), a native of North Africa, the Iberian peninsula and southern Italy. Cork pictures used to constitute one of the better bargains among tourist souvenirs of the Mediterranean countries, but they seem to have been priced out of existence by wage inflation. After all, it must have taken many hours of painstaking labour to construct even the more basic pictures, while the more complex examples probably took several months to execute. A somewhat similar art was practised in China and Japan, using the dried bark of the Abemaki tree. The pictures were mounted in shallow glass frames and depict landscapes and animated street scenes, historical tableaux and religious motifs.

COUPONS AND VOUCHERS

These two words, both French and capable of many meanings, are here used in the sense of a series of attached tickets or certificates which often require to be cut out or detached and presented as needed in exchange for goods or services. Like TICKETS, they are a form of ephemera which has attracted the attention of ephemerists in recent years. One immediately thinks of the ration books and points booklets issued during the Second World War, very few of which appear to have survived. Rationing of certain commodities continued in Britain as late as 1953 and in many respects was worse after the war than during it. How many people nowadays remember BUs – the bread units issued in 1947? Petrol rationing during the Suez crisis of 1956 brought a temporary issue of coupons, with highly ornate designs as

A retailer's sugar ticket from 1916 (Author's collection)

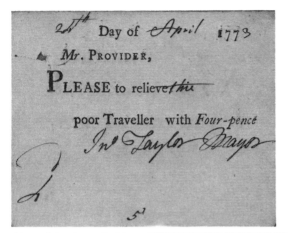

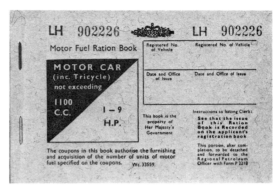

Above left: A meal ticket from 1773 (Author's collection) and *above right:* a motor fuel ration book issued in the petrol crisis of 1973 (Ian Fleming). *Right:* A charity lodging ticket of 1849 (author's collection)

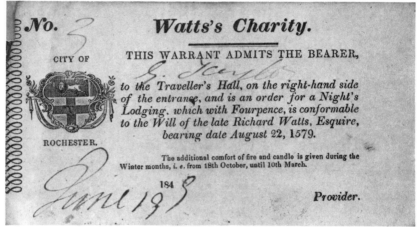

befitted security documents of considerable value. The aftermath of the Yom Kippur War of 1973 brought the threat of rationing, and an issue of petrol coupons which were never actually required. I wonder how many of these have been laid aside for posterity as potential collector's items!

Coupons and vouchers have been used in most countries at some time or another, and often relate to some national economic or political crisis that precipitated the shortage requiring a rationing system. The idea first became universal during the First World War, but much earlier there were coupons and vouchers distributed to the needy and exchangeable for flour, soup and other foodstuffs. Historically the most interesting are the meal tickets from the Irish Potato Famine of the Hungry Forties – a far cry from the meat tokens and food stamps of the present day.

CRESTED SPOONS

This is the poor man's answer to the Apostle spoons and seal-topped spoons which are now the closed preserve of the millionaire collector. As a tourist souvenir they had their origins in the second half of the nineteenth century when another of those forgotten geniuses suddenly hit upon the fact that every city, town, borough and municipality of any size or importance had a badge or coat of arms and this seemed an admirable ornament to put on such small, saleable mementoes as caddy spoons, teaspoons and coffee spoons. The same train of thought obviously influenced W. H. Goss and his competitors but which

A regimental shooting spoon
(Army & Navy Stores Ltd)

came first – crested spoons or crested china – I have not been able to determine.

For the most part, the crests were manufactured separately, cast and then enamelled in the civic colours, and finally soldered to the flattened ends of the handles. Some of the earliest spoons had the crests worked directly on the handle and these are now highly desirable. The majority of spoons are produced in electro-plated nickel silver but they may also be found in gilt-metal, Britannia metal, white metal and other alloys. The more elaborate varieties have enamelled decoration on the stems and bowls as well. The crested spoon mania, as a world-wide phenomenon, attained its zenith in the years immediately before the First World War, and the finest examples belong to this period. They have continued to appear right down to the present time, though most of the specimens I have seen from 1950 onwards seem tawdry by comparison, with poor quality chrome finish. These enamelled crests may also be found on other small souvenirs, such as paper knives, ASHTRAYS, bill-folds and STAMP CASES.

CRIMPING IRONS

Under this heading I have grouped an entire arsenal of small irons which were used by the housewife (or her servants) in days gone by. Heavy and relatively clumsy flatirons were all very well for the routine ironing of linen but a variety of more delicate instruments was required for the subtleties of lace collars, ribbons, ruffles and cuffs. The tiniest of these was the lace iron with a delicately curved bottom to avoid snagging threads. Then there was the finishing iron which smoothed the edges of garments once they had been ironed by more conventional means. A variant of this was the Italian iron which specialized in smoothing silk ribbons and bows. These slim, cigar-shaped irons were heated in the fire, then placed in a cylindrical sheath fitted to a long handle before being run over the ribbons. Goffering irons, goffering stacks, fluting irons,

Opposite: A goffering iron with 3 charcoal irons (Clark, Nelson Limited)

crimping boards and rollers fall into the category of crimping irons proper, designed to preserve the characteristically corrugated appearance of ruffles and pleats. Some of these resembled miniature mangles, with ridged rollers rotated by a handle. Others consisted of ridged boxwood boards and wooden rollers, like tiny rolling pins with horizontal ridging. The collar was laid on the board and the crimping roller moved back and forward until the desired effect was achieved. Towards the end of the nineteenth century, when frills and furbelows were fashionable, the range of crimping irons was greatly extended, and there were many patent irons on the market with pulleys and crankshafts and other mechanical contrivances intended to improve their efficiency. They disappeared overnight during the First World War, when dress trimmings became plainer, and the advent of man-made fibres has ensured that they will never be revived.

CRUMB TRAYS AND BRUSHES

Changes in eating habits, rather than improvements in table manners, have led to the disappearance of the crumb tray and its matching brush. They belong to the era of damask table-cloths and formal meals in the dining-room, and have no place in the modern casual atmosphere of breakfast bars and TV dinners. They seem to have come into widespread use in the second half of the last century and continued till the early 1950s, so there is plenty of scope here for the collector. Actually there were two distinct schools of thought. There were those who favoured the use of the curved-back crumb brush with its matching fluted tray, like a miniature dust-pan. Others used a crumb scoop with an elegant handle, and deposited the crumbs into its matching waiter, as these distinctive oval trays were called. The finest sets were manufactured in silver, but silver-plate and EPNS were more common, and lower down the scale there were sets in brass, bronze, copper and chrome-plated steel. Brush-backs, trays and scoops were invariably

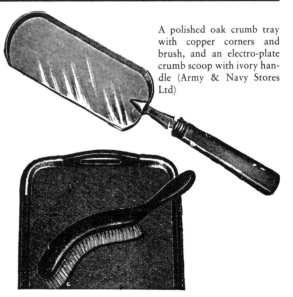

A polished oak crumb tray with copper corners and brush, and an electro-plate crumb scoop with ivory handle (Army & Navy Stores Ltd)

decorated in the most extravagant manner, with a welter of arabesques, gadrooning, scallops and foliate patterns. There were even crumb trays for the nursery, decorated with fairy-tale characters and scenes in brightly coloured enamels.

CUSTARD GLASSES

In the Middle Ages custard was a kind of pie, but by the late seventeenth century it had come to mean a pudding made with milk and eggs. From this period date the earthenware and stoneware custard pots in which custards were oven-baked. New recipes developed in the nineteenth century, however, resulted in a whole new range of utensils. The preparation of a more liquid form of custard led to the use of custard jugs from which individual portions were then poured into small custard glasses. The jugs can be found in all the prevailing patterns, from pressed and moulded glassware to cut glass, and in the different kinds of glass, from plain clear glass to opaque and coloured glasses. The custard glasses themselves followed the same styles, as they were often produced in matching suites. The glasses may be found in many shapes. A large group resemble squat glass cups, fitted with handles and supplied with matching saucers. Others have conical or fluted bowls mounted on short

Three crystal custard glasses (Army & Navy Stores Ltd)

stems and a wide foot. Others are like flattened bowls, with scalloped rims, fluting and deeply indented sides. In the early years of this century many novelty shapes, including animals, birds and human figures, were used – probably designed for the juvenile market with a view to making custard (and similar milk puddings) more palatable. Individual custard glasses may be picked up for next to nothing even yet, in second-hand shops and jumble sales, and are a compact and inexpensive way of illustrating trends in the design and manufacture of glassware over the past 150 years.

DARNERS

These are another thing of the past, rendered obsolete by the use of modern, artificial fibres for hosiery that are run-resistant and never spring holes till they are worn out anyway. When socks and stockings, gloves and mittens had to be laboriously repaired by hand, the darner or darning egg was indispensible. Any round object, such as a potato, would do the trick, but most households had darners produced specifically for the purpose. The majority of them consist of wooden hemispheres mounted on a handle and are attractive examples of TREEN. A few were decorated with carving or pokerwork or had brass hoops. In the nineteenth century there was a vogue for darning eggs in glassware, porcelain, earthenware, ivory, silver or electroplate and these were often enamelled or painted with pictures or floral patterns. Much sought after nowadays are the patent darners of the period 1870–1900, with tiny needle compartments in the handle.

DENTAL EQUIPMENT

This and the next subject will appeal mainly to members of the dental profession, who alone will appreciate the finer points of instruments which the rest of us would tend to view with horror. In the Middle Ages any old pair of forceps or pliers would do for the extraction of teeth, which had to be pretty loose anyway before the owner would part with them. From the early fifteenth century onwards, however, special instruments, such as the dreaded Pelican or the Turnkey, were devised and continually improved on, the subtle refinements in their design being aimed at eliminating the unfortunate tendency to damage adjoining teeth during the process of extraction (and remember that all this took place without the comfort of an anaesthetic). It was not until the 1830s that forceps were scientifically designed and adapted to the teeth in different parts of the jaw and thereafter the range of instruments rose dramatically. Orthodontics and cosmetic dentistry are relatively new branches of this science, though there are some fearsome appliances still extant from the late eighteenth century which were used to move teeth from one part of the jaw to another.

These crude attempts at transplants were sometimes successful! The nineteenth century witnessed the growth of orthodontics and many weird and wonderful appliances, but only since the pioneering work of Angle in this field in the early years of this century has orthodontics become an exact science. His inventions between 1910 and 1930 rendered all previous unsystematic instruments and appliances obsolete. Since the Second World War the greatest advances have been in the drilling machines themselves. The treadle-driven wrought-iron drills of not so long ago are now classed with the other dental curios of the past.

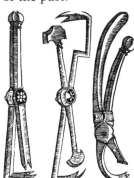

Three instruments used for pulling teeth in the 16th century (Routledge & Kegan Paul)

DENTURES

I must confess that the prospect of serried rows of false teeth, grinning fixedly in limbo, is more than somewhat unnerving; but I can understand their fascination for the members of the dental profession.

Individual false teeth, ligated teeth and bridgework have been in existence for almost three thousand years and examples of finely wrought gold bridges have been discovered in the archaeological sites of Etruria. No attempt seems to have been made to supply sets of dentures, either partial or complete, till the mid-seventeenth century. The base-plates were carved from bone, ivory, close-grained hardwood and even the tusk of hippotamus, while the well-to-do could afford dentures of solid gold – which were often pawned because of their intrinsic value. Partial dentures were held in place by fearsome metal clasps which encircled (and swiftly rotted) neighbouring teeth.

For the entirely toothless, however, the problem was immense. George Washington was not the only martyr to his dentures, but one of the best-known, thanks to Rembrandt Peale's sensitive portrait. Complete sets of upper and lower dentures were held, more or less, in place by elaborate devices of coiled springs. George Washington soaked his dentures overnight in port wine; but though they were doubtless rendered more palatable little could be done to make them more comfortable. Rembrandt's son, Charles W. Peale, was also a portrait painter but deserves to be better known for having made himself a set of silver dentures and was the first to experiment with artificial teeth made of porcelain, in 1807.

It was in the United States that the more scientific approach of modern dentistry began in the 1790s. At last some attempt was made to fit dentures to the mouth of the wearer. Impressions were taken in beeswax and moulds made therefrom in plaster of Paris. First porcelain, then vulcanized rubber or vulcanite, were used for better-fitting base plates; and by 1850 the extension of the base

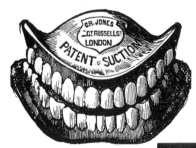

Right: Ivory dentures on a holder with Prince of Wales feathers, *c.*1805 (By courtesy of the Wellcome Trustees). *Above:* A full set of dentures from a testimonial advertisement of the late 19th century (Mary Evans Picture Library)

plate in the upper denture to cover the hard palate did away with the need for cumbersome springs. Vulcanite dentures were in use from about 1860 to 1935 but all-metal dentures also had a wide following in Europe and survived the Second World War. For a time in the early years of this century celluloid plates were used, but tended to turn from a healthy pink to a ghastly green and were highly inflammable. The late Sir Compton Mackenzie used to tell of a friend of his whose teeth caught fire when he fell asleep with the end of a lighted cigarette between his lips. Fortunately synthetic resins and acrylics have eliminated that hazard.

The early dentures were equipped with real human teeth, stripped from the corpses on the field of battle or the cadavers in mortuaries. The poor but dentally healthy would even resort to selling their teeth and endure the torture of primitive extraction without anaesthetics for a few paltry sous, as witness the ordeal of poor Fantine in *Les Miserables* (1862). Porcelain and vulcanite dentures may not have done a great deal for your smile, but at least you were comforted in the knowledge that you were not chewing on someone else's misfortune!

DIVER'S HELMETS

The earliest diving apparatus on record was the *Colimpha* in which Alexander the Great is reputed to have descended to the sea-bed in the fourth century BC, and in *De Re Militaria* by Vegetius (1532) we actually have a picture of a diver wearing a close-fitting leather helmet and breathing tube. The forerunner of the modern diver's helmet was invented by Repton in 1617 but leaked so badly as to be quite useless. He adapted it from the armour of the period. A century later John Lethbridge of Devon invented a leather suit with half a hogshead capacity of air, and is said to have made a fortune from it. Kleingert of Breslau produced an egg-shaped metal helmet in 1798 which came down over the wearer's torso. Air was inhaled through an ivory tube in the diver's mouth, attached to a hose kept afloat by means of a buoy.

The diving industry was revolutionized, however, in 1819 by Augustus Siebe who invented the metal helmet of copper, attached to a tunic of waterproof leather. Though primitive by modern standards it was far in advance of anything else then on the market and established the firm of Siebe Gorman, still in the forefront of industrial safety to this day. Numerous improvements were patented by Siebe up to 1872 but the external design of diver's helmets remained little changed from

A Churchman's series of cigarette cards of 1937 shows a diver in a magnificent helmet at work on the sea bed (Ian Fleming)

1830 till the 1950s. The fact that the helmet and corselet (the piece resting on the diver's shoulders and chest) were invariably constructed of highly planished tinned copper explains their main appeal to the collector. With a bit of elbow grease they take a high polish and make an ideal ornament for anyone inclined towards the nautical in interior decoration. Modern diving techniques call for much more sophisticated equipment and consequently many of these copper helmets have come on the market, to be eagerly snapped up by collectors of marine memorabilia.

DOOR BELLS

These do not seem to have received the same attention as the older door-knockers and yet they are just as collectable and have a much wider range of technical features. The ancestor of the door-bell was a spiral rod of wrought iron with a vertical base-plate affixed to the front of the door. A metal ring with a short handle encircled the rod and when lifted up and down smartly produced a ringing tone. In my native Scotland this action was known as 'tirling at the pin', and I daresay the

Sassenachs had their own name for it also. Only the other day I saw a traditional tirling pin made recently by a contemporary blacksmith, so perhaps we are about to witness a revival of this charming custom.

The earliest door-bells operated on a somewhat similar principle, involving the rattling of a clapper against a metal container. Out of this cumbersome contrivance developed the patent rotary door-bell of about 1880, in which the bell was rung by turning a large key.

Rotary door-bells of this type survived well into the present century, and some are still in use. They were made of iron, with cast ornament sometimes inlaid with brass and were designed for decorative effect. A parallel development was the door-bell with a brass plunger or pull mounted on a plate attached to the door-post. Pulling or pushing this handle (as the case might be) operated a rod or cable attached to a bell in the interior of the house. The name of the householder was

A collection of Victorian bell-pulls, with other door furniture (Christies, South Kensington)

frequently engraved or punched on the surrounding plate. Many of these old-style, pre-electric door bells have come on to the collector market in recent years following the demolition of old houses and form an attractive addition to any collection of ornamental brassware.

DRAWER PULLS, HANDLES AND KNOBS

Long after the drawers which they adorned have been broken up for firewood, these useful but decorative features of old-fashioned furniture tend to have been preserved. For many years out of keeping with the severely practical styles of modern furniture design, they were overlooked but now they have acquired a period flavour and are even being reproduced. Drawer pulls are plates with a semi-circular raised portion so that you can

get your fingers underneath. Handles come in many shapes and forms, but the most attractive are the little drop-handles which may be found in glass, enamels and porcelain as well as brass and electroplate. Drawer knobs range from the plain brass to the highly ornate examples with animal masks, floral patterns and vine clusters – very pretty to contemplate but not terribly practical when it comes to cleaning and polishing.

DRAWING INSTRUMENTS

Instruments for the mathematician and technical draughtsman have probably existed since Pythagoras devised his theorem but the majority in collectable condition date only from the seventeenth century. Not surprisingly, the early instruments are very rare and extremely expensive, but fortunately there are plenty of examples from the early nineteenth century onwards which can still be picked up quite cheaply. They include drawing pens

with ivory or hardwood handles or an all-metal construction, from silver and electroplate to nickel and stainless steel; spring bows, compasses, callipers and dividers, produced in most alloys from electrum to stainless steel. Late nineteenth-century refinements included screw sheaths and ball-bearing self-centring heads, and there are curious hybrids which combined pen, pencil and divider in a single instrument. Rulers, scales, protractors, set

A No. 4 geometry set in tin box, comprising pencil compass, divider, boxwood rule, 2 celluloid set-squares, drawing pencil and a piece of india rubber (Army & Navy Stores Ltd)

squares and semi-circles come in a surprisingly wide range, being made of silver, Sheffield plate, electroplate, brass and steel, or in semi-transparent substances such as mica, ivoride and celluloid. Boxwood was also widely used for rules and squares, occasionally with a metal strip along the drawing edge. Folding rules, slide rules, parallels and pantographs (for enlarging or reducing drawings accurately) all date from the 1830s and may be found with calibration in many different measures, before standardization in inches and centimetres prevailed in the 1860s.

The cases of drawing instruments, often beautifully constructed from closegrained boxwood, with velvet or plush lining, or covers of shagreen or leather, are collectable in their own right.

DRESS ACCESSORIES

Buttons have been an established collectable for many years, but there are many other forms of dress accessory which are worth considering. BELTS and BELT-BUCKLES, GARTERS and GARTER-CLIPS, HATS and CAPS, HATPINS, RIBBONS and RIBANDS, TIE-PINS and SCARF-PINS are the major categories which have now attracted the attention of specialist collectors and there are many other items which are of interest to the student of costume. The collector of lace will find considerable scope in collars, cuffs and trimmings. Even such minor but indispensible articles like safety pins have yielded a great many collectable variants since their invention exactly a hundred years ago. This is a subject which appeals mainly to the ladies, yet mere males will find that a study of neck-ties over the past century and a half is a fascinating subject.

Costume itself is such a vast subject that the beginner is best advised to concentrate on a fairly limited aspect or leave it well alone, since the proper care of old garments is fraught with many problems. Underwear is a ticklish subject (no pun intended) but one which would repay research. I only discovered recently that the brassiere was invented by a

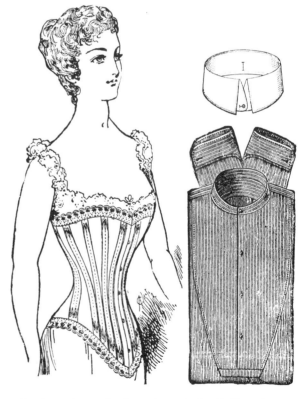

An elegant long-waisted corselette edged with Sévres lace, from an 1890's newspaper ad, and a shirt and collar from a 1902 brochure (Author's collection)

'Ties of all shapes' from the 1902 leaflet catalogue of J. Wood & Co., Silloth (Author's collection)

lady with the appropriate name of Caresse Crosby, better known as a sculptress in bronze. Old-fashioned foundation garments tend to resemble the products of constructional engineering rather than the fine arts. The wooden stay-busks inserted down the front of a corset to flatten the stomach were frequently carved and decorated by sailors and presented to their wives and sweethearts as a form of LOVE TOKEN.

DRESSING TABLE SETS

Greater attention to personal appearance from the mid eighteenth century onwards resulted in the manufacture of a whole host of articles intended for the dressing-table. The basic set might consist of little more than hair and clothes brushes, COMBS and looking glasses, but by the late nineteenth century the range of toilet articles had been extended to include scent bottles and atomizers, nail polishers, soap jars, powder puffs and boxes, button-hooks, jewel caskets, VANITY CASES, SHOE HORNS and shoe lifts, GLOVE STRETCHERS and a host of small boxes and jars for rouge, mascara, pomades, dentifrices and face creams.

The materials employed are infinite in variety. The backs of brushes range from polished hardwood, through ebony, ivory, horn and tortoiseshell to the early PLASTICS such as Erinoid, pigskin and shagreen. PIN TRAYS and brush trays were made of coloured or opaque glass, or in metals from silver-gilt to electroplate. The suite of brushes and mirrors

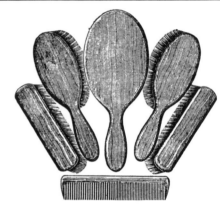

A ladies ivory toilet set offered by the Army & Navy Stores in 1939-40

might be decorated in restrained engine-turned silver, but elaborate *repoussage* was more fashionable at the turn of the century. After the First World War there was a vogue for delicate shades of transparent enamels on a silver deposit. Other articles associated with the dressing-table, such as HATPIN HOLDERS, RING TREES, STUD BOXES and UNION CASES, are discussed later in this book.

EGG COLLECTABLES

Boiled eggs have been one of the staple breakfast foods for centuries and have indirectly produced a formidable array of collectables associated with their consumption. Probably the oldest and most enduring is the egg-cup, examples being known in various forms of earthenware from the sixteenth century down to the present day. More elegant egg-cups have also been produced in silver, Sheffield plate and electroplate as well as a wide variety of base metal alloys, while painted or carved wooden egg cups are a popular tourist souvenir in many parts of the world down to the present day. Rather elusive, but worth looking for, are the egg-cup stands which were fashionable from about 1770 to the end of the nineteenth century. They comprised a central pillar surmounted by a handle, with a circular stand or wire basket with apertures for four or more egg cups. The more elaborate stands of the nineteenth century even had recesses for egg spoons and a salt cellar of Bristol blue glass in the centre. Canoe-shaped stands, with lavishly ornamented scroll-ends were briefly in vogue in the early 1800s, and other unusual shapes include ovals, triangles and lozenges. The Victorians preferred stands resembling shallow bowls raised on four feet, decorated extravagantly with bird and floral motifs and pierced trellis work.

The mid-nineteenth century was the zenith of inventions associated with boiled eggs. The most interesting are the various egg boilers and coddlers, complete with sand-glass and spirit lamp. Boilers had been in existence from the 1790s, but the contraptions of the 1840s were often masterpieces of technical and mechanical ingenuity, ranging from the simple three-minute coddler to the complex multiple boiler. Chromium-plated electric egg boilers were manufactured in the United States in the 1920s but never really caught on with the public. They incorporated a tiny bell which rang when the eggs were boiled.

From top: An egg decapitator; an egg steamer available in silver or electro-plate; an electro-plate egg stand and spoons; an electric egg boiler; and two egg poachers (Army & Navy Stores Ltd)

So far as I can gather, poached eggs were a much later fashion altogether, and special pans and dishes for this purpose, often termed cocottes, seem to have been manufactured from about 1860 onwards. Egg poachers with individual egg dishes and a spirit lamp date from the turn of the century and may be found in silver or electroplate.

Apart from the controversy in *Gulliver's Travels* between the Big-endians and the Little-endians over which end of the boiled egg should be cut, there are opposing schools of thought to this day, as to whether an egg should be cut or have its shell broken by tapping with the spoon. Adherents of the former were helped in their task by a device patented under the gruesome name of egg-decapitator. This alarming instrument resembled a pair of scissors joined at the tips, with the blades curved to form a circle and twin rows of spikes placed on the inner sides. The decapitator was placed over the egg and a brisk squeeze of the scissors pierced the shell and removed the top – rather a messy operation if performed by unskilled hands.

ELECTIONEERING ITEMS

Collectors of Bristol delftware have long had a keen appreciation of plates bearing such slogans as 'Fortescue & Harris For Ever, 1754' or 'Creswell Esqr. For Ever'. These are electioneering plates, produced in connection with the parliamentary elections of the 1750s. They may be found with the names of candidates for many of the West Country constituencies and the fact that the names often go in pairs is a reminder that, before the Great Reform Act of 1832, English boroughs returned two members apiece.

Nineteenth-century elections seldom raised the same enthusiasm – at least among the pottery manufacturers. Instead, electioneering has left its mark in more ephemeral articles, such as printed kerchiefs extolling the merits of parliamentary candidates. Politics tended to become more serious after 1832 and affected much larger sections of the community, with the result that the holiday atmosphere evident in the earlier delftware gave way to the more prosaic propaganda of the broadsheet and pamphlet. These make attractive pieces of ephemera, often put together hastily by a jobbing printer in a variety of founts, lampooning or attacking the rival candidates with blithe disregard for the laws of libel. The burning issue of the day, so vividly depicted in these leaflets and broadsides, seem unimportant today. Recurrent themes, however, include women's suffrage, Irish home rule, Chartism (in Britain), abolitionism, federalism and states' rights (in America) and they provoked brilliant rhetoric and scurrilous invective in both words and pictures.

Something of the holiday atmosphere of election time survived in America, where campaign badges and pins, sashes and favours of all kinds provided a wealth of ephemera from the 1840s onwards, and this tradition has continued to the present time in car stickers and plastic pin-backs. In Europe election propaganda has included satirical medalets, in bronze, brass, pewter, white metal or aluminium. Placards and posters extolling the merits of parties and individual candidates form a large section of election memorabilia. Why not make a start by collecting the ephemera associated with elections in your own locality?

ELECTRICAL APPARATUS & GADGETS

We tend to think of electricity as one of the wonders of the twentieth century, yet domestic current was being supplied in New York and London almost a century ago. Admittedly, it took many years to win widespread acceptance and it is only since the late 1920s that its fans and oscillating fans, often using materials such as BAKELITE which were developed in the electric era. Bakelite was used as an alternative to enamelled or chromed metal in the earliest hairdryers, dry shavers, curling irons and food mixers. These articles, which were often regarded as ahead of their time, now seem curiously dated. They are usually much more cumbersome than their modern counterparts, having to incorporate a device known as a resistance which had to be adapted to the voltage and current (both varying considerably from place to place).

Early lamps offered limitless scope for artistic expression, particularly those of the Twenties that combined modern materials with attempts to convey the essence of modernity – Art Deco at its best. Do not overlook the possibilities inherent in old electrical accessories, the transformers, lamp-holders, adaptors, plugs and pressel switches in bakelite or proto-plastics such as ivoroid.

Above: An Ediswan Dowsing's patent electric fire with 4 250-volt tubular lamps, *c.*1920 (Christies, South Kensington)

full potential has been realized. The largest range of collectables are those associated in some way with sound reproduction and these include GRAMOPHONES AND PHONOGRAPHS, RADIO AND TELEVISION and TELEPHONES.

The oldest electrical gadgets were those which contained a heating element and they date from the early 1880s. They include warming plates and food servers, chafing dishes and flat irons. Electric toastracks date from 1900 and electric kettles and tea-making machines were in use before the First World War. These gadgets were marketed in nickel-plate, chromium-plate, stainless steel or polished ALUMINIUM – all metals which seemed to epitomize the spirit of the age.

A later development was the electric motor, and between 1910 and 1930 countless variants were devised, miniaturized and adapted to every conceivable situation. This was a period of great inventiveness as more and more applications for electricity were found. Among the earliest were electric air purifiers, exhaust

ELECTROLUX

So quiet!
it wouldn't wake a sleeping baby

Above: An advertisement for an Electrolux vacuum cleaner in the 1939 Army & Navy catalogue – 'There is also an attachment to destroy young moths and their larvae'. *Left:* An early electric kettle.

ENAMELLED COINS

This is a minor art form which flourished for about half a century (1887–1925) and has made a remarkable come-back within recent years. It seems to have originated in Birmingham in 1887 when the Jubilee coins, with their intricate armorial reverses, challenged the skills of W. H. Probert and Edwin Steele. The crowns, with their spirited motif of St George and the Dragon, were ideally suited to watch-chains, while the tiny armorial sixpences made excellent cuff-links. The different elements in the design were picked out in contrasting colours, in the same manner as the small enamelled BADGES which were the main stock in trade of the Birmingham manufacturers. This profitable sideline died out at the turn of the century, but it lingered on in France and Italy till the Twenties. On the Continent the favourite coin for the enamelled treatment was the handsome Peacock rupee of Burma, which provided the enamellers with immense scope for their talents. Other coins which were

Two enamelled crowns, issued by the Pobjoy Mint, one on behalf of the Queen's Silver Jubilee Appeal, 1977, the other being the Jacobite pattern crown of 1716

enamelled included the French 5-franc silver pieces and other dollar sized coins of the major European countries.

In recent years a revival of interest in these old coins has encouraged several companies in Britain and America to try their hand at decorating contemporary coins. The Kennedy and Eisenhower coins of the United States and the handsome commemorative crowns of Britain and the Isle of Man seem to be the prime choice for this unusual treatment.

ENVELOPE AND STAMP MOISTENERS

These desk dampers and moisteners might never have been invented, had it not been for Sir Rowland Hill and his postal reforms of 1840. Not only was he instrumental in the adoption of adhesive postage stamps, but his scheme of Uniform Penny Postage made the use of the new-fangled envelope feasible. Hitherto an envelope counted as an additional sheet and double postage was charged, so this militated against its widespread acceptance.

An envelope damper and sealer, which was simply filled with water (Army & Navy Stores Ltd)

The fixative used on early postage stamps – disconcertingly referred to by the Post Office as 'cement' – was viewed by the public with some suspicion. Though assured that it was made from edible starch (from Irish potatoes, no less) the letter-writing public was not easily convinced, and this inspired the invention of the stamp moistener.

Actually there were many different kinds of gadget designed for this purpose. There were squat little glass bowls containing a piece of wet sponge; they had very thick bases which gave them stability and enabled them to double as paperweights. Then there were the drum-shaped moisteners with a perforated disc on top; the stamp was placed on this, pressed down slightly and the sponge underneath released a minute quantity of water. The larger desk models consisted of troughs of glass or pottery with a roller of similar material that picked up moisture as it rotated and facilitated the moistening of envelopes. A later variant of this dispensed a gummed strip, ready dampened, and was ideal for sealing parcels. At the other end of the scale were the tiny pocket moisteners, resembling a FOUN-TAIN PEN, with a reservoir of water and a felt tip. In between came the Stubby hygienic damper, with a pad of porous rubber or sponge on top and a BAKELITE body. This type was immensely popular in the 1930s. Dampers and moisteners may be found incorporating rulers, inkwells and even STAMP BOXES.

EXHIBITION SOUVENIRS

I cannot over-emphasize the importance of old exhibition catalogues as source material for the antique collector. Indeed, many of the catalogues of the great nineteenth-century exhibitions have now been reprinted wholly or in part. The London exhibitions of 1851 and 1862, the Glasgow exhibitions of 1888, 1901, 1911 and 1938 and the Wembley exhibition of 1924–5 are the more outstanding British examples. The Paris expositions from 1867 to 1937 and the American world fairs, from the Columbus Exposition of 1892–3 to Hemisfair 1968, and the other major world exhibitions from Brussels 1912 to Osaka 70, have all provided their quota of catalogues and hand-books which will stand the test of time as permanent reference works on developments in the arts and sciences.

The mementoes of exhibitions, from the great world fairs to the local agricultural show, include the medals and trophies awarded to exhibitors, tickets of admission, and the galaxy of promotional literature and other ephemera produced by the standholders, from leaflets and labels to car stickers and PICTURE POSTCARDS. Special stamps and coins have been issued in connection with many of these exhibitions since 1892 and form a distinct branch of philately and numismatics.

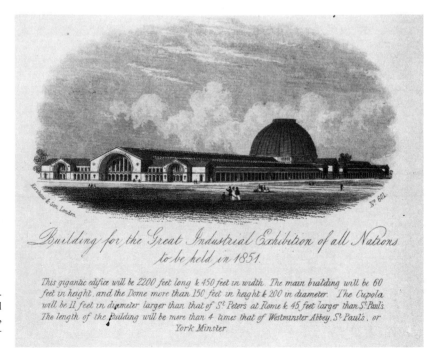

Headed notepaper commemorating the Great Industrial Exhibition of All Nations, held in 1851 (Author's collection)

FERNWARE

This appears to have been a peculiarly Scottish form of decoration and was invented in 1900 by William Smith of Mauchline, Ayrshire, as an alternative to transfer-printing for ornamenting the small wooden boxes popularly known as Mauhline Ware. The ferns were gathered in the island of Arran by the female members of the Smith family and laboriously applied to a wide variety of wooden articles, ranging from snuff-boxes and napkin rings to BLOTTER-HOLDERS and even draught-screens. When demand exceeded supply the Smiths resorted to simulated ferns, using paper with an embossed pattern to decorate their wares. Simulated fernware is regarded as inferior by the purist, but is quite scarce for all that. The business came to an abrupt end, however, when the factory was destroyed by fire in 1933. The Mauchline Museum has a splendid collection of fernware articles.

FOOD MIXERS AND BEATERS

Until the middle of the nineteenth century food was laboriously mixed by hand and beaten with a fork or spoon. Patent mixers and beaters were among the many labour-saving devices which eased the lot of the housewife from 1850 onwards. The earliest, and still the most basic, form of beater was the egg whisk made of loops of wire gathered in a metal or wooden handle. Nowadays an all-steel construction is favoured but a century ago whisks were made of nickel-plate, electroplate or tinned wire. Rotary beaters came into use in 1899 and varied in size and complexity, depending on whether they were intended for whipping cream and eggs or cake mixes. About the same period even larger and more elaborate gadgets were being produced which combined the functions of a GRINDER with a blender and mixer. Mounted on a board, they consisted of a metal drum containing blades and cutters rotated by means of a crank-handle. These mechanical food choppers were the ancestor of the modern electric mixers which were themselves patented in the 1920s in America, though they did not become widespread in Europe till relatively recently. Among the more specialized forms of mixers and beaters may be mentioned the various

A Kenwood Major, 1951 (Kenwood)

cream makers developed at the turn of the century. They invariably had glass containers and a system of rotating blades operated by diverse plungers, fly-wheels and cranks. Old mixers, like other household gadgetry of the past, were often quite decorative, with polished wood surfaces and gleaming brass and copper replete with ornamental moulding.

FOOT AND HAND WARMERS

Like HOT WATER BOTTLES, these relics of an era before the dawn of central heating were to be found all over the Northern Hemisphere and come in many different shapes, sizes and materials. The basic principle of the foot warmer was a container of bronze, brass or copper, holding a quantity of coal or charcoal. The glowing cinders were placed in a metal box which itself was inserted into the outer casing. Occasionally the outer sheath may be found with rows of perforations, but generally the conductive properties of copper were regarded as quite sufficient. The more elaborate warmers were covered with upholstery. Variants found in Eastern Europe had an outer case of carved, pierced or fretted wood, often gaily painted in traditional patterns.

Miniature versions of these warmers were produced for the hands. Flat or cylindrical warmers were intended to be placed by ladies inside their muffs, while circular examples, known as chafing balls, were kept by gentlemen in their pockets on a cold winter's day. Apart from copper and brass, these hand

A 17th-century foot warmer.

warmers may be found in silver, Sheffield plate or electroplate. They often held boiling water rather than hot coals, and several devices were patented in the late nineteenth century which used chemicals to produce heat.

FOUNTAIN PENS

The evolution of writing instruments has moved so rapidly that many of them have had a relatively short life. Just as the steel PEN NIB ousted the QUILL, so the ballpoint, brainchild of the Hungarian-born inventor Biro, has ousted the fountain pen after an active life of less than a century. Personally I abominate ballpoints and will continue to use a fountain pen so long as I can find a supplier of liquid ink for it!

Many attempts were made in the mid nineteenth century to devise a pen that would not have to be dipped into an INK BOTTLE every other second, thus interrupting the writer's concentration, but it was not until 1883 that Lewison Edson Waterman produced his Ideal Safety pen which overcame the distressing tendency of its rivals to leak in any position other than an upright one. The earliest pens had a glass barrel or reservoir which had to be laboriously filled using a glass tube with a tiny rubber bulb. By the end of the century, how-

A selection of fountain pens dating from 1885 to the present day (Christies, South Kensington)

ever, self-filling pens had been devised, using a small lever in the side of the pen to depress a rubber sac. Later variants dispensed with the lever and relied on manual squeezing of the sac to fill the pen. Other refinements were rotary plungers and suction devices, refills and cartridges. Fountain pens are deceptively simple to the untrained eye. A good pen involved over 200 operations in its manufacture, the nib alone requiring 80 separate stages in its development.

Aside from the technical features, fountain pens were quickly recognized as objects meriting decorative treatment. The cases were originally made of wood or vulcanite but early forms of plastic such as BAKELITE were favoured in the period up to the Second World War. An infinite variety of moulding, ribbing and engine-turning was applied to the surface, inlays of gold, silver, mother of pearl and enamels were popular and the most sumptuous pens were of an all-metal construction, rolled gold being a favourite material. Manufacturers such as Waterman, Swan, Conway-Stewart, Pelican, Onoto and Parker produced literally hundreds of different pens, each graced with an exotic name befitting its distinctive character. From the Onoto 'Magna' to the Swan 'Visofil' and the Conway 'Duro', they became virtually household brands. Waterman's 'Lady Patricia' was a veritable aristocrat among pens, while the same company's 'New Art' of 1904 was an expression of Art Nouveau at its best.

FREEMASONRY ITEMS

Only the most credulous would accept that Grand Master Moses organized the Israelites into masonic lodges, that Solomon and Nebuchadnezzar were Grand Master Masons, that Cyrus appointed Jerubbabel Provincial Grand Master of Judah and that Charles Martel was Right Worshipful Grand Master of France – statements proclaimed with all the force of Holy Writ by the Rev. James Anderson who compiled the earliest history of Freemasonry in 1723. There is no doubt, however, that Freemasonry as a secret society goes back to the mists of pre-history. Anthropologists have traced parallels between the ancient rites of the masons and the initiation ceremonies still practised in China and the remoter parts of Asia and Africa. The oldest relics of Free-masonry include manuscripts dating from the fourteenth century, now in the British Library, and several of the oldest lodges, notably in Scotland, have records going back to the sixteenth century.

Inseparable from the rituals of Freemasonry are the insignia and regalia associated with the various chapters and degrees, from the richly embroidered aprons to the medals, jewels, badges and chains in gold and silver, decor-ated with precious stones and sumptuous enamels. Many lodges continued to function outwith the organization of the grand lodges (which date from the early eighteenth century only), and there have been numerous insti-tutions of a similar nature, such as the Grand Order of Knights Templars, the Order of the Eastern Star, the Ancient Arabic Order, the Mystic Order of Veiled Prophets of the Enchanted Realm and the Tall Cedars of Lebanon. European Freemasonry has had a somewhat chequered career, often proscribed by the Catholic Church which banned mem-bership of secret societies, and persecuted in more recent years by totalitarian govern-ments. The regalia of the French *Corps d'Etat* and *Grand Orient*, the German *Steinmetzen* and similar institutions in other countries are also worth looking for.

FRUIT BOWLS AND BASKETS

Another object in the 'every-home-should-have-one' category, the fruit bowl, like the CAKE STAND used to be an indispensible feature of lounge and dining-room, reposing on every dresser and sideboard with its medley of fruits. A popular standby for wedding presents over the past two centuries, fruit bowls and baskets have been produced in a wide range of materials, from turned woodware and col-oured glass to earthenware, porcelain and metalwork. The last named, in particular, gave tremendous scope to the craftsman working in silver, Sheffield plate and electro-plate. Bowls were fluted, scalloped or gad-rooned, and baskets pierced and fretted or constructed entirely from wire. Fruit baskets with wire-work sides and foot rings came into fashion in the 1790s, solid handles eventually giving way to openwork designs about 1800. The earliest shapes were round or oval, but rectangular forms came in about 1805. A liner of blue glass was an optional extra. Solid fruit baskets in silver or electroplate were also a favourite line in presentation pieces and may be found with inscriptions commemorating long and faithful service and other marks of worthiness that add a touch of human interest.

From top: A pierced silver fruit dish (Army & Navy Stores Ltd). a George III silver fruit basket, *c.*1851, and a Victorian silver embossed fruit stand (both Lyle Publications)

GAMBLING EQUIPMENT

Gambling is one of the oldest human vices and the equipment associated with it dates back to pre-history, judging by the primitive dice and counters recovered from archaeological sites. There are numerous biblical references to the casting of lots and the story of the Roman soldiers who gambled for the clothing of Christ is well known. The dice, jetons, knucklebones and counters associated with games of chance are known from every part of the world and a most interesting collection could be formed along ethnographical lines. Gaming tokens date from the Middle Ages and range from the jetons of Nuremberg to the fake spade guineas of the eighteenth century and the satirical Cumberland jacks of the 1830s. Modern gambling tokens date from the 1960s when the scrap value of silver dollars exceeded their face values. The handsome dollar-sized tokens struck by the Franklin and Pobjoy Mints for casinos as far afield as Nevada and Tasmania are an unusual sideline of numismatics. Roulette wheels and gaming boards may be found in many kinds of material, but dice cups provide the greatest range of decorative treatment over the past three centuries, being found in leather, carved or turned wood, pewter, pottery or even silver.

GARDEN FURNITURE

Who, I often wonder, was the author of this quatrain:

> The Kiss of the Sun for Pardon,
> The Song of the Birds for Mirth,
> One is nearer God's Heart in a Garden
> Than anywhere else on Earth.

Some nameless bard who scraped a living composing stanzas for tombstones and Christmas cards, no doubt. His (or her) verse does not seem to have been copyrighted, since it crops up all over the English-speaking world, usually engraved or carved into the top back rails of garden seats and benches made of well-seasoned teak, or cast in iron for the more robust furniture of that material. I have even come across it on sundials and bird baths; and somewhere doubtless there are garden gnomes with this doggerel lurking under their beards. Though simulated stonework in fibreglass and other plastic materials are making rapid strides in garden wares there is still plenty of life in the more traditional articles, the rustic log seats and wrought iron tables, the lead

From left: A 'Park' sundial, a stoneware 'Wendy' and a wicker garden table (Army & Navy Stores Ltd)

planters, urns and statuary and fountains. They usually come on the market as a result of country house sales, and many nurserymen and builders' suppliers stock them occasionally.

GARTERS AND GARTER CLIPS

Like brogues and whisky, garters are of Celtic origin, being derived from the ancient Irish word *gairri*, meaning the calf of the leg, and described the ribbons wound round the legs of kilted warriors to keep their socks up. As the menfolk of most other races did not wear skirts, garters were relegated to the fair sex and at an early point in their development seem to have acquired some erotic overtones, as witness the manner in which England's premier order of chivalry, the Garter, is alleged to have been founded in 1346. The Victorians, for all their prudish exterior, delighted in frothy confections of ruched silk, secured by clips in silver, silver-gilt or electroplate in the form of barred gates, cupids, hearts and lovers' knots and this style, with variations, has continued down to the present time. Despite the widespread use of tights or pantie-hose there will doubtless always be a place in the arsenal of female blandishments for the decorative garter. Garters for keeping men's shirt sleeves neat tend to be more sober in construction, though there was a fashion in the 1900s for clips with sporting motifs.

GAS MASKS

To most of us, who associate such things with the horrors of trench warfare in 1915–18, air raid precautions propaganda in the late Thirties and riot control at the present time, respirators seem a strange thing to collect. But, next to BADGES, HELMETS AND HEADGEAR and UNIFORMS, they are now one of the most widely collected form of MILITARIA and are also of great interest to collectors of equipment associated with the fire services and industrial safety. A century ago, one of the requirements for recruits to the fire brigade was a six-inch

A photograph by the US Army Chemical Corp., 1918, of 19 of the gas masks used in World War I by American, British, French, German, Russian and Italian forces.
American: 2, 4, 5, 6, 7, 19
French: 11, 12, 13
Russian: 15
British: 3, 8, 9, 10, 17
German: 1, 14, 18
Italian: 16

beard which could be soaked in water and wrapped round the nose and mouth as a primitive smoke filter. Augustus Siebe, whom we have already encountered under DIVER'S HELMETS, devised several types of self-contained breathing apparatus for firemen and miners, and respirators with anti-gas filters were in use before the end of the last century. These early gasmasks, of oiled leather with mica windows and brass or copper filters, are exceedingly rare.

The earliest gasmasks used by troops in wartime, by contrast, were very simple affairs of impregnated gauze, known as the Veil Respirator or Black Widow. Later masks consisted of flannelette hoods impregnated with chemicals that neutralized the effects of chlorine and phosgene. The Germans had masks of oiled leather, or rubber sheeting from the captured French dirigible *Alsace*. The Italians had a mask of ALUMINIUM while the French had a type with a face-piece of cast iron. The majority of gasmasks since 1918 have been constructed of moulded or sheet rubber. The advent of total war, in Manchuria, Abyssinia and Spain, in the early 1930s led to the manufacture of gasmasks for civilians and even special types designed for babies, young children and hospital patients. There were gasmasks designed for horses, dogs and carrier pigeons and the Germans (who thought of everything) even equipped the Afrika Korps with gasmasks for camels!

GLOBES

Christopher Columbus may have got the idea that the world was round from seeing the terrestrial globes produced by German cartographers in the late fifteenth century, but similar spheres had been in existence ever since the time of Crates of Mallus who made globes in the second century BC, with the world divided into four quarters. In a more stylized form this became the orb surmounted by a cross, the medieval symbol of regal power. The earliest terrestrial globes were produced in brass, copper-gilt or painted wood but their manufacture was greatly simplified in 1507 by the technique of overlaying a papier-mâché base with printed sheets of paper cut to shape. Naturally early globes do not come cheaply these days, but there is still plenty of scope for the collector in the commercially produced globes from the beginning of this century onward. You only have to consider how the political map of the world has altered in the past eighty years or so to realize the potential in this subject. Transfer-printed tinplate globes date from the early 1900s and hollow composition or papier-mâché globes from the same period. Nothing illustrates the changes of this century more vividly than a series of globes showing the African continent − first largely blank then dominated by a broad swathe of pink from Cape to Cairo and now a patchwork of many colours, not to mention more than a score of new names in the past two decades alone as decolonialization and the 'wind of change' have swept over the continent.

Celestial globes are also available, though less prone to change. Lunar globes, however, must have seen some dramatic changes since the Apollo spacecraft orbited the dark side of the moon.

GLOVE STRETCHERS

I do not imagine that the reason for these gadgets was really to stretch the fine kid, pig-skin or goatskin gloves, since a tight fit was desirable. More probably they were designed

to be placed inside gloves so that they retained their shape, without wrinkling, when not being worn. They consisted of two arms joined at the tip, with handles at the other ends and sometimes some form of spring device to separate them and keep the glove taut. They were widely used in the nineteenth century and survived as late as the Second World War. The best ones were beautifully carved in ivory or ebony, but polished boxwood, horn, tortoiseshell and bone were also used.

GORGETS

In medieval times the gorget was either a crescent-shaped piece of iron between the helmet and breastplate, or a part of the wimple covering the throat – depending on which sex you were. After armour went out of use the gorget survived as a form of ornament mainly worn by officers, suspended from the collar by short chains. Gorgets were decorated with regimental insignia and were often cast in silver or silver-gilt. Though seldom worn by NCOs and other ranks, gorgets are known in base metal, usually brass or bronze, with the badge mounted in silver or white metal. They went out of use in the mid nineteenth century and are remembered today only in the red gorget tabs on the collars of uniform worn by officers of the rank of colonel and above.

European armies, however, continued to make considerable use of gorgets as a form of insignia. Perhaps the best-known are those known as *Ringkragen* which were worn by certain officers and NCOs of the German Army till the collapse of the Third Reich in 1945. These emblems were mainly worn by military police and the equivalent of the American honour guards, and they are now much sought after by collectors of Nazi relics.

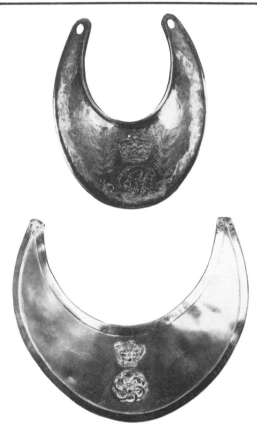

A Sheffield plate gorget of the 14th Foot (Christies, South Kensington)

GRAMOPHONES AND PHONOGRAPHS

Such are the differences between American English and English English that I am forced to use both terms in this heading. They are now synonymous and are still widely used on respective sides of the Atlantic to denote what is now more commonly called a record-player.

Originally, however, *both* terms were American and were jealously protected by the law of copyright, being the terms patented by Thomas Edison (1877) and Emile Berliner (1887) and denoting instruments which played recorded sound by means of cylinders and discs res-

pectively. The Berliner system was far superior to Edison's and by the beginning of this century cylinders had largely given way to discs – though Edison had the last laugh since it was his name that has survived in the land which gave birth to sound recording.

Above left: A Columbia type AB Graphophone (Christies, South Kensington); *above right:* A Victor's Horn Type talking machine of 1906, showing refinements and Morning Glory Horn (R.C.A.); *Left:* An Edison Amberola 75 phonograph (Christies, South Kensington); *right:* The first 'talking' machine with concealed horn, 1906 (R.C.A.)

They have all been swept aside, for practical purposes, by modern hi-fi-stereo systems using long-playing records but it is not too late to salvage the best of them before they are consigned to the junkyard. The centenary of Edison's invention has stimulated interest in early phonographs and this attention has also been focused on any recording or record-playing instrument down to the last of the horned table models of the 1930s. While cognoscenti concentrate on such technical features as early Columbia interchangeable rotating arms, triple-spring motors, all-metal

or celluloid diaphragms and tapering tone-arms, the layman will probably be more intrigued by such curiosities as the 'Puck' with its lyre-shaped base, the tiny Mikiphone, the clumsy Graphophone, the Tempophon which had a built-in alarm clock, children's toy phonographs or even the Stollwerck chocolate phonograph. The last named was a give-away dreamed up by a chocolate company about 1902 and came with discs of chocolate whose foil wrapper could be played like a RECORD.

GRATERS AND GRINDERS

Like FOOD MIXERS AND BEATERS, these gadgets developed considerably in the second half of the nineteenth century and were widely used till the all-purpose electric mixers and blenders were developed in the 1930s. Surprisingly enough, many housewives still prefer a hand grater since they are often less troublesome, and easier to clean, than the attachments on electric machines.

There was, in fact, a large family of handy little devices, designed to ease the lot of the housewife or her cook, and often tailored to meet the peculiar requirements of many different kinds of foodstuff. The best known in this category are the marmalade cutters which made their debut about 1900 and were designed to chop up oranges, though more often than not they reduced the fruit to a pulp. Apples, being easier to handle, provoked a range of parers and corers operated by rotary blades. Mechanical corers and parers date from the 1870s and were mostly of American invention. Raisin-stoners and cherry pippers date from 1898 and 1860 respectively, both operating on the principle of feeding the fruit through a hopper and separating the flesh from the seeds by means of rollers and blades.

Among graters proper, pride of place goes to the nutmeg grater, produced in many shapes and forms from the seventeenth century onwards and usually designed to be carried in the pocket. A touch of ground nut-

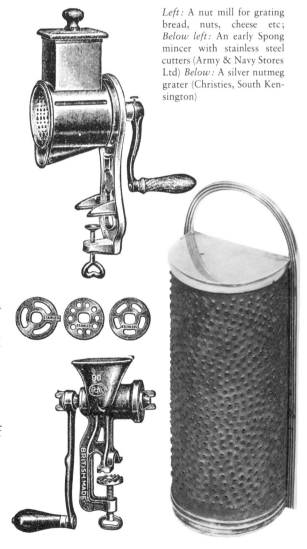

Left: A nut mill for grating bread, nuts, cheese etc; *Below left:* An early Spong mincer with stainless steel cutters (Army & Navy Stores Ltd) *Below:* A silver nutmeg grater (Christies, South Kensington)

meg or mace added flavour to meat and drink alike. Kitchen graters range from the small upright cylinder to the large horizontal box, with pierced surfaces designed for breaking up fruit, vegetables, bread, cheese and other substances into tiny fragments. The grating surface was usually of iron or tinned copper but nickel-plate was used in those cases where the acid in fruit would be likely to corrode the metal.

Pestles and mortars are the oldest form of grinder, used by the apothecary and the housewife alike in an age when spices, nuts, sugar and other foodstuffs were not retailed reduced to a manageable powder. These may be found in stoneware, wood, marble or various metals, such as iron or brass. COFFEE MILLS AND GRINDERS are a special class by themselves, but there were also rotary grinders for making sausage-meat, the earliest kinds being constructed of maple-wood lined with pewter. Cast iron mincers, clamped to the edge of the table, date from the mid-nineteenth century and were patented by Messrs Spong who also invented a number of rotary cutters and slicers for fruit and vegetables.

GREETINGS CARDS

Christmas cards and Valentines have received the attention of collectors for many years, but other forms of greetings card have been relatively neglected till recently. Though never rivalling Christmas as an occasion worthy of exchanging cards, Easter has had cards of its own since the latter part of the nineteenth century. These cards, decorated with Easter lilies, decorated eggs and hares (a European symbol for this season) were produced in Europe and America with chromolithographed scraps, embossed card and embroidered ribbon and are highly prized. From the early years of this century, however, they were superseded by more prosaic printed cards in the form of PICTURE POSTCARDS, with sepia illustrations and rather insipid tints.

I have not been able to discover when birthday cards came into fashion but they were certainly being manufactured in the 1880s if not earlier. Like Easter cards, the earlier collages of scraps and embossed paper gave

A British get-well card of the thirties (Ian Fleming)

Above: One of the first Mother's Day cards of 1927 (Hallmark Cards Inc., Kansas City). *Right:* A card for Grandparents Day, instituted by Hallmark Cards Inc. on 10 September 1978, the first major card-sending occasion in over 50 years (Hallmark)

way to postcards at the turn of the century. This type survived into the 1940s, but long before that time the more conventional fold-over card had been devised in America and spread to Britain and Europe in the late 1920s. America was also the birthplace of cards for many other occasions, from Mother's Day to Jewish New Year, and suiting every conceivable event of a more personal nature, from engagements and marriage to passing examinations and getting promoted in one's job. Pre-war examples of these cards are decidedly elusive, but of the more modern examples there is seemingly no end.

H

HAIR JEWELRY

Down the ages, bald men have made good the deficiency of nature with a variety of wigs, toupees and hair-pieces held in place by diverse fixatives. Ladies, on the other hand, have seldom required such drastic treatment and resort to transformations (a euphemism for wigs much used at the turn of the century), postiches, wavelets, pin curls and plaits when they were bored with their hair-do and could not wait till their locks grew of their own

Above and right: A 'transformation' and a pin curl offered in the 1939–40 Army & Navy catalogue. *Left:* A pair of Victorian hair earrings (Christies, South Kensington)

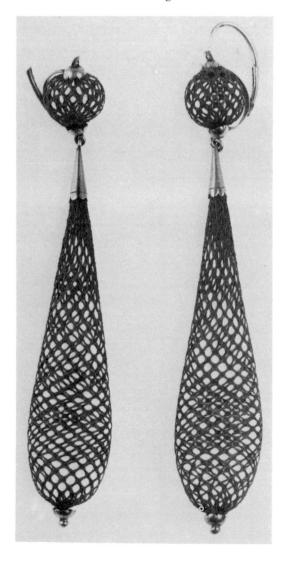

accord. The positioning and securing of these adornments required an array of COMBS, pins, grips and slides. Real tortoiseshell or jet were fashionable a century ago, and are now much sought after. Erinoid was used from the 1860s onwards as a tolerable substitute for tortoiseshell and is, itself, now quite scarce, though later forms of PLASTIC are much more plentiful. Elaborate hairpins in die-stamped and electroplated alloys, often decorated with semi-precious stones, paste and enamels, may be found with many unusual and novelty shapes.

Jewelry made of hair stems from the mourning rings and brooches, containing a tiny lock or curl of hair from the head of the dear departed, which became fashionable in the late seventeenth century. From these developed the sentimental jewelry and courtship rings and lockets containing hair. In the eighteenth century rings, ear-rings and even necklaces were composed of intricately woven strands of hair, much of the raw material being allegedly exported from certain villages in Austria where the women were renowned for their thick, wiry tresses. Watch chains, muff chains, bangles and bracelets were produced in plaited hair, bound with gold or silver and this art attained its height in the first half of the nineteenth century. Quite small pieces of hair were painstakingly assembled into tiny pictures and mounted in glass, additional embellishment being provided by tiny seed pearls and gold wire. If you want to learn more about this strange art, the Maidstone Museum has a fine collection.

HATBOXES AND BANDBOXES

These drum-shaped containers first came into prominence in the middle of the eighteenth century. The earliest ones were quite plain, constructed of carton, but it was not long before milliners recognized the value of decorating them with a covering of fancy paper. European hatboxes tend to be fairly straightforward in design, with the name, address and advertisements of the milliners and little attempt at floral or pictorial design. American hatboxes, usually known as bandboxes, however, soon became a prime subject for decoration in the most extravagant manner. Both the lid and the sides were frequently covered with scenic panoramas, portraits of contemporary celebrities and depictions of historic events. Particularly desirable are the patriotic bandboxes of the Civil War period (1861–5). Pictorial bandboxes went out of fashion towards the end of the century, and hatboxes since then have been rather prosaic.

Two American bandboxes of *c*.1830 (Reproduced by permission of the American Museum in Britain, Bath)

HATPINS AND HATPIN HOLDERS

Changing fashions in ladies millinery have accounted for the rise and fall of the hatpin. It first came to prominence in the last quarter of the nineteenth century when hats became increasingly large and perched precariously atop enormous coiffures. It was not uncommon for hatpins to be six to twelve inches in length, the pins themselves being of gold, silver, electroplate or nickel-plate, decorated with pearls, precious or semi-precious stones, jet, amber, tortoiseshell, carved ivory, shell cameos, and cut or moulded coloured glass. The fashion reached its height at the turn of the century and the Edwardian era witnessed numerous novelty shapes, with tiny figures of animals, birds, reptiles and humans. Good luck charms abound and there was even a passing phase when livery and regimental buttons were mounted as hatpins. Regimental hatpins, in fact, became *de rigueur* during the First World War. As large, wide-brimmed hats gave way to the close-fitting cloche in the Twenties the need for hatpins declined considerably. The pins used in the Thirties were necessary again as the fashion for little hats perched on one side of the hair-do became popular. Pins of this period, however, were much smaller, with an average length of three or four inches. Apart from purely aesthetic factors, there are technical features that hatpinologists enthuse over, such as swivel shanks, bayonet points and point protectors.

Hatpin stands, in a wide variety of metals, pottery, porcelain and polished woods, are also eminently collectable, and provide admirable display stands for one's collection. They resemble tiny vases, conical stands or miniature umbrella stands with holes or rings in the top to hold the pins. The most desirable examples are those with civic crests on the side, produced by Goss and other makers of souvenir china.

HELMETS AND HEADGEAR

This is an enormous field of MILITARIA and collectors usually specialize in one or other of its many aspects. Iron or steel helmets forming part of the armour worn by soldiers up to about 1670, when firearms became so accurate that little protection was offered by them, are among the more expensive of the established military antiques, so the collector seeking a field which is still relatively cheap will have to concentrate on something more modern. Armets, salades, sallets, burgonets, morions and cabassets have now moved into the millionaire class and even the pikeman's pot of the Civil War period (1642–9) will set you back about £100 ($200) these days.

Ceremonial headgear of the nineteenth century has likewise become expensive, though alberts, shakoes, bearskins, schapkas and busbies with regimental insignia in brass or white metal (worn by enlisted men) can occasionally be picked up for a modest sum. Forage caps, side caps, pill-boxes, Broderick caps, glengarries and tam o' shanters dating from the 1880s down to the present time are often quite decorative, with dicing, piping and ribands as well as regimental BADGES. Peaked caps, Service Dress caps, the wide-brimmed hats worn by American, Australian and New Zealand forces, the kepis worn by officers in some European armies and the pith helmets worn with tropical kit are in the medium price

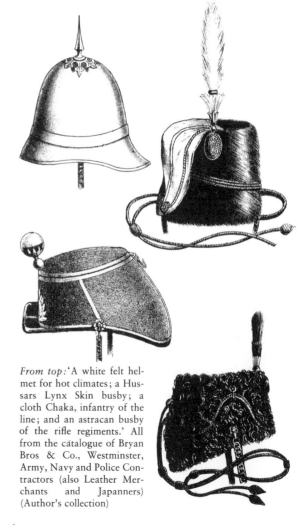

From top: 'A white felt helmet for hot climates; a Hussars Lynx Skin busby; a cloth Chaka, infantry of the line; and an astracan busby of the rifle regiments.' All from the catalogue of Bryan Bros & Co., Westminster, Army, Navy and Police Contractors (also Leather Merchants and Japanners) (Author's collection)

range. Head-dress of these types is best displayed on polystyrene wig stands to retain their shape.

Helmets as a head protection were revived as a result of the trench warfare of the First World War, when shrapnel and shell fragments became as much of a hazard as bullets. The Germans abandoned their spiked *pickelhaube* in 1916 for the *stahlhelm*, and various forms of steel helmet were produced by the British and French and adopted by their Allies. Distinctive national styles evolved in the 1930s and appeared in many subtle variations during the Second World War. Apart from technical differences, there is a multitude of decals, badges and painted patterns which make for a formidable array of collectable items. Beware of German helmets in fibre glass – 'reproduced' in recent years to supply the insatiable demands of the motion picture industry and subsequently leaked on to the collector market.

HOT WATER BOTTLES

There was roughly a hundred years' gap between the copper warming pan and the modern electric blanket and this was filled by the hot water bottle. During that period there were many different kinds, many of which are quite collectable. Stoneware bottles were produced by most potteries and were often decorated with their brand name and trademark, with coloured glazes ranging from deep brown to cream or white. Metal bottles were developed at the turn of the century and came in many different shapes. Some followed the traditional cylindrical pattern of the stoneware bottles, but others had dimpled sides, a triangular or conical section, or resembled flattened ovals and rectangles with rounded corners. Filler caps of brass and casing of copper make for an attractive contrast, especially when brightly burnished. From the beginning of this century date the flat-bottomed circular bed warmers in similar materials. In the 1920s heavy cast 'solar' ALUMINIUM was briefly in vogue but was largely superseded by moulded rubber hot water bags which have continued down to the present day.

A selection of hot water bottles, made of copper, tin, aluminium, stone and rubber (Army & Navy Stores Ltd)

ICE PICKS

Not at first glance the most promising subject – unless you count the macabre association with the notorious, such as the weapon used to assassinate Trotsky in Mexico in 1940; but there has been a surprisingly diverse range of such implements over the past two centuries, since ice was first marketed commercially. The simplest consist of steel spikes set in a wooden handle, but the United States was the home of various patent devices, such as the 'Reliance', with its spring-loaded sliding spindle, and a multiplicity of axes, chippers, chisels, shavers and awls, all designed for hacking blocks of ice into manageable chunks. There were even rotary ice-breakers, with vicious steel combs that reduced even the most obdurate block of ice to slush in no time at all. Though not prone to decorative features, ice-picks of the late nineteenth century may be found with animal masks and embossed motifs on the brass tang ends which secured the blade in its handle.

INDOOR GAMES

How did people while away their leisure time in the Dark Ages before the invention of television? When tasked with this question, my elders glower reprovingly and hint darkly of 'making their own amusements'. This, I am sure, covered a multitude of diversions, from PLAYING CARDS to PUZZLES, and included a wealth of indoor games which are of interest to the social historian and the collector alike. Apart from the games of chance discussed under GAMBLING EQUIPMENT there were numerous board games from the 1820s onwards, designed to impart knowledge and skill while combining the element of luck on the throw of

'British Sovereigns', a table game, by Wallis, 1837 (Christies, South Kensington)

a dice. Moneta, the ancestor of Monopoly, imparted commercial and financial skill, while Logos was a word game anticipating the modern Scrabble. There were military games, such as 'L'Attaque', 'Ship-Ahoy', 'Dover Patrol' and 'Tri-Tactics', often combining counters and dice with cards and a board. Then there were the board games for those with an addiction to the turf and the casino, such as 'Totopoly', 'Good Going' and 'Carlette'. Miscellaneous games in this genre included 'Buccaneer' with pirates and buried treasure to add excitement, 'Americana' and 'Wintersports' which enjoyed a brief popularity for a season or two in the pre-war period. There must have been literally thousands of board games in the past 150 years.

Games of skill included carpet bowls, 'Hocquette' (said to combine the thrills of ice hockey with that of croquet!), magnetic fishponds (an old-established favourite), table skittles, pin-ball and its numerous variants, and bagatelle. It is surprising how much variety there is to be found in such traditional stalwarts as darts and shove ha'penny. Early

The first game that George S. Parker, founder of Parker Brothers, invented and published in 1883 (Parker Brothers, Massachusetts)

specimens of the latter, for example, were of engraved slate with an ornate brass band and played with brass counters rather than real coins. Then there are the more sedate amusements, such as Snakes and Ladders, Ludo and Tiddleywinks, all of which have been going strong now for more than a century and provide many interesting variants, especially in the gaudily chromolithographed boards of the late Victorian period.

INK BOTTLES

The bewildering variety of shapes used for ink bottles has one common factor – invulnerability to accidental spillage. This explains the characteristic squat, dumpy appearance of ink bottles and their broad, solid bases. Apart from these criteria, however, the limits of human ingenuity have been stretched in producing circular, conical, rectangular and polygonal bottles, in coloured glass, with ribbed or fluted surfaces. There are boat shapes, dimpled ovals, and patent bottles with names such as Easifil, Tip-fill and Last-Drop designed for the loading of FOUNTAIN PENS without wasting a single drop. Other unusual features include grooves which could be used as penrests, and novelty shapes, such as tents, cottages, igloos, tea kettles, spinning tops and bird-cages and – most desirable of all – bottles moulded in human or animal form. Though the more successful commercial brands came

Four glass ink bottles (Army & Navy Stores Ltd)

in a clear glass bottle, collectors prefer bottles in shades of green, blue or brown – the darker the better.

Ink bottles were also made in stoneware and range from the tall cylindrical variety to the tiny drum-shaped or conical bottles. Stoneware bottles range in capacity up to two pints (about a litre) intended for the bulk supply of offices, and examples of this kind were in use until relatively recently.

INKSTANDS

If ink bottles can be regarded merely as a form of packaging, inkstands represent the more artistic receptacle for that liquid writing material now almost entirely superseded by the ballpoint pen. At one end of the spectrum are the modest pots and stands designed for the schoolroom and office, and manufactured in pottery, porcelain, pewter or brass, occasionally with liners of earthenware or glass, and sometimes fitted with circular slots for resting QUILLS and pens. Interest is added, however, if they bear the name or identifiable initials of school boards, government departments and similar institutions and their value is greatly enhanced by the inclusion of a date.

Among the more functional varieties were the Improved Non-spill Inkstand patented in the Twenties and made in Marbelite and other proto-plastic materials. Its screw-off top held the pen rests while the concave base allowed ink to be used to the last drop. Double inkstands for office use had a pen tray with containers for blue and red ink at either end, and may be found in silver, electroplate, glass or BAKELITE. The more elaborate stands were produced in the finest cut crystal, with silver or silver-gilt caps and mounts, and strawberry, hobnail or star-cut bases. In the Twenties there was a fashion for chromium inkstands mounted on a black glass base. More traditional stands were manufactured in pottery and porcelain and Wedgwood even produced

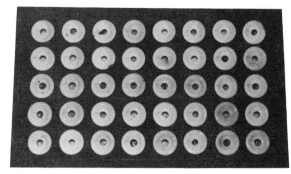

A school ink monitor's tray (Stanley Shoop)

inkstands in their famous blue and white jasperware.

In an era when wildlife conservation was unheard of, hunting trophies were often converted into useful articles, and inkstands come high on the list. While the head of the unfortunate beast gazed back at you from its wall mounting, its hoofs, tastefully decorated with mounts of silver or polished brass, made a capital inkstand for your desk. Digressing slightly, I have seen similar confections as match stands, letter balances, candlesticks, table CIGARETTE LIGHTERS, trinket boxes, snuff mulls and door porters. The feet of the larger animals, such as rhinoceros and elephant, were often used as UMBRELLA STANDS but they have also been noted in the form of tobacco jars and liqueur stands. Other bizarre uses to which all creatures great and small have been put will be found under STUFFED ANIMALS AND BIRDS.

A black basalt Egyptian style inkstand, c.1815 (Wedgwood Museum)

IRON STANDS

Before the advent of the electric smoothing iron, with its ability to stand vertically when not in use, it was necessary to use a small stand, like a trivet, to prevent the iron scorching the surface of the ironing board or table. Steel plates, roughly the same shape as the iron, were equipped with spring-clips and acted as protective shoes into which the iron could be placed. The majority of these devices belong to the present century, though the original patent was taken out as long ago as 1806, and early nineteenth-century examples in polished brass are much sought after.

The vast majority of iron stands – and there are literally thousands of different patterns – were made of brass, with a handle of the same material or sometimes in turned wood, and three short feet on the underside. The earliest examples were hand-worked from sheet brass and are relatively plain, such ornament, apart from simple chasing and piercing with hearts and diamonds, being mostly confined to the handles. By the early nineteenth century, however, iron stands were being commercially produced and more intricate patterns were cut or stamped in brass sheet. Cast brass was increasingly popular and it was then that the iron stand became a highly decorative article, with all kinds of pictorial ornament. There were even commemorative iron stands, with the portraits of Queen Victoria and King Edward VII, celebrating their diamond jubilee and coronation, in 1897 and 1902 respectively.

A 19th-century brass iron stand, and an 18th-century brass box iron and its stand (Lyle Publications)

Though heart and spade shapes were the commonest, many were produced in the form of horse-shoes or crescents. Elongated stands in cast iron and other alloys, with floral decoration, were produced to accommodate the patent spirit flatirons of the late nineteenth century. Highly prized are the stands with patriotic motifs, incorporating military badges, trophies of arms and national emblems, most of which date from the First World War, though one of the gems from the turn of the century depicts 'A Gentleman in Khaki', from the well-known bronze figurine of a British Tommy of the Boer War. The symbolism on iron stands includes LOVE TOKENS, often with naïve hand-wrought inscriptions of affection, and the emblems of FREEMASONRY. Many of the more modern examples, in wrought or cast iron, bear the trademark and brand name of famous hardware manufacturers or multiple stores.

JELLY MOULDS

Jelly and other gelatinous puddings have been on the menu for well over two centuries and the moulds associated with these confections have usually been in unusual shapes, designed to make the pudding more attractive to the children for whom they were mainly intended. Jelly moulds of tinned copper date from the early eighteenth century and were relatively plain, slightly conical vessels at first. It was the custom to serve jellies in individual moulds and these are best collected in matched sets, preferably with the original wooden stands. The shape of copper moulds became much more varied at the beginning of the nineteenth century and this custom has continued down to the present day, with pyramids, towers, geometric patterns, birds, flowers, animals, fishes and human figures of all kinds. Many of those sold today, I suspect, are never used for jellies but make ideal wall decoration for kitchens. The more serviceable moulds were made from about 1850 of tinplate, electroplate, and later nickel-plate, enamelled iron and even ALUMINIUM but are less attractive to the collector than the brightly burnished copper ones.

Moulds were also produced in many different kinds of pottery, from stoneware and

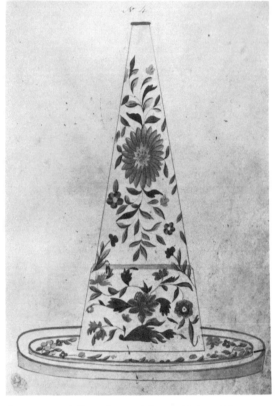

An ornamental Queen's ware jelly mould, late 18th century (Wedgwood Museum)

Left: A selection of moulds for jellies and entrées showing the various shapes, mostly in tin and copper (Army & Navy Stores Ltd)

ironstone, to Queen's ware, creamware, pearl-ware and transfer-printed earthenware. The more delicate examples may even be found in bone china. Brown saltglazed stonewate moulds were produced in the shape of farm-yard animals, appropriate to the cottage kitchens they equipped. Glass moulds range from simple geometric cones, pyramids and fluted domes to all the fancy shapes of animals

and birds. Britannia metal enjoyed a measure of popularity for jelly moulds in the late nine-teenth century. Pewter moulds were produced for butter and ice-cream and should never be used for jelly because of the poisonous proper-ties of the lead constituent. Metal moulds in the shape of tongues, chicken, lobster, cutlets and fishes are not jelly moulds at all, but were intended for the serving of jellied meats.

JETONS AND COUNTERS

These are usually associated with GAMBLING EQUIPMENT, but are, in fact, derived from the medieval forms of accountancy using a chequerboard. Sums were computed on these boards using metal discs in lieu of real coins. The special counters known as jetons (from the French word *jeter*, to throw) were a speciality of the metalsmiths of Nuremberg. The earlier examples, portraying the kings and queens, dukes and princes of Europe, are now becoming elusive and expensive, but examples of counters from the eighteenth century on-wards are still plentiful and an interesting collection can be formed at no great cost. Individual counters, in copper, bronze, brass, white metal and pewter, may often be picked up among the miscellaneous bric-à-brac on junk stalls. Unlike coins and tokens, they are often uniface. Among the notorious excep-tions are the brass imitations of Georgian

Two typical modern counters

spade guineas, but the substitution of 'In Memory of the Good Old Days' in place of the usual coin legend should not confuse even the newest recruit to coin-collecting. More modern counters bearing the names of gambling casinos, pictorial motifs and advertisements are worth looking for.

JUICE EXTRACTORS

The earliest squeezers and fruit presses were entirely wooden in construction and are among the more interesting and technically complex forms of TREEN. The fruit was fed into a hopper and the juice extracted by a variety of lever or screw devices. Presses of cast iron had wooden squeezers and glass-lined containers for the pulped fruit and the juice extracted from it, since the acid in the juice would have quickly corroded the metal.

The lemon squeezers used in the nineteenth century were fluted cones of polished hard-wood, often fitting into high-domed recep-tacles of the same material and the more elaborate varieties had a screw attachment. Squeezers of ironstone, stoneware and por-celain date from the second half of the nine-teenth century and pressed or moulded glass squeezers from the turn of the century.

JUKE BOXES

Etymologists have traced the origin of this word from *juke* meaning disorderly, in the dialect of the Gullah Negroes inhabiting the offshore islands of Florida and Georgia, and link it with *dzugu*, meaning wicked, in the Bambara language of West Africa. Just how this word came to be attached to the coin-operated purveyors of mechanical music in the late nineteenth century I cannot ascertain. The term is certainly much older than most people would have thought. Coin-operated machines were in existence long before Edison patented the PHONOGRAPH and range from the serinette, chamber barrel organ, stringed musical clock and reed organette of the mid-nineteenth century to the mechanical pianos of the 1890s known in England as pub pianos and in America as pennyanos.

Disc musical boxes were developed between 1882 and 1914. The first patent was taken out by Miguel Boom of Port au Prince in 1882 and the disc box or polyphon must be the only contribution of Haiti to modern technology. Actually the name by which these contrivances are now known was in fact the trade name of one particular type, the Polyphon produced by Gustave Brachhausen from 1890 onwards. Other famous makes at the turn of the century include Symphonion and Regina. The nickelodeons of the cafes and beerhalls in the early years of this century included disc orchestrions, the multiple-disc Eroica, the Sirion double-tune box, the Gambrinus or King of Beer and the Rococo, both by Symphonion, and the Desk and Drum Table Model by Regina. The latter company also produced the Disc Machine Gramophone, an early (and exceedingly rare) attempt to combined the steel discs of the musical box with the grooved records of the gramophone. Improvements in record-players in the Twenties, however, led to the decline of the disc boxes and the ultimate supremacy of the juke box in its modern form. From the outset the casing of these machines was a characteristically extravagant feature, resplendent with chrome plating and jazzy enamelling in the true spirit of Art Deco. The

A Chantal Meteor 200 jukebox (Christies, South Kensington)

more recent machines tend to have a rather more sober design, but they are today the last bastion of Art Deco at its most vulgar. In their heyday in the 1940s, however, juke boxes often plumbed the depths of KITSCH. With the passage of time they have acquired respectability and it is not so long ago that a Chantal Meteor 200 of the immediate postwar era came under the hammer in the august salerooms of Christie's.

KEYS

In cleidology and cleidophily we have the latest recruits to the growing army of pseudo-scientific terms, coined from classical Greek to denote the new collecting hobbies. They indicate respectively the study of and the love (or collecting) of keys. Since the Greeks had a word for it, we must assume that they have been around for a very long time, though the *kleis* referred to by Aeschylus was some kind of hook or catch securing or releasing the door-bolt rather than a key as we understand the term. The Egyptians had massive wooden keys many centuries before Christ, and the Romans had elaborate bronze and iron keys. One of the problems facing the collector is the fact that many patterns have been in continuous use for several centuries and it is possible to purchase keys in France, Italy and Germany today which are almost identical to keys used in Renaissance times. Age alone, therefore, is not much of a guide, unless a key has a well-established pedigree or provenance. The European key market was dominated by the French whose finely chiselled steel keys, with their elaborately fretted tops and intricate wards (the part which activates the lock), have never been surpassed. German keys tended to be heavier, with a ponderous repetition of the ward pattern. The shafts of keys vary enormously in length and shape, from a plain rod to fluted and spiral patterns. The most artistic keys belong to the eighteenth century, and were frequently topped by tiny cast figures and other ornaments. The most desirable examples have wrought monograms and crowns on the ends and from their having been produced in silver or silver-gilt it seems that they were more in the nature of badges of authority than meant for actual use. Finely turned baluster stems and elaborate bowed ends were fashions which carried forward into the nineteenth century. There were many technical improvements such as the Bramah key patented in 1784 and the mortice bolt with

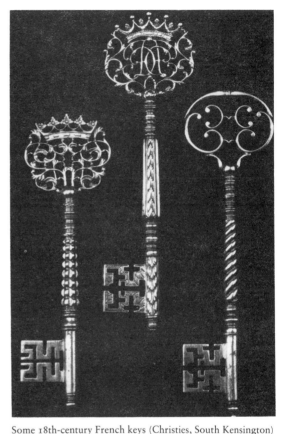

Some 18th-century French keys (Christies, South Kensington)

its grooved stem. Spade-shaped latch-keys were invented by Odell in 1792 and the lift-up key with its pivoted ward appeared a few years later. The quest for security led to the distinctive key patented by Linus Yale in 1844 and subsequently modified and improved right down to the present time. The flattened surface of these keys has permitted a considerable amount of decoration and inscription over the years.

Keys come in all shapes and sizes, from the massive door-keys of the eighteenth and nineteenth centuries, to the diminutive cupboard and box keys. The keys designed for winding up clocks and watches are yet another distinctive type, with countless variations in their composition and decoration.

KITSCH

This German word meaning tawdry has come into vogue in recent years to describe the more tasteless and vulgar offerings of the Twenties and Thirties, but it can be expanded to include any bric-à-brac of any period in poor taste or lacking a fine aesthetic sensibility. What exactly constitutes kitsch will, naturally, vary from person to person. I would place in this category those bronze and ivory figurines of girls in erotic situations, so fashionable in the earlier part of this century, but now that the prices for good examples by Preiss, Chiparus and Zach have soared past the four-figure mark I shall have to revise my ideas as to what constitutes good art. These chryselephantine figures (to give them their posh name) were extensively imitated in other materials, from ALUMINIUM and BAKELITE to chrome-plate and chalkware with gaudy enamelling or cheap glazes in primary colours, and these figures, which unconsciously parodied the idiom, most certainly would be considered kitsch today.

Then there are all the rather jokey items of the Twenties, from table CIGARETTE LIGHTERS disguised as Negro cocktail barmen to risqué ASHTRAYS and many of the novelty shapes used for cocktail decanters, beer-mugs, LAMP-SHADES, CAR MASCOTS and BOOK-ENDS. But remember, that what seems hideous today may become highly desirable tomorrow, and

An art nouveau bronze and ivory dancer supporting a clock.

the astute collector is the one who is probably examining the current range of cheap holiday knick-knacks and seaside souvenirs and assessing which of them will win an honourable place among the kitsch of the future.

KNIVES

So much has already been written on the subject of knives that I would like to concentrate here on some aspects of them which have been previously neglected and which therefore offer some chance for the newer collector. For this reason I shall ignore the entire gamut of flat-ware (or table cutlery to the layman) and the smaller edged weapons, such as daggers and dirks. This leaves a couple of very attractive groups associated with the writing desk. Paper knives first evolved in the seventeenth century when it was no longer the done thing for gentlemen to carry daggers around with them. The earliest knives resembled miniature daggers, and this is a form which continues to the present time. The paper knives of the eighteenth and early nineteenth centuries had very slim blades with a delicate point, indispensible for the slitting open of letters with the minimum of damage to the wax seals, in an era before envelopes were widely used. Later knives had broader and shorter blades and decoration of both blades and handles became much more extravagant. Paper knives from the second half of the nineteenth century were produced in polished hardwood, ivory, tortoiseshell, horn, bone and silver, and the lower end of the market was supplied by a wide range of die-struck metal knives in bronze, pewter and electroplate. Semi-precious stones, paste jewels and mother of pearl were extensively used as decoration. Apart from slitting open envelopes these knives were used to slit the uncut sheets of books which were often bound with the folds untrimmed.

Penknives originated in the scriveners' knives of the sixteenth century, with their delicately tapered handles and fixed blades. Considerable skill was needed to cut a QUILL PEN and as this was the only method of writing until the advent of the steel PEN NIB in the middle of the nineteenth century, penknives were a necessary adjunct to every writing desk. Joseph Bramah, better known for his KEYS, invented a pen machine which was a very elaborate form of penknife with a metal template for the quill which was cut to the required shape by depressing a lever and operating the blade. Pen machines were fashionable in the second quarter of the nineteenth century, and may be found with wood, bone or ivory shafts and brass or steel templates. Desk knives with fixed blades were often ornamented with carved wood or ivory handles, mother of pearl, agate, malachite, transfer-printed porcelain or enamelling. Spring-action folding penknives date from the late eighteenth century and emanated from France, though eventually their manufacture was worldwide. The French, however, produced the best folding knives with fancy or novelty shapes – fishes, birds, ladies legs, violins and banjos are among the more popular – and also went in for multi-bladed knives. Folding knives with

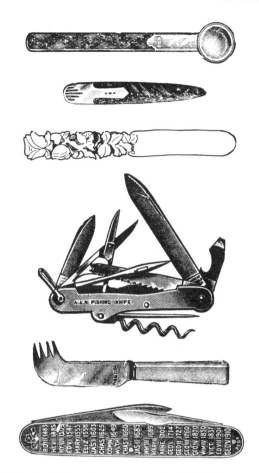

A selection of knives. *From top*: a tortoiseshell and silver paper knife with reading glass; a paper knife and book marker combined (Army & Navy Stores Ltd); an ivory Victorian paper knife (Lyle Publications); an Army & Navy Special Fishing Knife with every possible attachment for the angler; a combined knife and fork; and a Historical Knife showing the dates of the Kings and Queens of England (Army & Navy Stores Ltd)

casing of brass, white metal, pewter or bronze were die-stamped with portraits and motifs commemorating every celebrity and event worthy of note up to the First World War. In more recent years transfer-printed decoration has been applied to penknives used as tourist souvenirs.

L

LABELS

Some twenty years ago, while walking on a lonely Hebridean beach, I found what appeared to be an unopened bottle of beer, with its crown cork still intact. On opening it, however, I found no liquid contents, but a parchment certificate from King Neptune permitting the House of Guinness to cast these bottles on the sea in commemoration of their bicentenary, and a specimen bottle label with a bicentenary overprint. 'This is to acquaint you with the science of labology' stated the parchment, but this term, dreamed up by a Guinness copywriter, has not appeared in any dictionary so we are stuck for the moment with the longer if more explicit term of label-collecting.

Labelling is the oldest aspect of PACKAGING and dates from the late seventeenth century when printed labels were affixed to MEDICINE BOTTLES AND BOXES and PILL-BOXES. The typography of these early labels often matched the extravagant claims made by the promoters of these quack medicines and even when patent medicines became respectable and subject to drug legislation and other controls, the styling of labels continued to be quite florid. As brand names and trademarks developed in other fields of consumer goods in the mid nineteenth century, labelling became more widespread. As mass-production techniques hit the bottling and canning industries, labels were applied to all manner of goods, from beers, wines and spirits to foodstuffs, stationery and household commodities. Only tobacco, cigarettes and confectionery resisted this trend, their containers generally contin-

Heinz ketchup labels over the years 1880–1910 (H.J. Heinz Co. Ltd)

1880–1905   1889–1894   1887–1895   1889–1910   1906–1910

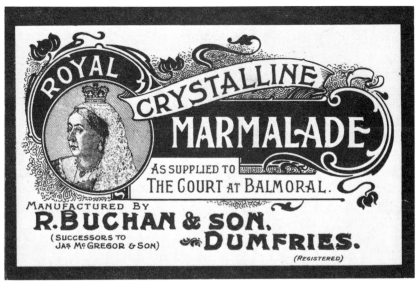

Above: An H.B. Foster's label, a beer company now defunct (Young & Co.). *Right:* A proof of a label for a pot of marmalade as supplied to the Court at Balmoral (Author's collection)

uing to have printing applied direct. Conversely cigar labels, both for the individual cigar bands and also for the boxes, constitute one of the most popular aspects of labelling, with their attractive vignettes and profuse colours. Labels from bottles, particularly beers, wines and soft drinks, are the most widely collected, though modern tendencies towards the use of rubber fixatives have made it difficult to acquire specimens in undamaged condition.

Labels denoting the prepayment of a charge date from the 1690s and range from the revenue tax labels applied to all manner of goods that have been taxed at some time or another (gloves, dice, hats, tobacco, patent medicines and PLAYING CARDS) to the luggage and parcel labels of the present time. Postage stamps – now the largest collecting hobby of them all – are basically a form of label, while phillumeny is the name given to another specialized form of collecting covering all aspects of matchbox labels. Other kinds which have their ardent devotees include the circular labels from cottonreels, car stickers, airmail labels (known as etiquettes) and commemorative labels (erinnophily).

LAMPSHADES

At one end of the spectrum we have those magnificent wistaria glass mosaic shades, resembling stained glass windows in miniature, which Louis C. Tiffany manufactured for the well-to-do at the turn of the century and which now fetch thousands in the salerooms. At the other end, however, there are the countless varieties of novelty shapes in plastic materials which can be picked up for a song at jumble sales. Many of the latter, of course, are pure KITSCH, but those designed for nursery lights are worth considering, particularly if they are decorated with characters from nursery rhymes and fairy tailes, or even

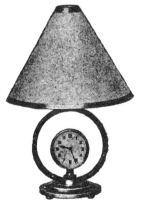

A lampshade of the 30's atop a combined clock and reading lamp (Army & Navy Stores Ltd)

motion pictures and cartoons of the Twenties and Thirties.

Apart from the very expensive glass mosaic shades which are now outside the reach of most collectors, there are numerous lampshades from the 1870s onwards that offer scope for collection. Moulded or pressed glass shades, with delicate frosting and colour blending are beginning to rise rapidly in price, especially if they can be attributed to one or other of the famous makers of fancy glass. Similarly, shades with porcelain panels known as lithophanes, which reveal motifs, like a watermark in paper, when illuminated, are decidedly scarce nowadays. This still leaves the enormous variety of shades in parchment, vellum, embossed leather, painted or enamelled glass and textile materials produced in the first half of this century. Bronze, white metal, nickel-plate and chromium-plated steel were widely used in the Art Deco period, when electric lighting was still considered something of a novelty, and these shades often adopted bizarre forms which are now much sought after.

A typical Tiffany lampshade and base (Sotheby & Co.)

LETTER RACKS

This form of desk equipment seems to date from the 1840s, when the change from letter sheets to envelopes revolutionized the filing system used in most households. Hitherto letters were opened out, folded vertically into three and then bundled together with pink ribbon. Most homes, in which the receipt of a letter was a rare event of some importance, kept letters in small racks, displayed proudly on mantelpieces for all to see, and thus the letter rack developed out of a handy receptacle into an ornament in its own right. Many different varieties were produced in cast or sheet brass, decorated with horseshoes, hearts or the stylized outlines of envelopes themselves and inscribed 'Letters' or its equivalent in other languages. Similar contrivances were produced in various kinds of pottery, moulded glass, pewter, papier-mâché, carved horn or ivory, and wood decorated with marquetry

inlay or chip-carving. Others were designed as wall ornaments, with an embossed leather backing and three or more pockets edged with brass ornament. A large brass ring was attached to the top for suspension from the wall.

A blotter and stationery rack covered in cretonne and a stationery rack available in oak or walnut (Army & Navy Stores Ltd)

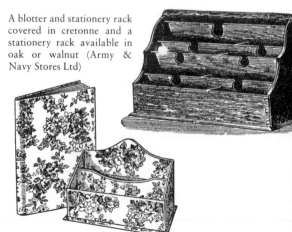

These homely letter racks were designed for the cottage mantel or inglenook. The letter racks intended for the roll-top bureau or escritoire farther up the social scale were of a much more impressive construction. The usual pattern was a cabinet of polished wood with a sloping top which opened to reveal several compartments, occasionally labelled as in a filing system. These racks were used both to file letters and to store writing materials. Stationery racks of this kind were sometimes covered with boulle ornament and, in silver, made a handsome presentation piece.

LOCKETS

This form of adornment probably originated in the seventeenth century out of the small padlocks used to secure the chain fastenings on cloaks and chatelaines, but soon developed into a form of jewelry in their own right. They have been made in all kinds of metal, from gold and silver to pinchbeck, electroplate, pewter, brass and copper, often decorated with filigree work, enamels and precious stones. Hearts are the most popular shape, though shields, ovals and elongated octagons are also plentiful. The locket was hinged and fitted with a clasp or catch. The inner sides were glazed and contained locks of hair or tiny portrait miniatures. From 1860 onwards photographs became the most popular form of portraiture.

LOCOMOTIVE MODELS

In every grown man is a small boy crying to get out – which explains the perennial popularity of toy trains ostensibly purchased by adults for their children but secretly intended for their own amusement. Many collectors of the present generation speak glibly of their deprived childhood during the Second World War when toys were hard to come by, but it seems to me that no excuse is needed. The paterfamilias of mid-Victorian times could unbend occasionally and play with his children's steam 'dribbler' without dredging up the privations of the Napoleonic Wars as an excuse.

Within a decade of the first passenger train model locomotives were being produced in

A No. 1 gauge 4-4-0 clockwork locomotive and tender painted in the Midland Railway colours (Christies, South Kensington)

A 3½ in (9 cm) gauge working steam model of a Duchess class locomotive and tender in maroon livery, and a working brass railway tank engine with steel wheels (Lyle Publications)

Birmingham. They were made of brass and ran on primitive steam engines fired by tiny spirit lamps and leaked all over the carpet like an untrained pup. Out of these mass-produced dribblers came the locomotive models designed on more scientific lines, with technical features such as slip eccentric valve gear or Stephenson's link motion. They were first copied, then greatly improved upon, by manufacturers in France and Germany and many of these were exported to the United States at the turn of the century. After the First World War they developed even further and became masterpieces of model engineering, reproducing in miniature the features of real locomotives. As such, they are among the more expensive of modern collectables and the larger salerooms now hold specialized auctions devoted to them.

The original dribblers, regarded purely as a toy, were superseded by the tinplate model powered by a clockwork motor. Many different kinds have been manufactured all over the world since 1900 and many of them can still be picked up quite cheaply. Electric motors were fitted to toy locomotives about 1910 but are rare before 1925. Examples after that date are reasonably plentiful at no great cost.

LOVE TOKENS

Under this heading come all the marks of affection that have been exchanged by lovers over the centuries. The commonest form is the Valentine card which has been in commercial production since the 1830s and is an important collectable in its own right, with a wealth of specialized literature devoted to it. Analogous to Valentines, however, are the handcrafted objects which were often given to wives and sweethearts on St Valentine's Day. The most desirable are the small boxes decorated with beads or shellwork, often in the form of a heart, containing personal inscriptions. Another popular pastime of young men in love was the defacement of coins by laboriously pin-pricking sentiments of love and affection on them. The large copper pennies were the most popular medium and the much more valuable silver coins were seldom treated in this fashion. Coins bearing names and dates, usually of betrothal or marriage, are highly prized. Carved wooden stay-busks and SCRIM-SHAW decoration on walrus tusks have long been collected, but the intricately carved wooden spoons, which were a speciality of the

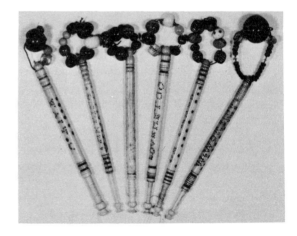

Descriptions on these lace bobbins read 'Love Me', and 'Love Buy the Ring' (Christies, South Kensington)

Welsh, are being produced to this day. I suspect that many of the more modern examples have been designed for the tourist rather than the girl-friend, but they are most attractive none the less. Carved or painted wooden spoons have also been produced as love tokens in many other parts of Europe, from Scandinavia to the Balkans.

MAGIC LANTERNS AND PROJECTORS

The optical principles behind the magic lantern were propounded by Friar Roger Bacon in the thirteenth century but the invention of a projector capable of throwing an image on to a wall is credited to Athanasius Kircher in the mid seventeenth century. As its name implies, the magic lantern was used mainly by charlatans to trick the unsophisticated and the simpleminded into believing that they could conjure up ghosts and spirits at will. It was not until the development of photography in the second half of the nineteenth century that magic lanterns were taken seriously and their educational and entertainment value appreciated. The earliest commercially produced lanterns consisted of a japanned canister, not unlike the watering cans of the period, with a large curved handle at the rear and a tapered protuberance at the front. The can contained a candle or lamp and was surmounted by a chimney to carry off the smoke. Lenses were fitted at the junction of the 'spout' and the can and also near the front of the spout – the condenser and projecting lenses respectively. A later development was the Sciopticon which could be fitted to an Argand fountain OIL LAMP and gave a much more steady projection. Some Sciopticons at the turn of the century contained a specially constructed paraffin lamp with three parallel wicks set edgeways to the condenser. Other variants patented between 1880 and 1910 include the oxy-calcium lantern, the oxy-hydrogen lamp, the clockwork-driven magnesium lantern and the heliostatic lantern which utilized sunlight.

For the more technically inclined there was a vast range of lanterns which could produce special effects. Some were fitted with lever slides, by means of which motion pictures could be simulated, the movement being achieved by a primitive jerking device. The Chromatrope used circular discs of contrasting colours, contra-rotated by means of a handle to produce a dazzling colour effect. Dissolving views were produced by a duplex lantern with twin projectors, patented by

A child's magic lantern with circular and rectangular slides (Christies, South Kensington)

Childe in 1811, while the Phantasmagoria was a lantern mounted on wheels so that it moved rapidly back and forward and the image made to grow or diminish in size and intensity. The Lantern Polariscope produced a dazzling kaleidoscopic effect, using selenite or some other doubly refracting crystal and a Nicol's prism. The glass slides themselves, ranging from the tiny multiple strips of four or five images, to the large single pictures, up to five inches square, are also becoming collectable.

MAPS

Cartography is a vast subject with a long tradition of antiquarian interest and early manuscript and printed maps are among the more expensive collectables. Moreover, there is a considerable volume of literature devoted to maps and map-collecting, and several specialist dealers of international repute in Britain, America and Europe. So what does this leave for the collector seeking something off the beaten track? Map-collectors have tended in the past to limit their interests to hand-coloured maps, printed from copper or steel engraved plates. Maps produced by lithography or letterpress have been largely ignored, and as these are the methods by which most of the maps published in the past 130 years were printed there is enormous scope for the beginner working on a modest budget. My own predilection is for early editions of the various Ordnance Survey maps and over the years I have picked up a large number, dating from the 1850s, for next to nothing. They may not be as decorative as the county maps of the seventeenth and eighteenth centuries but they contain a wealth of information which enables the local historian to trace the growth of his particular locality.

There are different types of map which will appeal to collectors whose principal interest

A map sampler of the Mediterranean by Elizabeth Warren, 1804 (Christies, South Kensington)

lies in other areas. Thus collectors of MILITARIA will want campaign maps, battle plans and even those location maps printed on silk for the use of airmen in case they had to bale out over enemy lines. Maps showing the circulation of letters are of consuming interest to postal historians and philatelists, while railway maps are among the most sought after of RAIL RELICS. Brightly coloured maps were a popular subject for early PICTURE POSTCARDS in many parts of the world. There are even locational maps and street plans printed on TRADE CARDS and ADVERTISEMENTS, tourist publicity broadsheets, posters and other ephemera.

MARBLES

Although marbles made of glass are known to have been produced in Venice as long ago as the fourteenth century, they seem to have attained the height of their propurality in the second half of the last century and to this period, from 1860 to 1890, belong some of the finest examples ever made. Marbles have been made of many materials but never, so far as I can ascertain, from the rock from which they derive their name. The Venetians were adept at making beautiful marbles from solid glass rods containing spirals of coloured or opaque glass. Small pieces were broken off, mixed with sand and charcoal in an iron container and then rotated in a furnace at high temperatures to produce complete round globules. After cooling they were cleaned and polished. In the nineteenth century marbles of glass were blown, moulded or pressed and range from tiny balls about a centimetre in diameter, to giants up to two inches across. Dutch (or Deutsch) stonies were a speciality of the Coburg stone quarries. Marbles were also made in various ceramic materials, ranging from the distinctive Chinamen with their black and white horizontal bands, to the plain taws of cream-coloured stoneware. Blood alleys were a form of taw with red streaks. Steel balls from Pennsylvania and Connecticut enjoyed a measure of popularity at the turn of the century, but lack the variety and interest of the glass and ceramic marbles.

MARROW SCOOPS ETC.

I don't know why marrow scoops are singled out by writers on silver and Sheffield plate, unless it is because they conjure up a picture of a vanished era of polished era of leisurely meals with ten or a dozen courses and between the serving of the entrees and the puddings you whiled away the time by extracting the marrow from the discarded bones. Certainly the tool provided for this purpose is the nearest thing to a surgical instrument ever to grace a dining table. Most marrow scoops are double-ended with a baluster handle in the centre and scoops of differing diameters at either end. They were produced in silver, silver-gilt, Sheffield plate and electroplate and such decorative touches as they possessed were confined to the central stem.

Infinitely more interesting to my way of thinking, however, are all those other fiddly bits and pieces which never rate a mention, but which every well-appointed household required to maintain its well-appointed status. There were ice tongs and hammers in silver or electroplate, with vicious claws and spikes, or a more natural effect achieved by using finials of birds' feet or clam-shells. Meat skewers had spindly shanks or double-edged blades, with a ring at the end. Cheese scoops may be found with handles of polished wood, ivory or mother of pearl and the scoops may be completely circular in section, more generally semi-circular, or even like a very shallow trowel in miniature. Chutney scoops resemble

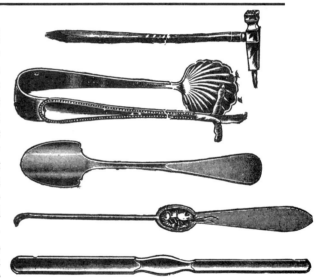

From top: an ice hammer, ice tongs, a cheese scoop, a lobster pick and a marrow scoop (Army & Navy Stores Ltd)

tiny ladles with a relatively long stem and a spatulate handle. The stems were frequently twisted, wrought or decorated with tiny ornament, sometimes produced with matching pickle forks which had barbed trident tines. The ultimate *sine qua non* in the scoop family was the lobster pick. Like the marrow scoop, this was a double-ended weapon, with a wicked looking curved probe at one end and a broad, slightly concave blade at the other. The centre portion was usually round or oval and a common form of decoration was a cast or die-stamped outline of lobsters and crayfish. TONGS are a diverse category which merit their own separate treatment.

MATCHBOXES

John Walker of Stockton-on-Tees knew a snappy title when he saw one, which is why he called his invention 'sulphurata hyperoxygenata'. Even the Greeks, whose language he so flagrantly exploited, prefer the word 'spirto' which almost conveys the sound of a match being struck. Walker's first friction matches consisted of slivers of wood three inches in length, tipped with a witches' brew of antimony sulphide, potassium chlorate, gum arabic and starch. Ignition was effected by drawing the match swiftly between folded emery paper and this produced a shower of sparks and the release of gas of such toxicity that every box was made to carry a Government health warning! Things have improved immeasurably since 1827. Once phosphorus was substituted for antimony sulphide matches became both safer and less of a health risk and their popularity then grew enormously. They became smaller and were sold in small tins or cylinders containing about half a dozen matches. It was not long before silversmiths were producing more elegant containers and these elegant objects of vertu were fashionable from about 1840 till the First World War. The finest examples were made of gold, silver-gilt or silver, decorated with enamels and precious stones. Further down the scale they were made in pinchbeck, Sheffield plate and electroplate, and towards the end of the century in nickel-plate, brass and other alloys.

The basic shape was that of a small book whose binding opened to reveal the matches. A serrated 'fore-edge' provided the striker for ignition, while the spine and covers were lavishly decorated in the manner of contemporary bookbinding. Some boxes even had tiny compartments inside the back cover for postage stamps. Other boxes may be found in shagreen, leather, polished wood, horn, ivory or porcelain. There was also a brief fashion in the early 1900s for novelty shapes, discussed in greater detail under VESTA BOXES.

The next stages in the development of the matchbox was the invention of the safety match by J. E. Lundstrom of Sweden in 1855.

A selection of match containers and matchbox cases in a variety of materials and shapes from the Army & Navy Catalogue of 1939–40.

Safety matches did not become widespread till the 1880s and to this period belong the earliest examples of the silver cases with an aperture down one side to expose the patent striking surface of the matchbox. Like many other small bibelots, silver matchboxes disappeared during the First World War, though they have, from time to time, been revived as novelties and souvenirs in unusual shapes. With the rise in the popularity of MATCH BOOKLETS, special match covers were designed in the Twenties and Thirties and these, like the earlier matchboxes, may also be found in precious metals and enamels.

MATCH BOOKLETS

Philadelphia lawyers have acquired an international reputation for shrewdness and an ability to exploit the finer points of legal technicalities, but it was one of their number, Joseph Pusey who, in 1892, added another dimension to their ingenuity by inventing the match booklet. Paper book matches to give them their proper title were designed from the very outset as an advertising medium and in the land of their birth they are given away by the million every day of the week. The advertising matter on the cover and inside the flap covers the cost of production. They were slow to catch on at first, but by 1920 they were well established on both sides of the Atlantic and have since spread into every corner of the globe. Outside the United States they are mainly confined to hotels, bars and restaurants, but have also been produced as fundraisers for charity, and have largely taken the place of the commemorative medal as a popular memento of events and personalities of passing importance.

A modern match booklet advertising a somewhat exclusive establishment in New Orleans.

MEAT CLEAVERS

Pre-packed and 'convenience' foods have done away with the need for a whole host of useful articles which are now enjoying a new lease of life as kitchen collectables. In particular, the preparation of meat yields a formidable array of choppers, mincers and cleavers, distinguished by their heavy broad blades. Quite a variety can be found, with different types of handle, or with decoration along the brass guard running along the top of the blade.

Meat jacks have long been collectable because of their gleaming brass cases and interesting clockwork mechanism. They were suspended from a hook over the open hearth and rotated slowly so that the joint of meat would roast evenly. They were the forerunner of the modern electric rôtisserie and survived in rural districts well into this century.

A meat chopper, a mincing knife, a mincer (for cutting parsley, mint, almonds etc) and a meat skewer (Army & Navy Stores Ltd)

Not at first glance a very promising subject, the meat skewer is today little more than a little spike of stainless steel. The dressing of meat and poultry, however, is an age-old practice and the skewers used over the past four centuries alone present quite a range of designs and materials, from silver and Sheffield plate to wrought iron, with straight, spiral or broad-bladed shanks. The ring at the end was frequently decorated. There were also special skewer holders, consisting of racks fitted with small brass hooks from which the skewers were suspended, or stands of polished wood or pottery into which the points of the skewers were inserted.

MEDICAL ANTIQUES

In an era before such blessings as a National Health Service or Medicare were conferred on civilization, medicine and even minor surgery was often of the do-it-yourself variety and most households possessed a medicine chest and a variety of surgical instruments and appliances. Judging by the ADVERTISEMENTS in newspapers a century ago, home medication was a booming industry and many were the weird and wonderful (though not always effective) gadgets foisted on the health-conscious Victorian public. Many of these contrivances might be purchased in the heat of the moment, tried once and then relegated to a cupboard – which explains why so many of these patent gadgets have survived in pristine condition.

From the enormous range of inhalers, pomanders, carbolic smoke balls and respirators one tends to form a picture of the Victorians being obsessed with their breathing, but we have to remember that tuberculosis (commonly called consumption) was a prevalent killer and the atmosphere often smoky and insanitary. Enemas, syringes and irrigators are another enormous category which reflect the Victorian pre-occupation with what they termed the 'lower bodily functions'. Glassware accounts for many of these medical antiques, from graduated measures, jugs and tumblers, dredgers and drying bottles to eye-glasses, eye droppers and eye baths, nasal irrigators, nose and throat atomizers and sprays. Even THERMOMETERS, for bath, food and·clinical purposes, may be found in a wide variety of sizes, shapes and gradations.

Then there are all the quasi-medical contraptions which utilized that wonder of the

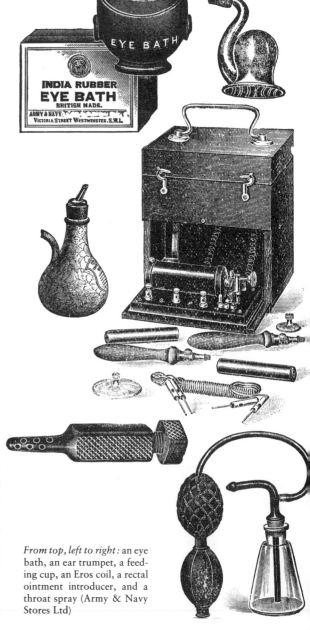

From top, left to right: an eye bath, an ear trumpet, a feeding cup, an Eros coil, a rectal ointment introducer, and a throat spray (Army & Navy Stores Ltd)

age – electricity. At one end of the spectrum there are the fairly harmless faradic coils which gave the victim a shock that was supposed to tone up the system, but at the other extreme were many devices, emitting currents or rays, which could be lethal in certain circumstances. Fortunately most of these devices were intended to work off the wet cell batteries of the period and the voltage was usually fairly low. The late-Victorian and Edwardian fascination for electricity (of which many people had heard but few had experienced at first-hand) inspired a host of pseudo-medical articles, from corsetry to socks and hairbrushes utilizing static atmospheric electricity for the benefit of the user.

MEDICINE BOTTLES AND BOXES

Allied to the gadgetry outlined in the previous entry were the myriad preparations and nostrums which, prior to the introduction of drug legislation in most countries at the beginning of this century, flourished like the green bay tree. Their uncertain efficacy in practice was more than amply balanced by the extravagant claims of their manufacturers. Many of these panaceas came into the category of all-purpose cures which could be taken externally or internally and would remedy most if not all the ailments which prey on man and beast.

Backing up the ADVERTISEMENTS for these medicines was the actual PACKAGING of the wares. No expense was spared in making the presentation as attractive as possible, and every technique from chromolithography to intaglio engraving was used in the design and printing of labels and wrappers. Apart from the labels, however, both bottles and pillboxes were often constructed on unusual lines.

Prescriptions would give much more pleasure if they were still given in envelopes like this (Author's collection)

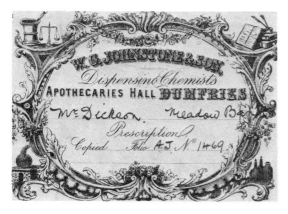

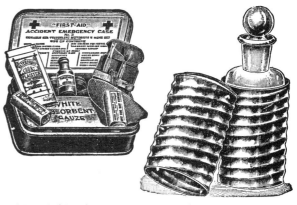

A First Aid Accident Emergency Case and stoppered bottles in spiral metal cases (Army & Navy Stores Ltd)

The bottles which contained patent medicines, embrocations, cough-cures, gripe water, balsams and bitters were usually in distinctive shapes and colours, dark green, blue and brown being popular. The trademark or name were often pressed into the sides and collectors prize such long-forgotten medicines as Dr Steer's Opodeldoc, Daffy's Elixir and Bronnington's Irish Moss. Warner's Safe Cures used bottles shaped appropriately like home safes, while Radam's Microbe Killer came in bottles impressed with a skeleton hitting a man over the head with a club. Poison bottles were invariably distinctive in shape and colour, triangles, hexagons and polygons distinguishing them from the usual cylindrical forms. Ribbing, fluting and moulded decoration showing a skull and crossbones also helped to make poison bottles more prominent. Hop bitters were usually sold in tall rectangular bottles, but one variety much sought after is Dr Soule's, which came in bottles shaped like tiny log cabins embossed with hops.

MENUS

How the French word 'minute' or 'detailed' passed into the English language to denote a list of the courses in a restaurant is curious. The custom of setting out the details of a meal began in France in the early years of the nineteenth century at a time when Napoleon's armies were sweeping victoriously across Europe. Cards setting out the bill of fare were embellished with patriotic motifs and tiny vignettes of battle scenes. The martial flavour swiftly disappeared after Waterloo but the habit of decorated cards lingered on and soon spread to other parts of Europe and eventually came to America in the 1830s. European menus up to the time of the First World War, however, continued to draw inspiration from topical events for their decoration and were often strongly political in their pictorial composition.

Elsewhere a more restrained form of ornament prevailed, a common device, then as now, being a picture of the hotel or restaurant as a heading. Menus have been lavishly produced on embossed card, and even printed on silk to honour banquets and other important occasions. As such they have often been retained as mementoes and have survived in appreciable numbers. Apart from the commemorative menus, there are numerous attractive examples produced by hotels and restaurants all over the world, by shipping lines, railway companies and airlines. I have a sneaking feeling that the more exotic menus in the latter category are deliberately designed to atone for the shortcomings of in-flight cuisine!

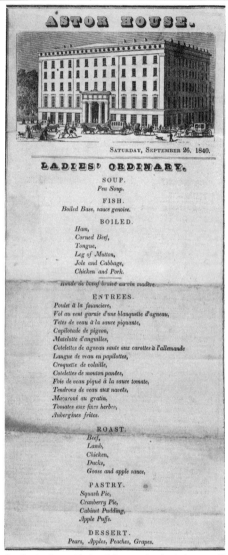

Not for the 'ordinary' lady of the 1970's who is forever dieting!
(Author's collection)

MENU HOLDERS

Nowadays menus are either free-standing or are held upright in insignificant plastic stands, but before the Second World War no self-respecting restaurant would have permitted anything other than a menu holder of silver-plate and the hostess worthy of her salt would have matching sets of menu and place-card holders in sterling silver to grace her dining table. I do not know whether they were ever produced in Sheffield plate; if any do exist they must be rare since this form of close-plating was being superseded by electroplating at a time when menu holders were coming into fashion. Holders in solid silver, electroplate and nickel plate became increasingly popular as the nineteenth century drew to its close and range from the plain circular stands to elaborate confections wreathed in the tendrils and lily pads which characterize Art Nouveau. Of particular interest to the collector of MILITARIA are the holders decorated with regimental insignia. Others may be found with die-struck or cast ornament showing animals and birds. They were often produced in sets with a common theme but varying subjects, such as different breeds of dogs or game birds, either with a solid or pierced backing. Less frequently menu holders were made of pottery, porcelain or glass.

Three different types of menu holder, in silver and glass, offered by the Army & Navy Stores in 1939–40

MICKEY MOUSE ITEMS

If we accept the rigid definition of an antique as anything a hundred years old, then Mickey Mouse, most famous of all cartoon characters, is merely halfway there, having made his squeaky debut in 1928. The celluloid antics of Mickey and Minnie Mouse soon eclipsed that earlier and rather lugubrious character, Felix the Cat, and captured the imagination of the world. Eternally dapper in his white gloves, he has masqueraded under many names in many languages but the image (like that of Charlie Chaplin) is universally recognized. Mickey Mouse has appeared on children's mugs and plates, as enamelled decoration on children's cutlery and even as a whistle built into the handle of children's toothbrushes. He has appeared in the form of figurines in all manner of materials, from porcelain to soap, he has decorated ASHTRAYS and COMPACTS and for many years his elegantly gloved hands have told the time on children's watches. The prototype GASMASKS designed for young children in the United States in 1940, when war seemed imminent, were intended to make the wearer look like Mickey Mouse and thus allay the child's fears. Though they never subsequently went into production the name was taken up by the British for the brightly coloured respirators

A toy lantern outfit made in England under licence, c.1937 (ⒸWalt Disney Productions)

issued to under-fives. Nowadays the term 'Mickey Mouse' has come to be synonymous with anything insignificant or lacking in importance, which conveys a totally wrong impression so far as Mickey Mouse collectables are concerned. Walt Disney Productions have always strictly controlled the licensing of the image to manufacturers and ensured that a high standard was maintained. Mickey and Minnie have even appeared on postage stamps, and their golden jubilee has been celebrated by medals, plaques and other commemorative wares.

Mickey and Minnie Mouse dolls made by Charlotte Clark, c.1930 (© Walt Disney Productions)

MICROSCOPES

The Roman philosopher and arbiter of elegance, Seneca observed the magnifying powers of a simple flask filled with water almost two thousand years ago but it was not until about 1660 that Antony Van Leeuwenhoek of Delft produced the first practical microscope. The earliest microscopes were usually of brass with fittings of hardwood and ivory. The compound microscopes had tubes of card covered with leather and these are exceedingly rare. They were succeeded about 1725 by an improved design known as the Culpeper type, distinguished by its tiny concave mounted on the base. Twenty years later John Cuff produced a microscope of brass in which the body tube and stage were overhung from a square brass column. Cuff microscopes were mounted in polished wooden cases with a drawer underneath for accessories. From then on brass became more common and the older leather-

A high-grade school apparatus offered by the Army & Navy Stores in 1939-40

covered card was phased out. Microscopes became more complex after 1800 and many technical refinements were introduced as the microscope gradually became the indispensible tool of the serious scientist and ceased to be merely an object of curiosity.

MILITARIA

This term has come to mean anything connected with military and para-military forces, police, fire brigades and security services and consequently the scope for the collector is almost limitless. Many collectors prefer to concentrate on every aspect of arms, equip-ment, insignia and ephemera associated with a single army or air force, or study the material connected with a single war or campaign. Others, however, study variations in one particular field, irrespective of the country of origin. Certain kinds of militaria which lend

A French printed handkerchief of 1893. 'Le Mouchoir d'instructions militaires' (Christies, South Kensington)

ards, cuff tiles, aiguillettes, lanyards, shoulder boards and sword knots, chevrons and rank badges. Increasing attention is also being paid to the non-personal items such as bayonets, inert grenades and mortars, trenching tools, range-finders, field TELEPHONES, wireless equipment, compasses and binoculars. One advantage which the militaria collector has over most other collectable fields is that the material he studies is invariably marked with dates, ordnance serial numbers, national emblems and even the names or initials of government contractors – all features which makes classification and identification much easier.

A levee sporran of the Queen's Own Cameron Highlanders (Christies, South Kensington)

themselves to the latter treatment, have a wide following and separate entries will be found in this book for BADGES, BELTS AND BELT-BUCKLES, GASMASKS, GORGETS, HELMETS AND HEADGEAR, MODEL SOLDIERS and UNIFORMS. Several other entries, from CHINA FAIRINGS and CIGARETTE CARDS to WHIPS and WHISTLES, can be found with a military connection.

This still leaves us with a pretty formidable field. Under the heading of miscellaneous equipment, for example, are all the accoutrements from the ceremonial sabretaches of the cavalry to the more prosaic pouches and cross-belts of leather or webbing used by modern armies. Among the minor accessories are regulation footwear and underwear, eating irons, mess tins, field dressings, identity discs, repair holdalls and cleaning equipment. Military ephemera includes pay books and training manuals, warrants, commissions, passes, invasion and occupation money and military payment vouchers. Insignia includes brass-

MINERS' LAMPS

Retrenchment and rationalization of the coal-mining industry in many countries in recent years has brought a great amount of collectable material on to the market. Miners' safety lamps are unusual in appearance and, with an abundance of copper and brass fittings, highly

attractive. Most of the features incorporated in miners' lamps were invented between 1815 when Sir Humphrey Davy patented his gauze cylinder lamp, and 1882 when the French scientist, J. B. Marsaut devised the gauze cap chimney. In between there are numerous variations, many of which survived in use till recently. These lamps have patent numbers, dates and makers' names inscribed, usually on brass plates, and it is not too difficult to assemble at least a representative collection of lamps with such names as the Improved Davy, the Clanny, the Muesler-Marsaut, the Gray, Elion and Boty. At the moment the strength of the market lies in the more recent (and more decorative) examples, though collectors with a more scientific turn of mind would profit from tracking down the more mundane but technically interesting lamps from the period 1860 to 1920.

MODEL SOLDIERS

Boys have played with toy soldiers for centuries and among the great strategists who were introduced to military science in this manner were Frederick the Great and Winston Churchill, both of whom had large collections of soldiers. *Kriegspiel* or wargaming is a worldwide hobby which had its scientific origins in the rules formulated by H. G. Wells and Jerome K. Jerome at the turn of the century and published by the former in his delightful book *Little Wars*.

The soldiers used in the time of Frederick the Great were *zinnsoldaten* – tin soldiers, essentially two-dimensional in appearance though often incredibly detailed and beautifully painted. These 'flats' were a speciality of the Nuremberg toymakers, though by the mid-nineteenth century the market was dominated by two companies, Hinrichsen and Heyde in Dresden. The French produced larger figures and the major manufacturers, Lucotte and Mignot, exported their wares to Britain and America. In the 1890s a British firm emerged and soon revolutionized the market. William Britain invented a form of hollow casting which gave his figures a rounder, three-dimensional appearance without increasing the cost of raw materials.

Britain gave his figures a much more life-like appearance and infinite variety by the adroit use of movable limbs. In the three decades up to 1914 his company produced regiments of soldiers for most of the armies of the world and was quick to add to the range whenever and wherever war broke out. Thus the Britain catalogue for 1913 includes models of Turkish, Italian, Serb and Bulgar troops and Mexican revolutionaries. Britain's soldiers swept the world in the interwar period and were produced in various grades and sizes. The most desirable are the compound sets, such as the balloon team, the pontoon bridge builders and the horse artillery gun crew.

Lead soldiers were gradually superseded by plastic figures in the 1950s but since then there have been many small companies specializing in the production of superbly hand-crafted metal figures. These are available already painted but the true *cognoscente* prefers to do this for himself, spending hours in producing a miniature work of art, correct in every detail.

MOTION PICTURE SOUVENIRS

Few collectors would go so far as to include examples of camera and projection equipment from the pioneer days of the film industry. Cumbersome contraptions with Greek names, like Edison's kinetescope, Latham's panoptikon and the eidoloscope, together with the early bioscopes, vitascopes and theatrographs with which the commercial cinema was launched, are probably all in museum collections by now.

This leaves a considerable amount of collectable material, most of which is more manageable anyway. ADVERTISEMENTS and POSTERS for early motion pictures have been reprinted in recent years but it should not be too difficult to distinguish these reprints from the much more desirable originals. Magazines for cinemagoers and movie buffs date from the Twenties and early examples are extremely rare, but there is plenty of material dating from the late Thirties. This was a period when the star system was in the ascendant and the great Hollywood studios expended vast sums on publicizing their actors and actresses. PICTURE POSTCARDS, signed photographs, books and brochures on individual stars and the major pictures abound. Later spin-offs of the silver screen include RECORDS of the theme music and excerpts from the soundtrack and these are keenly sought after, particularly when they relate to the careers of certain singing stars. Programmes from premieres, the

A cigarette card of Dick Powell from an album set called *Film Stars* issued by Players in the mid 30's (Ian Fleming)

special handbooks associated with the release of the great screen epics, and old annuals are among the more collectable motion picture items. A few stars have inspired a whole host of articles portraying them. Charlie Chaplin statuettes, Shirley Temple dolls and Jackie Coogan paint-boxes are much sought after, but whether the same interest will be shown in present-day toys based on the heroes of television and the cinema remains to be seen. The breaking up of many of the old Hollywood studios has brought a great deal of material on to the market. Props and costumes from the great historic, biblical or western dramas of yesteryear have come under the auctioneer's hammer of late and added a new dimension to movie memorabilia.

A film poster of Jayne Mansfield (Christies, South Kensington)

MOTORING EQUIPMENT

Since the internal combustion engine does not celebrate its centenary till 1985 none of the articles in this category can be classed as antiques in the strict sense. But motoring more than any other human occupation has always suffered from the malaise of built-in obsolescence, so that last year's model is *passé* and anything more than ten years old is positively outmoded. Ignoring the vehicles themselves, on the grounds of their size, we

are left with a considerable amount of collectable interest. CAR BADGES AND MASCOTS have already been discussed, but there is tremendous variety in the decorative radiator caps which were all the rage in the period from 1910 to 1940. Many of the examples produced in the Twenties and Thirties were minor works of art, ranging from the beautiful frosted glass figures by Lalique of France to the elegant ornaments cast in bronze, silver, brass and chromed iron by the foundries of Germany, Italy, Britain and the United States. Apart from these three-dimensional figurines and busts, there were plaques and bas-reliefs in bronze or chromium which were intended to be fitted over the radiator grilles.

The literature of motoring since the 1890s is vast and includes motoring manuals, touring guides and MAPS. The mass-production techniques pioneered by Henry Ford and later developed by Professor Porsche and Lord Nuffield, brought motoring within the reach of every class of society and this, in turn, inspired the wide range of popular motoring literature. Many of the motoring magazines of the 1930s are of considerable social historical interest today. Among the more ephemeral items are registration labels, licence plates, road fund licence discs, drivers' licences and log-books and even parking tickets. Fuel rationing in two World Wars and a host of minor crises has resulted in a wide variety of COUPONS from many countries. Car models have been produced as SCALE MODELS and tin toys, both of which have a steady following.

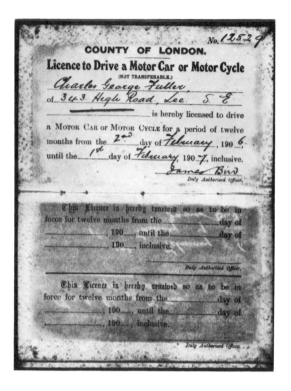

A 1906 driving licence (London Fire Brigade, Greater London Council)

MOURNING ITEMS

Vaccination, better housing and improved hygiene and nutrition have greatly lowered the mortality rate among the more civilized nations, so that death is not omnipresent as it was in the eighteenth and nineteenth centuries. The Victorians in particular seem to have been greatly pre-occupied with death and the hereafter, as witness the ostentatious appearance of their cemeteries. Death had an etiquette of its own, accompanied by the elaborate panoply of mourning cards and black-edged stationery. Black-edged quarto sheets with copperplate printed intimations of death and funerals were commonplace until the 1880s when they gave way to court-sized cards with tasteful symbols of death and mourning, embossed in white against a black background. This practice died out during the First World War when death became an all too familiar occurrence.

In Affectionate Remembrance of

SHADRACH GREGG,

Retired Iron Merchant,

Who died at Union Street, Wigton, on Saturday, January 14th, 1911,

Aged 72 Years.

———

To be Interred at Wigton Cemetery, on Wednesday, January 18th, at 2 o'clock, leaving residence at 1-30 p.m.

A mourning sheet, edged in black (Author's collection)

A beautifully printed black, grey and silver mourning card (Author's collection)

The etiquette of mourning also involved special articles of clothing, from crepe bands on headgear to the fashion for jet jewelry. Brooches and pendants containing locks of hair from the dear departed were also much in favour, and even HAIR JEWELRY itself, plaited from the tresses of the deceased. In more recent years mourning for national and international celebrities has assumed a more commercial aspect, with memorial items ranging from stamps and coins to medals, RACK PLATES, figurines and pendants.

MUSICAL INSTRUMENTS

It is with some trepidation that I even mention this subject, such is its tremendous scope, but if we stick to the modestly priced and relatively neglected aspects that will narrow it down considerably. The collector of humble means could not hope to aspire to the great names among violins, such as Stradivarius and Guarneri, but there are many kinds of stringed instrument which offer considerable interest and amusement for a small outlay. Early examples of strumps, poliphants, cit-

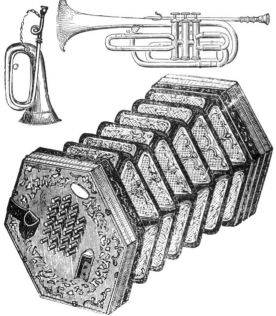

A bugle, trumpet and concertina from the catalogue issued by G. Butler's Manufactory (Author's collection)

terns and lutes have virtually disappeared into museum collections, but the early English guitars of the eighteenth century are somewhat neglected and overshadowed by their more flamboyant French and Spanish cousins. Spanish guitars of the early nineteenth century are quite plentiful and often elegantly decorated. Plain Spanish, Italian and French guitars from 1840 to 1920 are still reasonably cheap. Small lutes and mandolines of the same period were very popular in Britain up to about 1910 and many of them are languishing in attics to this day. For the more adventurous, there are the various hybrids produced in the nineteenth century by Edward Light, partly to increase the versatility of an instrument and partly to make playing easier for the beginner. These harp-lutes and harp-lyres were all the rage during the Regency period.

Banjos, ukeleles and their hybrids have always been regarded as the poor relations of the stringed family but there are many varieties and their decoration is almost a form of folk art.

Wind instruments have long been popular with the collector, partly because the brass instruments are very decorative in themselves and partly because there are many small instruments which take up little room. Among the latter is a vast range of flutes, recorders and flageolets, varying in the number and position of keys and holes – not to mention the materials used, ranging from polished hardwood, ebony and crocus-wood to ivory with gold or silver mounts. Many brass instruments have become rather expensive either because of their technical complexity or because they bear regimental insignia and therefore appeal to collectors of MILITARIA. The unconsidered trifles in this field include plain brass or silver-plated bugles without keys, cornets of the late nineteenth century and the simpler varieties of Kent bugles.

Among keyboard instruments, I am afraid that it is now too late for any bargains. Not so long ago German square or table pianos could still be picked up for a song, but they have become fashionable and are joining the ranks of the virginals, spinets, harpsichords, clavichords and early grand pianos among the more expensive instruments.

MUSTARD POTS

A selection of early Colman Foods mustard pots (Colman Foods)

Though mustard has been used as a condiment for two thousand years it was not until the 1720s that mustard was prepared in the form of a paste mixed with vinegar and spices. This created a need for special pots, both as containers used by grocers, and as an essential item of tableware. Mustard pots are among the earliest forms of commercial PACKAGING and some of them retain a hint of the eighteenth century in their underglaze decoration to this day. These pots may be found in earthenware, stoneware porcelain or glass, in many shapes and sizes. The pots intended to grace the dining table, however, were usually small drum- or boat-shaped silver vessels with a handle and a flat or domed lid. The mustard itself reposed in a glass container, Bristol blue being a favourite material which contrasted nicely with the fretting and piercing of the silver. These pots are best collected with matching mustard spoons. They may also be found in Sheffield plate, electroplate, glass or ceramic materials and in the earlier part of this century joined their better known cousins, the salts and peppers, as a popular tourist souvenir from many parts of the world, decorated with appropriate motifs.

NARGHILES

Nargil is the Persian word for a coconut and it was from this handy natural receptacle that the Persians and the Turks fashioned silver-mounted vessels mainly associated with smoking. The smoke from the tobacco pipe was conducted through the vessel filled with water and inhaled through a flexible tube. The name came to be applied also to any vessel of a similar shape, made in other materials.

Narghiles are usually found in opaque glass or tin-glazed pottery, decorated in the Islamic style. More recent examples, in inlaid brass, were probably designed for the export trade that developed in the second half of the nineteenth century. Somewhat similar tobacco vessels were produced in China in the distinctive blue and white porcelain and may be found in unusual animal shapes.

NAUTICAL MEMENTOES

Navalia is the maritime counterpart of MILITARIA and encompasses the arms, equipment, insignia and UNIFORM worn by sailors. There are many distinctive collectables associated with the sea, from BOSUN'S PIPES and DIVER'S HELMETS to SCRIMSHAW, while instruments like SEXTANTS and TELESCOPES often have a nautical connection. Perhaps the most popular of the nautical collectables are the SHIP MODELS, but apart from models there are items associated with the full-scale ships themselves. The more decorative objects include steering wheels, binnacles, compasses and telegraphs which, with their brass and copper casings, have an innate decorative quality. Ships' lanterns and navigation lamps with red and green bullseye lenses are much sought after.

Few collectors could afford the cost (or the house room) of ships' figureheads, but the more symbolic and heraldic aspects of navalia include many items, from crested crockery and cutlery to brass tompions which fitted over the muzzle of guns and were frequently decorated with the ship's name and badge. Painted wooden or leather buckets bearing naval insignia are also highly desirable. Then there are all those articles with a nautical flavour from RACK PLATES and mugs celebrating naval

A brass ship's engine-room telegraph (Christies, South Kensington)

victories and heroes, to commemorative medals and engraved glassware, Staffordshire figures and CHINA FAIRINGS; while ephemera includes ADVERTISEMENTS, POSTERS, MENUS and TICKETS of the shipping companies.

NEWSPAPERS

Who has not come upon an old newspaper, perhaps lining a drawer or underlying a carpet, and failed to be captivated by reading the stale news of long ago? Events which have long since passed into history are presented with all the urgency and up-to-the-minute quality which one associates with journalism. There is a considerable industry these days based on the reproduction of historic issues of newspapers bearing banner headlines like 'French Navy Defeated at Trafalgar', 'Lusitania Sunk' or 'Japanese Attack Pearl Harbor'. This is nothing new, however, and facsimiles of the London *Times* reporting the death of Nelson have plagued ephemerists and second-hand booksellers for many years.

Genuine old newspapers are worth keeping as examples of old-fashioned typography, journalistic styles of a more leisurely age, or merely for the unique insight they give us about the social and political conditions of the period. Of particular interest are the newspapers of many countries up to about the middle of the nineteenth century, bearing an impressed tax stamp. It was one such tax as this that helped precipitate the war between Britain and her American colonies, and examples of colonial newspapers of the 1770s with anti-British slogans on the masthead are among the most desirable items from the Revolutionary War period.

Since the mid nineteenth century many newspapers have produced special editions to celebrate coronations, jubilees, presidential inaugurations, the cessation of wars and important anniversaries. Such editions are often printed on a better quality of paper, decorated with coloured illustrations or even produced in miniature form.

NUREMBERG PLATES

Dinanderie or brassware took its name from the Belgian city of Dinant but after it was razed to the ground by Charles the Bold in 1466 the centre of this industry shifted to Nuremberg in Bavaria. The ingredients of the brass were cast and then beaten into sheets which were cut into circular discs. These were placed over a matrix and beaten with hammers until a *repoussé* motif appeared. Later the process was greatly accelerated by using massive punches and anvils which struck a relief design at a single blow. At the same time the brass sheet tended to become thinner and the design more stereotyped. Genuine Nuremberg plates continued in production well into the eighteenth century, but they have been reproduced elsewhere in more recent times, and it is now becoming difficult to tell a nineteenth-century replica from a latter-day original. Genuine old brass plates have an indefinable quality which only the true connoisseur can discern, but the later versions tend to be lighter in colour.

Biblical and mythological subjects were the most popular motifs, with St George and the Dragon at the top of the league and Adam and Eve close behind. Less common are the plates or roundels with heraldic motifs. The majority have no inscription, but those with edge inscriptions in German, Dutch or French are much sought after. Subsequent generations often lacquered these plates or coated them with a dull brown paint, so you might just be lucky and come across an otherwise nondescript example thus disguised.

OFFICE EQUIPMENT

Many categories of office equipment will be found in the pages of this book, from BLOTTERS, CASH REGISTERS and INKSTANDS to PAPER CLIPS, PENCIL SHARPENERS and PENWIPERS. There are STAMP BOXES and staple fasteners, all the collectables associated with QUILL PENS and steel PEN NIBS, not to mention WRITING SETS themselves. SCALES include numerous examples designed for weighing letters and packets, while ENVELOPE AND STAMP MOISTENERS come in many varieties.

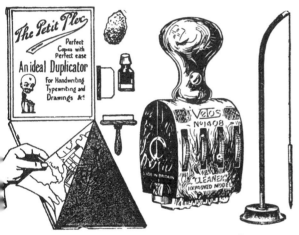

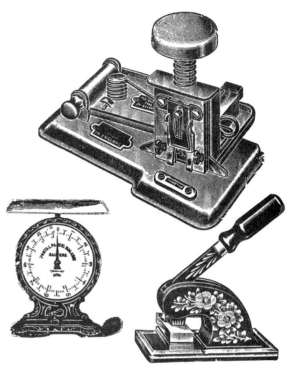

Top: The Longdon wire stapler. *From left:* The 'Petit Plex' duplicator 'for professional or occasional use'; the 'cleaner' dater; a captive pencil stand; a Salter's parcel post balance; and a postcard embossing press (Army & Navy Stores Ltd)

This leaves us with a miscellany of paperweights – not the ornate glass variety which are among the most cherished of bibelots, but the more functional types in hafnerware, tinglazed earthenware with relief moulding, or even in cast iron with leather padding. STRING-BOXES may be square, cylindrical, conical, globular or polygonal, and were often decorated with painting, pokerwork or transfer-printed motifs associated with Mauchline ware. And do not overlook early examples of adding machines, nor even the age-old abacus itself which I note is still widely used in Japan despite all these electronic pocket calculators!

OIL CANS

Lubricating oil – or 'liquid engineering' as one genius of a copywriter has dubbed it – has been keeping machinery moving since 1857 and it follows that oil cans have been around for the same length of time. The main function of these cans is to direct a fine stream of lubricant into the finest and most delicate of machinery and for this reason they are distinguished by long and slender nozzles. There have also been numerous patent devices controlling the rate of flow, and a considerable variety of shapes and sizes, as well as materials from polished brass and copper to lacquered tinware or painted toleware. The most desirable examples are those bearing the embossed initials or insignia of the oldtime railway companies. They range in size from the tiny glass phials with attached dropper used for oiling clockwork mechanism, to the giant brass oil cans used in lubricating marine engines.

OIL LAMPS

Vegetable and mineral oil has been used for lighting since time immemorial and the lamps have ranged from the primitive crusies of the ancient Irish and the handsome bronze and terracotta lamps of the Romans to the highly complex duplex lamps marketed in the early years of this century. There are curiosities like the wrought-iron Scottish two-valve crusies in use in remote districts until the 1890s, the tiny travelling lamps used to illuminate railway carriages a century ago, and the attractive children's night lights of the 1880s with their gaily coloured decorations drawn from nursery rhymes and fairy tales.

There are brass hand lamps and small tinplate oil burners, larger lanterns with glass chimneys, coach and carriage lamps and cylindrical lamps, with their metal parts of burnished brass or japanned iron. Interior decor was greatly enhanced by the siting and styling of oil lamps, ranging from the discreet wall lamps in their sconces and the elegantly bracketed piano lamps to the larger reading lamps and table lamps. The latter, in particular, form a large group with the greatest decorative appeal, since they were often designed as centre-pieces and have beautiful glass shades in every colour, mounted on lamps whose bowls were made of ornamental glass, porcelain and brassware. Quite apart from the decorative features of the LAMP-SHADES, there are many technical features of the lamps themselves which are worth studying. They range from the early Slip burners, through the myriad styles of Duplex burners and the types distinguished by such names as Argand, Carcel, Colza, Kronos and Candesco. The makers' names and emblems frequently appear in embossed brass on winder buttons.

From top left: A Duplex oil lamp with marble pillar and bronze or brass container; a Queen reading lamp in brass; a hurricane oil or candle lamp; a hand lamp (Army & Navy Stores Ltd); and an early Aladdin lamp (Aladdin Industries Inc)

Aladdin is still a household name in this field and there are clubs in America devoted solely to the study and collection of Aladdin lamps.

OPTICAL TOYS

Long before the doubtful blessing of television was conferred on mankind there were numerous visual gadgets for keeping children amused. Many of them come under the heading of peep-show and consisted basically of a box with a tiny viewing aperture, some form of lighting at the back and painted landscapes on the inner sides. The scenery and action was varied by the judicious insertion of painted glass slides to create moving or three-dimensional effects. A nineteenth-century variant was the perspective toy, consisting of a tube of cardboard or a concertina-shaped box, with scenery and figure mounted at intervals along its length, so that they appeared in perspective when viewed through a lense at one end.

These peep-shows suffered a major drawback; they were immobile, and even the most imaginative of children would soon tire of gazing at the same scene. That optical phenomenon, the persistance of vision, was scientifically explained in the 1820s and thereafter was applied to many optical toys, combining a revolving drum with strips depicting figures in slightly varying positions. J. A. Paris patented the Thaumatrope in 1825 and thenceforward many toys involving rotating discs and picture strips were marketed right down to the end of the century. They all had jaw-breaking Greek names, such as Strotoscope, Phenakistiscope, Phantasmascope, Praxinoscope, Kaleidorama or Zoetrope. The Praxinoscope even incorporated a series of mirrors which helped to project an image that

A praxinoscope by E. Planck (Christies, South Kensington)

appeared to move, and foreshadowed the development of the Kinora and the Kinetescope which was the prototype for true motion picture projectors. Then there was the Chromatrope whose pictures mounted on cards were flicked over very quickly by cranking a handle. This was the principle underlying the better-known fairground spectacle 'What the Butler Saw'. Stereoscopes permitted the viewing of still PHOTOGRAPHS in three-dimensional form and ranged from the elaborate table model to the small hand-held viewer, both in polished wood with brass mounts. In more recent times there have been children's versions of cinema projectors and numerous variations on the traditional peep-show theme, incorporating microfilm strips.

PACKAGING

We have already encountered some of the older, though not necessarily more honourable, forms of packaging under MEDICINE BOTTLES AND BOXES. Patent medicines were the earliest form of branded goods to be marketed on a large scale. So long as foodstuffs and similar perishable commodities were manufactured for local consumption little attention was paid to packaging beyond merely identifying the goods, but by the early nineteenth century some of the larger companies, notably the breweries and soap-manufacturers, were using distinctive LABELS and wrappers and there was extensive litigation between rival companies over the use of similar trademarks. The system was regulated by the Trademark Act of 1875 and on January 1st of the following year Bass launched their famous red triangle brand, to be followed shortly by Lever Brothers' Sunlight soap.

Other countries enacted trademark and pure food and drug laws and the brand name on consumer goods became a worldwide phenomenon. This stimulated the growth of an industry devoted to the labelling and packaging of goods of all kinds, the printing of inscriptions and pictorial vignettes on labels, boxes, wrappers and TINS. Many of these early examples of packaging echoed the typography of contemporary ADVERTISEMENTS and were designed to be as eye-catching as possible. They were frequently decorated with miniature representations, in gold ink of course, of the medals won at international exhibitions. Some companies still feature these medallic awards – even though the exhibitions and their royal patrons have long since been forgotten!

Apart from the plethora of fancy lettering, there were several gimmicks which were popular for many years. They included portraits of the proprietor (always a firm favourite with medical goods) and views of the

Two cardboard milk bottle tops (Clifford's Dairies Ltd)

ultra-modern factory premises, emphasizing cleanliness and efficiency. The more mundane the actual goods, the greater care was lavished on the packaging and one suspects that in many cases today the box or packet is worth more than its contents. Of all forms of packaging, the one which probably appeals most to the collector is the cardboard milk-bottle top. It had a fairly brief life, having come into use in the Twenties as the traditional churn-and-ladle era drew to a close, and was superseded in the mid-fifties by the foil top. During its 30 years' existence the milk-bottle top was used as a vehicle not only for advertising individual dairies, but the virtues and versatility of milk as a food, and there were even commemorative tops which celebrated contemporary events such as the coronations of 1937 and 1953 and the silver jubilee of 1935. Cigarette packets enjoy a modest following and paper wrappers of all kinds are now being avidly collected by ephemerists.

PAPER CLIPS

Few people, looking at the humble pieces of curved wire now in use, would ever imagine that a paper clip could be an object of beauty, but its ancestors of a century ago were just that. Spring-loaded clips, measuring several inches in length, were first marketed in the 1870s and considerable attention was paid to the ornamentation of the upper and lower blades. They may be found with embossed, relief or intaglio decoration, with tiny landscapes, figures of animals and birds or floral patterns. A popular style was shaped like a pair of hands, which held the sheaf of papers in a vice-like grip. Others depicted horseshoes and other talismans of good fortune. They were made of sheet brass, cast bronze, iron, steel, nickel-plate and less commonly of electroplate or sterling silver with dies-stamped ornament. They gave way to the bull-dog clip about 1910 and the wire clip soon afterwards, but they still turn up occasionally among the smaller bric-à-brac in antique shops.

PAPER FLAGS

Here is one of those instant successes which can be dated very accurately. The idea started in 1912 – June 26th to be exact – when charity collectors took to the streets of London to sell artificial paper flowers on the first of Queen Alexandra's Rose Days. Within days of the outbreak of the First World War in August 1914 the idea was extended to the sale of small paper flags to raise money for the Prince of Wales' National Relief Fund for the dependents of soldiers and sailors. From a modest beginning the flag-day grew into a great national institution and raised more than £15 million during the war alone. It spread to the other Allied countries and became the most important single fund-raiser. Its scope was extended to other charities once peace was restored and has continued down to the present day.

From paper flags the charity emblems developed into many other devices, printed on paper, card, silk or linen. Matchstick 'flagpoles' were often used when pins were in short supply and in recent years self-adhesive backing has been widely used. Though many other methods of fund-raising have since been introduced, the flag-day is still one of the traditional stand-bys and the flags and favours are attracting the serious attention of collectors.

A selection of charity paper flags

PATCHWORK

This traditional folk art of Britain and North America is enjoying a considerable revival at this moment and collectors are now seeking out good specimens of earlier work. Quilting was a widespread medieval skill, but the use of variegated patches of cloth to form unusual patterns was a New England speciality in the eighteenth century, and was brought back to the former mother country in the early nineteenth century. Haphazard patchwork of odd scraps of cloth is of little interest or value, but bedspreads and coverlets with intricate patterns skilfully designed and worked in small patches are now much sought after. Geometric patterns predominate, but there are unusual floral and figural designs. Since patchwork tended to develop patterns distinctive to certain areas they are of considerable interest to the social historian. Patterns even took on distinctive names, such as 'Birds in Air', 'Drunkard's Path', 'Goose Tracks' or 'Moon over the Mountain'. Generally speaking, the smaller the individual patches the more desirable the quilting, and some delicate mosaic effects have been noted.

A magnificent patchwork quilt top in a geometric pattern, from Massachusetts, c.1875 (American Folk Art Museum, New York)

PATTERNS AND PATTERN BOOKS

These may be regarded as the poor man's (and woman's) answer to the fashion plates, so esteemed by collectors and connoisseurs of costume over the past 250 years. The *nouvelles pauvres* who were the post-war counterpart of the *nouveaux riches* followed the maxim that 'to be poor and look poor is to be damned poor', and turned from the couturiers they could no longer afford to the new breed of low-price fashion magazines headed by McCall's and studied the dress patterns therein. Home dressmaking developed rapidly in the Twenties and the manufacture of fabrics and paper patterns flourished. Paper patterns were sold in the United States for 45 cents, and in Britain retailed for as little as a shilling, or were

Part of a page from Butterick Metropolitan Fashions for Spring and Summer 1877 (Christies, South Kensington)

given away free by the manufacturers of fabrics, such as Viyella, Courtauld, Ancos or Atlas. Vogue, McCall's, Weldon and Butterick were the best-known publishers of patterns and pattern-books on both sides of the Atlantic but there were many others.

Few of the paper patterns have survived intact but there is considerable interest in the multicoloured envelopes with their pictures of the finished garments modelled by svelte young ladies. The pattern-books – often consisting of stout volumes that resemble the contemporary mail-order catalogues – are an invaluable source of information regarding the fashions of the inter-war period.

PENCIL SHARPENERS

The earliest pencil sharpeners were the desk models clamped to the edge of a table and were relatively cumbersome, with their ornate japanned casing and heavy crank-handle. The delicate business of furnishing the pencil with a fine point was achieved by twin milling cutters of solid tool steel and various ingenious devices were patented in the late nineteenth century to ensure that cutting ceased at the right moment before the point was ground away to nothing. There was the 'Boston' pencil pointer, the 'Crown' sharpener and the 'Dominion' point regulator, not to mention the various models of Velos cabinet pencil sharpeners available in marbelite in a variety of colours.

The Boston and Dominion pencil sharpeners (Army & Navy Stores Ltd)

The Europeans, however, developed the small pocket versions in which the pencil itself was rotated against a narrow blade held in a metal frame. There were sharpeners with twin blades, designed to whittle the wood and lead point separately. From the collector's viewpoint, however, the interest lies mainly in the staggering variety of novelty pencil sharpeners which have been marketed over the past ninety years. They have been disguised as animals, human figures, birds, motor cars, windmills, gnomes and trolls, ships and aircraft, cigars and submarines and countless other objects, in brass, nickel-plate or brightly enamelled metal, and in more recent years plastic materials have been widely used.

PENS AND PEN NIBS

Long after the FOUNTAIN PEN had come and gone, the last stronghold of the steel pen nib was the British Post Office whose public writing benches were equipped with pots of a strange semi-liquid substance and a battery of wooden pens whose nibs pointed all ways at once and made form-filling more of a hazard than a chore. Thankfully, these old-timers have now been pensioned off, like their QUILL predecessors, and replaced by ballpoints that

STEEL PENS.

No.		Per box 6 doz.
1.	"The London School Pen," fine point, a good pen for scholastic use	1/6
3.	"The Commercial Pen," fine point; a good pen for general office work	1/7½
6.	"The Star Pen," fine point; a very flexible, easy writing pen	1/9

Two steel nibs from a vast selection offered by the Army & Navy Stores.

occasionally work. In his great masterpiece *Of Human Bondage* Somerset Maugham (thinly disguised as the hero Philip Carey) describes a game played with steel pen nibs which enjoyed brief popularity in the 1880s, as much depending on the quality and style of nib used as on the skill of the players. The J nibs which he describes were still doing yeoman service sixty years later and were one of the more popular styles produced by most pen makers.

Among the many varieties stocked by stationers in the early years of this century were the London School Pen, 'a good nib for scholastic use', the Star with its fine point and great flexibility, the Actuary, with a medium fine points, the Metallic Quill, the Rob Roy, the Peerage, with an extra broad J point, the Latem 'Countess', the Czarina (formerly known as the Duke), the Stub (formerly the Duchess), the Firefly and the Queen Mary (in white metal suitable for ladies' use). The Edinburgh firm of Macniven and Cameron produced a famous trio with an accompanying advertising jingle that can still be seen on some rusty enamelled signs in Auld Reekie:

'The Pickwick, the Owl and the Waverley Pen They come as a boon and a blessing to men.'

Anyone who doubts the variety of pen nibs should visit Philip Poole's stationery shop in London's Drury Lane, where his collection,

A selection of his wares being displayed by Philip Poole in his shop in Drury Lane, London (Tony Hutchings)

now in excess of 5,000 specimens, is displayed. Many of the exhibits consist of the elegant display cases once carried around by the travelling salesmen of such companies as Perry, Hinks Wells, Mitchell and John Heath. Even the nib boxes were as colourful a form of PACKAGING as any devised at the turn of the century and are becoming collectable in their own right.

PEN WIPERS

An adjunct to your collection of PEN NIBS, and ideal for keeping them in pristine condition, of course, is the pen-wiper. In its basic form, as I remember from my schooldays, it consisted of several small pieces of flannel or felt stitched together to form a little book. This was an article, however, beloved of the makers of fancy goods and in the interwar period you could buy pen-wipers bound in leather embossed with the crests of tourist resorts and tastefully lettered 'A Souvenir of . . .' There were also novelty pen-wipers in the shape of hats or helmets, the Arab fez being especially popular. The most elaborate pen-wipers had covers of

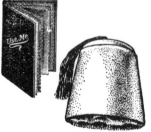

Two pen wipers, one in book shape made in real leather, and the other shaped like a fez (Army & Navy Stores Ltd)

wood, metal, ivory, glass or porcelain while others were decorated with beadwork or embroidery. An unusual table model from the turn of the century was made of glass and incorporated a patent sponge device for moistening the nib for easier cleaning.

PHOTOGRAPHS

It seems incredible that photography is now more than 150 years old, its birth being taken as the invention in 1826 of the first light-sensitive plate by the Frenchman, Nicephore Niepce. Niepce used a pewter plate coated with bitumen of Judaea dissolved in oil of lavender to fix the image of his courtyard after an exposure of eight hours. In the ensuing forty years there were numerous experiments and patent devices before photography became established as a pastime or skill within the capabilities of most people. In this early, experimental period the kind of photograph is of major importance and a great deal depends on the process used, the identity of the photographer and the subject, the condition and aesthetic appeal, in descending order of importance.

The best-known photographs of this period are the daguerreotypes on metal plates, often mounted in ornate framed and embossed leather cases. These UNION CASES are themselves highly collectable. Daguerreotypes were first produced in 1839 and continued till 1860 when they were superseded by cheaper processes. Calotypes (1841–55) used paper negatives and positives and enabled copies to be made from the original. Specialists distinguish the earlier salted-paper prints from the later albumen prints, but value is placed mainly on the artist-photographer, calotypes by David O. Hill, Joseph Cundell, John Forbes White, Thomas Keith and John McCash being among the more desirable. The wet collodion process patented by Frederick Scott Archer in 1851 used glass plate negatives to produce ambrotypes. This made street photography practicable, though most of the street photographers preferred an even cheaper process known as tintypes. Tintypes are usually of a very poor quality but well-preserved specimens up to about 1880 are worth looking for in old family albums. The inventions of George Eastman, whom we have already met in connection with CAMERAS, revolutionized photography and brought it within reach of the masses.

Purists tend to turn up their noses at photographs taken after 1880, but now is the time to

A fine example of pre-Great War studio photography by J. Douglas Ritchie of Paisley: Lieutenant Colonel Coats of the Argyll and Sutherland Highlanders and his wife in the uniform of the Voluntary Aid Detachment (Ian Fleming)

give consideration to *cartes de visite* and cabinet photographs of famous people of the late nineteenth century, good prints of animated street scenes and rural life of long ago, and early war photographs, particularly from the Boer War, the Spanish-American War, the Boxer Rebellion and other campaigns before the First World War. Early photographs of aircraft and balloons are of immense interest to collectors of AERONAUTICA and old photographs of locomotives and stations are among the more desirable RAIL RELICS.

PICKLE JARS

Special jars for sauces, preserves and pickles date from the early nineteenth century and were often produced in the shape of familiar utensils, like butter churns, small kegs and barrels. Greater variety was imparted by the frequent use of ribbing and fluting and by the 1860s jars were even being produced in moulded or pressed glass in fancy shapes.

Ornate moulding was not confined to the jars themselves, but often decorated the glass stoppers. Although the latter have now been superseded by the metal screw cap with its rubber seal, the shape and decoration of pickle jars and sauce bottles with impressed ornament continues in many countries to this day.

PICTORIAL BOOKBINDINGS

Prior to 1822 books were usually sold in paper wrappers, to be bound in leather or vellum of the customer's own choice, but in that year books were first offered for sale in an edition binding of cloth on board, decorated discreetly with gold blocking. The idea was slow to catch on but by 1840 it had become widespread in Britain and America. In the 1850s it spread to Germany but never secured much of a foot-hold in France or Italy. Gradually the decoration of the binding developed from a small vignette, perhaps derived from the frontispiece or a pictorial motif on the title page, into a full-sized picture whose lines were delicately picked out in gold or less frequently in silver. The first bindings with a coloured picture die-stamped on them appeared in 1854 but did not oust gilt decoration till the end of the century and were themselves superseded by pictorial dust jackets. Curiously enough, pictorial dust wrappers had appeared sporadically since 1860 when Longmans produced a cheap edition of Bunyan's *Pilgrim's Progress* thus encased, but they did not become widespread till 1899 and did not dominate the publishing scene till the 1920s.

Pictorial bindings on books dealing with history, travel and topography have been sought after for some years now, but other classes, such as boys' stories, light romantic fiction and prize books have been comparatively neglected. Even they, however, are now graduating from the bargain trays and shelves of secondhand dealers into the more prestigious booklists, but they can still be snapped up at jumble sales and church bazaars for a trifle.

PICTORIAL NOTEPAPER

This is an ancestor of the PICTURE POSTCARD which has tended to be overshadowed by its more ebullient offspring. Stationers began selling boxes of notepaper with a pictorial heading in the 1820s and the fashion seems to have reached its peak at the middle of the century and then tailed off by the 1870s. Perhaps the fact that it was increasingly used by hoteliers and tradesmen militated against its continuing acceptance by 'the quality'. Letter sheets were produced in boxes decorated with assorted views and were exquisitely engraved by the copperplate process. Recently students of nineteenth-century printing have stumbled on the fact that firms such as Lizars and Banks of Edinburgh, De La Rue and

A splendid engraving of Windermere heads this piece of notepaper (Author's collection)

Waterlow Brothers and Layton of London, sometimes used vignettes in these letter sheets which they also utilized in the manufacture of banknotes, and the hunt for examples of these related collectables is now on by notaphilists. I wonder whether the same practice was indulged in by Messrs Rawdon, Wright, Hatch and Edson – better known today as the American Bank Note Company?

Apart from the innocuous scenic motifs, there are stirring patriotic designs from the American Civil War period and political propaganda dealing with the burning issues of the day, from women's suffrage to Irish home rule. The majority of these nineteenth-century letter sheets were produced in black and white but a few were tinted by hand or chromo-lithographed. The idea was developed commercially by hotels, mainly in Europe, which had engraved or lithographed pictorial headings on their notepaper. Highly prized are examples which are mementoes of the great exhibitions in Europe and North America in the second half of the nineteenth century, from the Great Exhibition of 1851 to the Exposition Universelle of 1900 and the St Louis World's Fair of 1904. The matching envelopes are rare and have long since been boosted in value by philatelists and postal historians.

PICTURE POSTCARDS

The postcard as a convenient form of postal stationery was invented by Dr Emmanuel Herrmann of Vienna and pioneered by Austria in 1869. It quickly spread to several other European countries and was adopted by Britain in October 1870. At first only the official Post Office cards were permitted and had to bear the impressed postage stamp, but gradually the rules were relaxed and first private cards with trade advertising were permitted, then an element of pictorialism was allowed on the verso. Picture postcards were well established in Europe in the 1870s, but were not fully permitted in Britain till 1894. Generally speaking, any used picture postcards dating before 1900 are scarce and priced accordingly, but after that date they are still quite plentiful. The heyday of the picture postcard was the period up to the First World War. Drastic increases in postal rates during that war, as well as the increased cost of production, led to their decline and though cards are still sent by the many millions every year, mainly from holiday resorts, they have never regained their Edwardian pre-eminence.

The posh word for the study of postcards is deltiology and it has developed dramatically in the past decade alone. There are now several excellent catalogues and a number of periodicals devoted to the subject. Cards are collected according to the country of issue, the artist who designed them and the publisher; by subject matter or theme, and by composition and material. There are hold-to-lights which reveal a hidden motif when illuminated and the more sophisticated metamorphics, mechanical cards, fabs (with fabric surfaces) and reflectors, all-metal cards in ALUMINIUM or ZINC, cards in celluloid or woven silk. Some are intended to double as BOOK MARKERS; others have served as TICKETS or CALENDARS and there are even rarities designed as miniature gramophone RECORDS. The artistic cards of the turn of the century are highly prized and examples with the signatures of such maestros

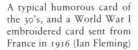

A typical humorous card of the 30's, and a World War I embroidered card sent from France in 1916 (Ian Fleming)

as Alfons Mucha, Raoul Kirchner and Louis Wain are keenly sought, as are the early comic cards of Donald McGill and Phil May. Few other collectables of comparable antiquity are available at such a low price, but the market is developing so rapidly that prices are escalating from day to day.

PIE FUNNELS

The secret of a well-baked pie, as any pastrycook will tell you, is a firm piecrust on top, neither sagging nor saggy. The secret of keeping the pastry clear of the meat or fruit filling lay in the expert use of a pie funnel. Often a cook will use an egg cup or a dariol tin but these never fulfil the function quite so well as the pie funnel which both supports the roof of pastry and has a vent in the funnel to carry off the steam as the pie is cooking.

Pie funnels designed for this purpose came into use in the second half of the nineteenth century and were made of earthenware, stoneware, ironstone or robust china. They may be found in plain funnel or conical shapes, but others have a mushroom flange for greater support and various dents or undulations on their rims to permit the free flow of hot vapours. At the turn of the century novelty designs became fashionable, and from this period date those rabbits and ducks, tortoises and elephants, dolphins and Chinamen, gnomes and chefs with holes in their hats through which the steam issued forth.

PIN TRAYS

Pincushions are a well-established antique which have been collected for many years, but scant attention has been paid to their relatives, the pin trays and bowls which served the same purpose a century ago when pins were comparatively expensive and not to be discarded lightly. The more elegant versions were designed for the dressing table and may be found in transfer-printed porcelain, coloured glass, papier-mâché or silver-gilt. Pin bowls were a favourite medium for the delicate lacquerware imported from China and Japan, or the intricately inlaid Moradabad and Bidri wares of India. Less decorative but of interest nonetheless were the various patent pin holders marketed at the turn of the century. There were magnetic pin cups and even automatic pin dispensers which guaranteed always to deliver each pin head uppermost so as not to prick the unwary hand.

An automatic pin box (Army & Navy Stores Ltd)

PIPES

The tobacco habit existed for countless centuries in America before the advent of Columbus and the so-called mound or platform pipes, carved from porphyry and other hardstones, are among the most interesting ethnographical remains of the earliest inhabitants of Ohio, Indiana, Illinois and Iowa. Baked clay pipes were also used by the Indians in pre-Columbian America and these formed the basis for the designs adopted by Europeans in the sixteenth century. Though pipe-smoking has been overtaken to a large extent by cigarette smoking, it has left us a rich legacy of collectables in the form of pipes and pipe-cases.

Many pipes, such as the Indian calumet or peace pipe, are of primary interest to the student of ethnography; others, such as meerschaums and the elongated porcelain pipes of Germany, are associated with specific localities. There are pipes with metal bowls and cane stems from Japan, and red clay bowls and cherrywood stems from Turkey, churchwardens from eighteenth-century England and corn-cob pipes from nineteenth-century America. Clay pipes embossed with regimental insignia are of interest to collectors of MILITARIA, while the hookahs and qalians of the East are similar to the NARGHILES of the

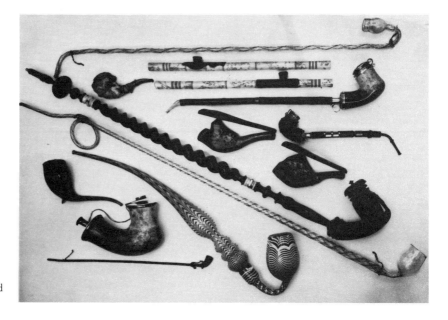

A selection of pipes long and short (Phillips)

A companion case of pipes and a 'Hurricane' pipe, ideal for sportsmen (Army & Navy Stores Ltd)

Islamic world. Even the briar pipes commonly used in Britain and the United States may be found in an infinite variety of style and quality, with vulcanite, amber or ivory mouthpieces and gold or silver mounting. Pipes were often sold in sets and come in special leather or shagreen cases holding two to four pipes. Look out for some of the more unusual kinds, such as the Hurricane, a pipe with a swivel-mounted bowl which could be concealed in a windproof shield in bad weather and was recommended for sportsmen and sailors.

PIPE STOPPERS

Though pipe-smoking is still a common habit it is curious that the pipe stopper, or tobacco tamper, is a thing of the past. Pipe-smokers today have to risk burning their finger in packing down the tobacco in the bowl to get an even draw, though some smokers' pen-knives and CIGAR CUTTERS have a tamper fitted on the end. An attempt was made in the 1930s to market a gadget called a Smoker's Companion and this consisted of a silver ring to which was fitted pricker, scraper, spoon and tamper, but from the fact that they are rarely seen today I deduce that sales were small.

In the eighteenth and early nineteenth centuries, however, you could purchase an amazing variety of small articles, usually made of brass, with a flattened disc on one end for tamping down the tobacco. These pipe stoppers were often shaped like horses' hooves or ladies' nether limbs. Others were in the form of literary or biblical characters, or

A smoker's companion (Army & Navy Stores Ltd)

had mounted small portrait busts or medallions of contemporary celebrities. Some were modelled in the form of tiny hammers, gavels or bottles, warming pans or cannon shells and the most desirable varieties had commemorative inscriptions. Look out for the pipe stoppers which also combine a tiny knife or corkscrew. Apart from the brass stoppers which are still fairly plentiful, there are elusive examples in turned or carved wood, ivory, amber, porcelain and precious metals. Perhaps the most prized examples of all are those intricately carved in ivory which contain tiny compartments holding miniature dice, dominoes, wine glasses and other symbols of the sweet life.

PLASTICS

Much as one may regret the passing of once familiar articles in wood or metal, pottery or glass, now superseded by similar objects produced in plastic, it has to be faced that we are living in the age of plastic. So if there is no

point in ignoring them, what is there about plastic materials that is worth collecting?

The answer is quite a lot, since plastics in one form or another have been around since 1862 when Alexander Parkes of Birmingham invented Parkesine, a polymer consisting of a mixture of cellulose nitrate and castor oil. Brush-backs, combs, plaques, medals, knife-handles and even bookbindings of Parkesine were displayed at the Great International Exhibition held in London that year. This plastic prototype was only in production for six years, however, and examples of it are consequently very rare. Improved cellulose nitrate compounds, such as Xylonite and Ivoride, were marketed in the 1870s but are just as scarce, being superseded by Celluloid which was patented in 1871. This remained supreme until 1926 when it gave way to the much safer, non-inflammatory cellulose acetate, marketed as Non-Flam Celluloid. These were versatile compounds, widely used in all manner of articles, both useful and decorative, from shirt collars to toy and fancy goods.

Shellac has been known for centuries as the basis of oriental lacquer, but its plastic properties were not fully explored till 1900 when it was used in the manufacture of gramophone RECORDS. In this form it reigned supreme till replaced in the 1950s by polyvinyl compounds. Casein, derived from sour milk and formaldehyde, has been used since 1900 in many articles, from parasol handles and brush-backs to buttons, BELT-BUCKLES, imitation tortoiseshell boxes and hair slides, toys and

An erinoid hairbrush, and a xylonite toothbrush holder (Army & Navy Stores Ltd)

fancy goods. It is better known under its trade name of Erinoid and objects of this material are still fairly common.

The most widely used plastic in the first half of this century was BAKELITE, which reached the acme of its popularity in the Art Deco period. It gradually lost ground to the urea compounds, first marketed under the trade name Aldur in 1928, and still manufactured in improved versions under such names as Scarab, Beetle and Plaskon. With the advent of the polystyrene, acrylic and polyvinyl plastics, developed during the Second World War and greatly extended since then, durability and flexibility have given plastics much greater scope. Much of the early plastic products may come under the heading of KITSCH but there is also a great deal of material that would repay serious study.

PLAYING CARDS

Like paper and paper money, playing cards are thought to have been invented by the Chinese. The earliest examples, dating from the tenth century, may have utilised contemporary banknotes in their design. Others are thought to have been a form of written notation for dice. European cards are known, from stray literary references, to have been in use in Venice in the thirteenth century, though the oldest pack extant dates from about 1440, the cards being of French manufacture. The collector is unlikely to come across any of these medieval rarities and for all practical purposes playing cards are available only from the early eighteenth century, and then only at

Transformation cards produced by MacClure, Macdonald and Macgregor of Manchester (Stanley Gibbons)

French suited hand-painted German tarot card (Stanley Gibbons)

century were often produced in series with an educational element in their illustrations. There are many novelty packs from this period, with humorous, satirical or political undertones. Highly prized are the so-called transformations, in which the pips on the face have been incorporated in ingenious little pictures. The fashion for highly decorative packs declined after 1850, but there have been many packs in more recent years worth watching for. These include the patriotic sets from the two world wars and packs with commemorative motifs on their backs celebrating royal anniversaries and outstanding international events. Apart from the conventional packs, which vary enormously from country to country, there are special sets for Piquet and Tarot – not to mention all the different packs designed from the early nineteenth century onwards for children's card games, such as Happy Families, Dr Busby and Animal Grab – and all of these are worth considering.

great price. As they frequently have attractive vignettes engraved on their backs they are quite collectable, though obviously not as desirable as complete packs.

Packs from the eighteenth and nineteenth

PLUMBING

It is two centuries now since Joseph Bramah (whom we have already encountered under the subject of KEYS) patented his improved water closet. Flush lavatories had been in existence for many years, ever since Sir John Harington, the Elizabethan poet and courtier, had published his *Metamorphosis of Ajax* in 1596. The title contained a pun of which even Shakespeare might have been proud: a jakes was the sixteenth-century slang word for a privy. Until a satisfactory water supply and a system of sewerage could be devised, however, water closets were the privies of the privileged few. Bramah closets coincided with vast improvements in urban water supply and they gradually became more fashionable. By the middle of the nineteenth century many boroughs in Britain had bye-laws insisting on the installation of proper water closets, and the industry of sanitary engineering grew at a meteoric pace. This was an era in which Royal Doulton and many other companies made their fortune in the production of lavatory

bowls in vitreous china and other hard-wearing ceramics. The earliest bowls were discreetly encased in cabinets of polished hardwood and the flush operated by handles or plungers of wood and brass.

Once the lavatory was freed from its wooden confines it became an object of ornament in true Victorian fashion and from about 1860

Late 19th-century Doulton Lambeth closets (Doulton)

PLUMBING GOODS AND SUPPLIES.

As space will not permit of listing a full line of these goods, we quote only such articles as are most commonly used in the country, but would state we can furnish anything you may wish in this line—Closets, Bath Tubs, Lavatories, Basins, Lead Pipe and Fittings, Soil Pipe, etc., and can guarantee to save you 75 per cent on same. We would be pleased to figure on outfits. If you are building, or contemplate doing so, send us your plans, giving exact measurements of all rooms, height of each floor and total height from roof to ground, also show exact location of tub, closet, lavatory, etc. State whether you have city water pressure or will get your water supply from a storage tank. If from tank, state where located, and, if possible, send specifications, showing how you would like your pipes, etc., laid out. State style and grade of plumbing wanted, and we will make you a net price which will include everything complete, and with the instructions we send any ordinary gasfitter or plumber can put them in.

Enameled Iron Hopper Closets.

No. 24R7500 Enameled Iron Straight Hopper, self raising seat, complete as shown in cut, no waste or supply pipes or tank furnished at the price. Price, each....$6.00

No. 24R7500

Frost Proof Closets.

Our Frost Proof Closets have frost proof brass valves, for outside and exposed places. The valve is below frost line, and is connected with hopper by a heavy chain, fastened to seat; when seat is depressed the valve is opened and hopper is flushed, when seat is relieved the supply is shut off and waste pipe opened allowing the water which is in pipe to drain direct into trap, therefore valve and pipe are at all times free from water. We furnish above complete with cast iron hopper, enameled inside, self-raising seat, frost proof valve, 5 feet length of pipe, cast iron P trap, complete with chain and lever. For cold or exposed places this outfit is the best on the market, water is always below frost line. It is easily connected, is substantially constructed and avoids rotting away of wooden supports as all water valves direct into sewer. No. 24R7503 Price, complete.....$10.75

Low Tank Wash Down Siphon Combination Closet.

No. 24R7504 Simple flushing valves. No float; nothing to get out of order. Gives a strong powerful flush, and a large positive refill. Bowls to rough in at 12 inches or 17 inches. Everything complete to properly set up closet. In ash, light or dark cherry plain oak, finished antique or plain varnish. Price, with plain bowl.....$16.00
Add for embossed bowl.....1.00

Hopper Closets.

No. 24R7506 Hopper Closets complete, as shown in cut, includes tall flushing rim hopper, single discharge siphon tank, seat and cover, nickel plated iron tank and seat brackets, flush and supply pipes, pull and chain, pipe holders with buffer and bolts. Price, complete with oval hopper.....$13.25

Acme Water Closets.

No. 24R7510 Our Acme Water Closet is by far the best finished and most up to date closet on the market. It has a round cornered natural oak siphon tank with double ⅜-inch sawed oak attached seat, 1½-inch nickel plated flush pipe and ⅜-inch nickel plated supply pipe, with No. 2 front wash-out with plain bowl. The bowl roughs at 8½ inches from final finish of wall to center of the bend. The chain and pull and all fixtures are nickel plated. Tank is copper lined, has patent float cut off with chain and pull to flush closet. It is made of the very best materials throughout and the workmanship and finish are perfect. Furnished complete, ready for use, no fitting or extras required. Price, each.....$13.50
No. 24R7519 Closet, same as No. 24R7510 only without supply and waste pipes. Price.....$11.50

Siphon Jet Water Closets.

No. 24R7514 Water Closets complete, as shown in cut. Outside made of quarter sawed oak; has siphon jet; embossed bowl; 1½-inch nickel plated flush pipe; ⅜-inch nickel plated supply pipe. Bowl roughs in at 12 inches from final finish of wall to center of the bend. Has double oak seat attached to bowl; chain and pull nickel plated. Furnished complete with chain, pull, striker and floor bolts. A very neat and substantial closet at a moderate price. Price, each.....$19.75
No. 24R7516 Closet, same as No. 24R7514, but without supply and waste pipes. Price, each.....$17.75

Part of a page from the spring 1902 catalogue of Sears, Roebuck & Co., 'Cheapest Supply House on Earth, Chicago'

onwards the more decorative bowls became

part of the repertoire of every pottery. To this period belong the elegant blue and white underglaze patterned bowls with tasteful Italianate ruins in the manner of Piranesi, the richly fluted neo-Baroque pedestals, the mock Grecian urns and the lavatorial extravaganzas decorated with water nymphs, dolphins and sea horses in keeping with the spirit of an age when Britannia ruled the waves. Of course they were dreadfully unhygienic and no amount of complicated valve and plunger mechanisms could compensate for their malodorous nature. They were swept away by improved models in the 1890s with high-level cisterns and CHAIN-PULLS. I should have thought that they had all been broken up long ago, but they keep appearing mysteriously in the junk stalls and shops around London's Portobello Road and are just as quickly snapped up by those who see their rich potential as conversation pieces and planters.

Personally, I prefer the ephemera of plumbing to such relics. Many of the bill-headings and TRADE CARDS of the plumbers and sanitary engineers of the nineteenth century are still plentiful and often bear pictorial representations of the latest line in wash basins, baths and lavatories, exquisitely engraved or lithographed.

PRISONER OF WAR WORK

Those exceedingly intricate SHIP MODELS, carved from scraps of bone and rigged with human hair, which were produced by the French prisoners at Norman Cross and Dartmoor during the French Revolutionary and Napoleonic Wars that spanned an entire generation, have stolen all of the limelight. These models, however, have long since been elevated to the more august salerooms and fetch four-figure sums. To chance upon one of these gems, unconsidered and unsuspected, in a jumble sale or junkyard today would be tantamount to winning the pools or the premium bonds.

There are many other examples, however, of the handicrafts practised by those whom

A model man-of-war in carved and painted bone, c.1800, in a contemporary straw-work box (Christies, South Kensington)

the fortunes of war have trapped in prison camps, internment camps and aliens detention centres. Straw marquetry, whereby small boxes were decorated with a mosaic composed of pieces of coloured straw, is one such example of a craft that flourished in these conditions and examples dating from the Napoleonic period still turn up from time to time. No craft was too painstaking for men who had any amount of time on their hands, and for this reason much of the craftwork they produced shows infinite patience, whether it be intricate chip-carving or pokerwork, or reliefs hammered in repoussage out of old tobacco tins. Scraps of bone and oddments of wood were often transformed into minor works of art, by men using little more than a penknife, a sharpened nail and a few other primitive tools. Work-boxes, sewing-boxes, ASHTRAYS, wall plaques and carved figures are among the objects produced by the captives and detainees of both world wars and sold for paltry sums to augment their meagre income. There is a certain poignancy and naïve charm about these articles which amply compensates for any aesthetic shortcomings.

PROPELLING PENCILS

Mechanical pencils date from 1822 when Samuel Mordan of London patented a device in which a thin length of graphite was raised inside a narrow tube by means of a simple slide and knob arrangement in the side. Mordan produced many variants of this in later years and marketed pencils in silver, rolled gold, electroplate, brass, tinplate, ivory and wood. Other manufacturers produced their own variations on the theme and by the 1840s the cases were being decorated with carving, engine-turning and die-struck relief. The propelling pencil in the true sense, with a lead raised by rotating part of the casing, was invented by Johann Faber of Nuremberg in 1863 and this type soon dominated the market, though slide-up pencils continued to be manufactured till the end of the century. Later developments included a more complicated spiral arrangement, using projections at either end of the pencil, and telescopic pencils which compressed to a length of no more than an inch or two and could be carried conveniently in pocket or purse when not in use.

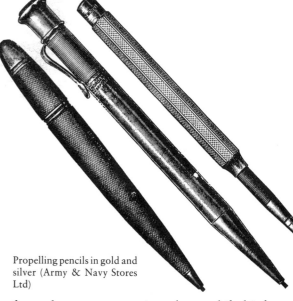

Propelling pencils in gold and silver (Army & Navy Stores Ltd)

Apart from the technical features and various materials, the interest in propelling pencils lies in the numerous novelty shapes and motifs which may be found. One of the more popular forms at the turn of the century was the pencil in the shape of a beer or wine bottle, sometimes with tiny labels worked in enamels. Others were fashioned after sports equipment, from shotguns to tennis rackets, while birds, animals and human figures are not uncommon. Egyptian mummies, skeletons, Cleopatra's needle, medieval battle-axes and characters from literature or the Bible are among some of the less common varieties. The most desirable of all are those pencils which combine tiny calendars, calculators, whistles, KNIVES, rulers, BOOK MARKERS and even SCALES AND BALANCES. The most unusual of all, however, was the Thornhill pencil shaped like a fish, with a pencil in its mouth, a whistle in the tail, and a penknife and nail-file emerging from its sides.

POSTERS

This is an enormous subject and it is difficult to confine my remarks to a few lines. There is a vast amount of literature on the subject, covering every aspect of the poster, commercial, military and political and some of the more recent publications are given in the Reading List. The problem facing the would-be collector is not so much how to collect but what to collect, for the range of different kinds is so great. Another problem which besets the beginner is the ability to distinguish reprints from originals and for this it is necessary to acquire a knowledge of the printing techniques used at different periods. Many modern reprints, for example, are produced by photogravure, whereas the originals were lithographed. As a rule, reprints bear some indication (however minute) that they are reproductions and it is advisable to study the small print on the bottom of the poster for such tell-tall signs. Of course, an unscrupulous dealer can always cut off such data. Generally speaking, it is the more artistic posters of the past that have been reprinted and these include the works of the great masters such as

A late 1890's poster for the thirsty traveller (Coca-Cola)

A woven theatre poster of 1852

Toulouse-Lautrec, Grasset, Cheret and Mucha. Many of the more commercial posters, however, have also been reproduced of late and one should be on one's guard when offered early posters of aviation meetings and famous sporting events, war recruiting and the great motion picture epics.

This probably sounds rather discouraging, but there is still tremendous scope among the more modest posters. Eighteenth- and nineteenth-century posters, entirely composed of letterpress in many different founts of type, advertising country house sales, turn up in lawyers' attics and are of considerable interest, both to the typographer and the social historian. It is amazing how many of these were filed away at the time and are now coming to light again. Posters of the nineteenth century advertising rail, coach and steamship services are most attractive, with their wood-cuts of vintage modes of travel, their ludicrously low charges and timetables of a more leisurely era. Moreover, these posters tend to be quite small and are more manageable than the later wall posters.

Theatrical posters and handbills range from the glossy productions of the West End and Broadway to the amateur productions in the village hall a century ago. For my money, the latter are preferable, especially if they were composed by the local printer and carry local advertising. Then there is the enormous range of miniature posters and leaflets dropped by aircraft over enemy territory in time of war. Although this form of psychological warfare dates from the Napoleonic period, when balloons were used to drop leaflets, the bulk of the material on offer dates from the Second World War when the USAAF was dropping seven million leaflets on enemy-occupied territory every week – compared with a total of three millions for the whole of the First World War.

PUZZLES

While a large part of the world was still at the cave-dwelling stage the Chinese were devising puzzles involving rods and cubes that locked together in an improbable tangle and yet could be taken apart with ease once the secret was mastered. Examples of these interlocking puzzles in wood, bone, pottery or metal have been dated as far back as 1,000 BC and are masterpieces of construction and ingenuity. They were not widely known in the West until the 1850s when many of these Chinese puzzles were first marketed commercially in Europe and America but since then there have been countless variations. The European and American toymakers often gave these puzzles a topical slant, using ancient Chinese principles in the manufacture of the Persian Shah, Egyptian Mummy and other puzzles popular in the early years of this century.

About 1800 an entirely new kind of puzzle was invented, in which small steel balls had to be rolled into holes set in a decorated board inside a glass case. These puzzles were square, circular or polygonal and although the principle was invariable the background setting was infinite in scope. Dating from the Edwardian era are the numerous word and number games using small pieces of wood, bone or plastic with letters or numerals on their surface, which slide vertically and horizontally to form words or arithmetic problems. Jigsaws, or dissecting puzzles as they were originally called, date from the late eighteenth century and were originally intended as an educational aid, with little effort required to assemble the pieces. Much of the board was taken up by a printed text and the picture was often of relatively minor importance. By the middle of the nineteenth century dissecting puzzles were being marketed purely as toys, often in the form of locomotives and other mechanical wonders of the age which had to be reassembled. Jigsaws with interlocking pieces did not appear till the 1870s but in the past century there have been innumerable designs, varying in size, complexity and quality.

The box from an early jigsaw (Christies, South Kensington)

Q

QUAICHS

Imagine the shallow depression in a bird's nest, and you have the perfect shape of the quaich – which is merely an anglicized form of the Scottish Gaelic word *cuach* meaning the hollow of a nest. This was the traditional vessel for sipping *uisage beatha* – 'the water of life' – rendered in English as usquebaugh or whisky. The traditional quaich was a shallow bowl with two simple handles projecting from the rim at right angles, often with a circular foot. Quaichs were carved out of a piece of wood in one piece, but in the eighteenth century a chequerboard pattern became fashionable, using interlocking pieces of wood alternately white and stained dark brown.

A typical Stuart quaich, c.1675 (Lyle Publications)

Horn was also used frequently and often decorated with silver rims, handles and feet. Later developments included a silver liner and eventually the all-silver quaich emerged, though most of these highly ornate specimens, with festoons of Celtic knots and tracery, date only from the mid nineteenth century – the Scottish answer to the Gothic and Romantic Revivals in England.

QUILL PENS, HOLDERS ETC.

Before the advent of the steel PEN NIB, and for many years after, the quill was the standard implement of writing. Indeed, the word pen comes from the Latin word for a feather. Not any old feather would do, and for all practical purposes the best quills were made from goose feathers whose horn-like stems were both hard enough and broad enough to make satisfactory pens. The end of the quill had to be cut carefully, at just the right angle, with shoulders of the correct shape and a slit running upwards from the point. A great deal of practice was needed before one could cut a quill to perfection – hence the numerous pen machines which were marketed to help the ham-fisted. Quill cutters were the ancestors of the modern penknife and may be recognized by their very small, narrow blades with sharp points necessary to perform the delicate operation. The cutters and pen machines, originated by Joseph Bramah and developed by others, are discussed under the headings of KNIVES.

One disadvantage of a goose or crow feather as a writing instrument is that it is too slender to give one a firm grip. To overcome this problem stationers marketed quill holders, resembling tubes which fitted over the stem of the quill, and had a tapered opening at one end to accommodate the root of the feather. These holders may be found in wood, bone, ivory, leather or papier-mâché, often with silver or gold bands. They have even been reported in Parkesine, one of the earliest PLASTICS and resemble the casing of the FOUNTAIN PENS which were coming into use about the same time. Quill holders for the desk or bureau were modelled in the form of paperweights or stands, with apertures in their top so that the points of the quills could be inserted when not in use. Many of these are quite decorative, being produced in pottery, soapstone, hardwood, glass, pewter, brass or bronze, and novelty shapes include books, cottages and animal figures.

RACK PLATES

Tales of blue dash chargers and Italian Istoriato faenza dishes making four-figure sums at auction tend to frighten off the would-be collector of rack plates, though the great majority of items now on the market are still available for quite small sums. There are certainly plenty to chose from and a collection can be tailored to any purse. Eighteenth-century West Country plates publicizing parliamentary candidates have already been mentioned under the heading of ELECTION-EERING ITEMS. Much more plentiful are the patriotic plates of the late eighteenth and early nineteenth centuries, celebrating naval victories of every campaign from the Seven Years' War (1756–63) to the Napoleonic period. Nineteenth-century plates of this type are more elusive, though quite a few charted the progress of the Crimean War and the Boer War. The fashion for rack plates declined after 1900 and was largely confined thereafter to the commemoration of royal events. This shift of emphasis was largely brought about by Queen Victoria's Golden Jubilee in 1887 which opened the ceramic flood-gates, and thereafter every coronation, jubilee and royal wedding was commemorated in this manner. Political rack plates exist with the portraits of contemporary politicians, both Disraeli and Gladstone being favoured impartially. Less common are the political plates which served as propaganda for such burning issues as Irish home rule, votes for women and reductions in working hours. One specialized form of rack plate which arose like a phoenix out of the ashes of this particular kind of commemorative ware was the Christmas plate, pioneered in Scandinavia in the 1890s, which has since spread via Germany to Britain and the United States. Another interesting group comprises plates featuring CALENDARS. Rack plates may be found in every kind of earthenware and porcelain, with paint-painted or transfer-printed motifs, with jasperware motifs or moulded reliefs tinglazed in majolica.

RADIO AND TELEVISION

Though hailed as one of the seven wonders of the modern world, radio – or wireless telegraphy to give it its original name – has had something of a chequered career, being almost totally eclipsed as the focal point of the household by its precocious offspring, television. Radio is still all-pervasive, but largely confined to tiny, transistorized portables that do not offer much scope for artistic expression. By contrast, the domestic radio set was often designed consciously as an object of great beauty and once it had graduated from the cat's whisker and crystal stage in the late 1920s it became for a time *the* most important article of parlour furniture. Millions of homes in Europe and America owned at least one set by the early Thirties and manufacturers vied with each other in producing models which were both technically superior and also aesthetically appealing according to the standards of public taste at the time. The leading cabinetmakers and furniture designers were commissioned to produce cases to suit all tastes. The plain wooden box of the mid-Twenties soon became an object on which was lavished all the skills of the carpenter and wood-carver. The loudspeaker grille in particular was a suitable case for the full artistic treatment, reflecting the styles of Art Deco and Art Moderne, but the cabinets in general were

Far left: R.C.A. Victor's first television receiver, introduced for public use at the New York World's Fair in 1939. It features a picture reflected from the top of the kinescope to a mirror in the underside of the cabinet's uplifted lid. *Left:* A highboy cabinet-on-cabinet style radio, *c.*1925 (both R.C.A., New York). *Below:* Two vulcanite crystal sets (Christies, South Kensington)

inspired by many disparate sources, from the clockcases of the Baroque to the architectural masterpieces of Sullivan, Wright and Peter Clark and the interior decor and furniture of Ruhlmann and Deskey. The most desirable radios are those whose cabinets were intended to blend into their surrounds, the teak and mahogany extravaganzas and the beautifully lacquered radios toning in with a *Chinoiserie* surround. BAKELITE and other early PLASTICS played a considerable role in the development of radio design in the Thirties and Forties and cabinets of this period range from the ultra-modern geometric models to the intensely naturalistic.

Pre-war television sets are of the greatest rarity nowadays. The Baird Televisor, with its severely functional metal case, is a far cry from the elaborate console models marketed in the brief period from 1936 to 1939 when tele-vision programmes were beamed for a few hours daily to households within a short radius of London's Alexandra Palace. Post-war models have undergone numerous changes and tended to become slimmer as electronics have attained a greater degree of sophistication, so that the cabinets of the 1950s have acquired an antique character already.

RAIL RELICS

Interest in the railwayana of the past increases as the mileage of the world's railways shrinks. The Iron Horse reached its peak during the Second World War, but since then each year sees the closure of more unprofitable lines and the retreat of the locomotive in face of competition from other forms of transport. This has thrown a lot of material on to the junk heap, but nowadays most railroad companies and nationalized lines operate collectors' shops and junkyards, turning surplus equipment into a handsome profit.

Collectors' Corner near London's Euston Station, is a typical example of the genre. A splendid wrought-iron staircase leads one into a warehouse which is a veritable Aladdin's cave of railway memorabilia. Pride of place is occupied by the ornate crests of the old railway companies, many dating back before the great re-grouping of the 1920s, followed by the nameplates from long vanished locomotives and stations, and the signs and headboards, smokebox plates and builders' workplates, often cast in gleaming brass or picked out in contrasting enamel colours. Signalling equipment, telegraphic instruments, station and waiting-room clocks, conductors' and guards' watches, ticket dispensers, punches and machines, not to mention the TICKETS themselves, WHISTLES, pay-checks and transport tokens, locomotive and station LAMPS and even the crockery and cutlery bearing the crests and initials of the railway companies are among the more popular collectables. Then there are all the UNIFORM items, from BADGES and buttons to the HEADGEAR, the grease-tops

A LNER locomotive nameplate, and a Great Central Railway coffee pot (both National Railway Museum)

of drivers and firemen and the gold-braided caps of stationmasters. Railway ephemera includes handbills and POSTERS, timetables and tourist guides, and many of the companies in Europe and America gave away vast amounts of promotional material, from PICTURE POSTCARDS to PLAYING CARDS and advertising novelties.

RECORDS AND RECORD SLEEVES

The battle between the Berliner and Edison systems of sound recording and reproduction, using GRAMOPHONES AND PHONOGRAPHS respectively, was not resolved in favour of the former till about 1910. After that date flat discs were preferred to the earlier cylinders and these are now among the most highly prized forms of record. They may be found in their original tin containers, with printed labels on the sides. Berliner's galvano-plastic records of the 1890s are major rarities today, but the later shellac and cellulose nitrate records are relatively plentiful and were adopted by most of the world's recording companies. Other early variants include records of non-standard speed, size and groove but from 1910 onwards records were gradu-

ally standardized at 78 r.p.m. in diameters of 5, 7, 10 and 12 inches. Flexible records made a brief halting appearance in the 1930s but did not really catch on till the 1950s when the first

A Queen Mary Doll's house miniature record sleeve (about 1½ in or 3 cm in diameter), and white Neophone record, c.1905 (Christies, South Kensington)

of the modern long-playing records were marketed.

Record sleeves are of fairly modern origin, but from the turn of the century onwards sets of records were sold in albums with suitable decoration on their bindings and covers. The flimsy paper sleeves of the Twenties and Thirties frequently carried advertising matter and from this gradually developed the glossy wrappers of the present day. The more attractive and informative sleeves coincided with the advent of long-playing records about 1955 and early examples of this type are now much sought after.

RIBBONS AND RIBANDS

Here is a compact collectable for those interested in textiles, offering plenty of scope in the embroidery, printing and weaving of silks and satins over the past two centuries. The finest ribbons were made in France and exported to every part of the civilized world, but from the 1830s onwards ribbons were produced locally in Germany, Italy, Britain and the United States and considerable ingenuity was shown in devising complicated patterns for the Jacquard looms on which continuous ribbons were woven. Plain silk ribbons were pleated and gathered by machines and took on an almost sculptural quality. Elaborate rosettes and quatrefoils of ribbon were fashionable between 1875 and 1910 and may be found among the remnants of costume and DRESS ACCESSORIES. Ribbons woven with floral or geometric patterns were used for hatbands and GARTERS, for straps and braces and dress trimmings of all kinds. Firms like Stevens (better known for their STEVENGRAPHS) and Cash of Coventry exported pictorial ribbons to every part of the globe from the middle of the nineteenth century onwards. These ribbons may be found with historical, biblical classical or patriotic motifs, or with the symbolism of love, romance and other sentiments.

Collectors of MILITARIA prize ribbons of various kinds, from the cuff-titles of German regiments to the hat bands worn by sailors of most navies, inscribed with the names of their ships, and the embroidered or woven name and unit tabs worn on the tunics above the breast pocket. Ribands, strictly speaking, are ribbons intended as a decoration and range from the favours and rosettes awarded to sportsmen, to the parti-coloured silk ribbons worn with medals and orders.

RING TREES

A few of them actually look like miniature trees in wintertime, with bare branches of gilt metal or sterling silver on which ladies hung rings and other trinkets rather than store them in a jewel box. The Victorians, who had a sometimes surprising love of novelty, were not slow in devising many other shapes and forms, such as animal and human figures with limbs outstretched in artful poses and cunningly serving as the projections on which the rings were hung. Other popular forms were an outstretched human hand, the fingers parted so that the rings could be mounted. Around the turn of the century there were various patent devices of a more functional appearance, and some of these also incorporated a watch stand. They were produced in wood, ivory, horn, pottery, porcelain, glass and various metals. Like a lot of other useful objects that vanished with the passing of the Edwardian era, ring trees have been revived in recent years and there are some delightfully wrought modern examples, richly gilt and enamelled, sometimes incorporating a tiny looking glass.

SALT BOXES AND JARS

In this wonderful age of food preservatives and deep freezes it is difficult for us to comprehend what a problem our ancestors faced in maintaining an appetizing diet all year round, or how valuable a commodity salt and spices were. Salt was indispensible for preserving many meats and vegetables and was also used liberally to season food that might have begun to lose its freshness and flavour.

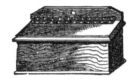

A wooden salt box (Army & Navy Stores Ltd)

The difficulties of keeping salt dry were overcome by storing it in special containers which were kept by the fireside or hung from the wall above the fireplace. Salt boxes were stout wooden cases with a wall bracket and a sloping lid made of oak. Since the usual iron or brass hinge and clasp would have corroded, these were replaced by ingenious wooden or leather hinges and straps. The surfaces of these boxes were frequently decorated according to the custom of each locality, by carving, pokerwork, or painting in traditional patterns. Salt jars, known also as salt kits or saut buckets, were made of earthenware or stoneware. They usually had a flattened back, with a ring at the top so that they could be hung on a hook at the fireside, and had a characteristic opening at right angles to the top. They were usually ornamented with white or coloured slip but may be found with tinglazed decoration in crude, vigorous patterns. The salt jar has been revived in recent years and is one of the useful articles so beloved of the craft potteries, decorated in their individual styles.

SALT AND PEPPER SETS

Salt cellars and pepper pots have been gracing the dining table for centuries and they rank among the smaller and less expensive items in the repertoire of the silversmith. They were produced en suite with MUSTARD POTS from the early eighteenth century onwards, and may be found with plain circular, conical or faceted surfaces, with piercing, gadrooning or bright-cutting, with foliate ornament and knopped finials. The collector of modest means, however, will probably settle for the numerous fancy and novelty shapes ranging from figures in national costume to an entire menagerie of wild animals, and from cannon shells to windmills (complete with rotating sails). They come in glass and porcelain, pottery of all kinds and various metals, BAKELITE and other PLASTICS. They may be found with civic crests after the manner of

Salt cellars, muffineers, a mustard pot and spoons in the 1939 Army & Navy Catalogue.

Goss china or with inscriptions implying a secondary role as tourist souvenirs from many parts of the world. It must be confessed that a fair proportion of them are pure KITSCH, but a large collection takes up little space and can look very attractive.

SCALE MODELS

This covers any replica reduced to scale but the most important categories, LOCOMOTIVE and SHIP MODELS are discussed separately. Many of the so-called APPRENTICE PIECES might more properly be regarded as scale models if they were primarily designed to demonstrate the working of a piece of machinery. Visual aids of this kind have been produced by industry for well over a century now and are of considerable interest to industrial archaeologists. Other models have been used as sales aids, a three-dimensional object being infinitely preferable to a two-dimensional drawing or photograph. Apart from models with working parts, there are many static models, ranging from the miniature aircraft used by tour operators and airlines, to the architectural models of houses, factories, public buildings and even entire towns and villages. Lego and other modern building systems have greatly simplified the art of

A scale model of the London to Brighton coach of 1888 (Christies, South Kensington)

model-building, but there are still a few hardy souls engaged in the time-honoured pastime of constructing models from used matchsticks. The secret lies in glueing the sticks together into more manageable lengths and blocks.

SCALES AND BALANCES

Now that weights have virtually been reduced to a single standard and metrication has triumphed, all those scales and balances which measured by the pennyweight and the drachm, the ounce and the pound, the stone and the hundredweight, have become obsolete. If no longer serviceable they are eminently collectable and join the ranks of all the weird and wonderful contraptions devised over the centuries for the measurement of weight.

The chief interest lies in the smaller scales, pride of place being given to the many patent devices used for checking the weight of gold coins. Even after the introduction of edge graining as a security device to prevent clipping, people still had a healthy distrust of coins they had not personally weighed. Pocket balances range from the simple brass gadgets with tiny pans at one end for sovereigns and half sovereigns (or guineas, ducats,

zecchini, napoleons or any other gold coinage) and a brass weight of the proscribed amount at the other. More elaborate balances had folding columns and arms that neatly stowed away into a tiny wooden case carried in the pocket.

The advent of uniform postal systems in the 1840s, with charges calculated according to the weight of the letter, gave rise to a large family of letter balances. Table models were designed like conventional scales in miniature, but there were many unusual devices of the arc and pointer type, or miniature steelyards that clamped to the edge of the desk. Letter balances are of particular interest to the philatelist and postal historian since they often show calibrated scales of postal charges and these enable the scales to be dated fairly accurately.

Apothecaries' scales and balances used by

A pair of brass scales in fitted walnut case (Christies, South Kensington)

jewellers and goldsmiths represent the acme of precision since they were required to measure the smallest variations in weight. They are delicate instruments finely made, with sets of tiny weights to match. The weights themselves are extremely interesting since many of them bear official emblems and stamps to testify to their true weight.

In the larger category are the commercial scales and balances used by grocers, butchers, grain and coal merchants, with weights of ponderous brass or cast iron. Other specialized scales include baby balances and penny-in-the-slot weighing machines, the earlier models being replete with cast iron ornament.

SCRAPS

One of my treasured possessions is a small leatherbound notebook of the mid-nineteenth century, picked up at a jumble sale for a few pence some years ago. It is crammed full of embossed crests and monograms cut from the flaps of nineteenth century envelopes. Some of the more pictorial examples have been cunningly worked into a series of watercolour landscapes. This is only one of the ways in which a craze known as decalcomania expressed itself in Victorian times. Even earlier, young ladies cut the illustrations from periodicals, bill-heads and PICTORIAL NOTEPAPER and pasted them in albums.

Inevitably stationers were not slow in catering to this craze and by 1840 were publishing sheets of scraps, chromolithographed, embossed and ready cut. Complete sheets of scraps from the Victorian era are scarce now, but similar scraps were being produced until quite recently and modern examples are quite plentiful. The scrap albums themselves are a

Victorian scraps pasted in an album

fascinating window on the past, particularly if they include cuttings from contemporary TRADE CARDS and ADVERTISEMENTS, especially the magazine inserts of the turn of the century. Scraps have also been used to decorate many objects, from pencil cases and WRITING SETS to draught screens and nursery furniture.

SCRIMSHAW

Otherwise known as scrimshander or scrimshouting, this is a folk art which is generally attributed to the whalers and sealers of Connecticut and Massachusetts, but was probably practised in some form or another by sailors in many parts of the world. It consists of finely engraving on such materials as whalebone and walrus tusk with the point of a knife or a sharpened nail and infinite patience was required to achieve some of the detailed landscapes and animated scenes found in this medium. The best of scrimshaw, dating from the eighteenth century, has long since vanished into museum collections, but there is a host of minor examples, in the form of powder horns, stay-busks and knife-handles, which were

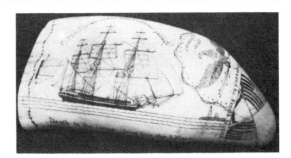

A scrimshaw, whale's tooth, 1829 (Reproduced by permission of the American Museum in Britain, Bath)

being carved and engraved up to fairly recently. Many of these have only the barest outline of a picture; others have highly detailed portraits and are highly prized if they also happen to have commemorative inscriptions.

SERVERS

The revolution in table manners which took place in the late seventeenth century made it bad form to stretch out and tear off chunks of meat with one's fingers. The refinement of eating habits that began with the introduction of the fork in the 1600s was completed with the invention of a whole host of serving implements, so that food was tipped on to one's plate without being touched by human hands. The first of the servers were the large spoons with ovoid bowls and plain stems that came into use in the reign of William and Mary. Gradually serving spoons and ladles were tailored to suit the needs of the soups and stews, meat and vegetables which they handled and by the 1730s servers were being produced to match the other items of cutlery.

Fish servers came somewhat later, and were originally known as fish trowels, with a very broad, pointed blade, curved where it joined the handle. By 1800 fish servers and slices had become longer, with narrower blades, often rounded or with an undulating edge. Servers were either flat-bladed or had a slightly concave curve, and the piercing to permit juice

A server in electro-plate (Army & Navy Stores Ltd)

and gravy to drain away gave ample scope for decorative treatment, either circular perforations arranged in attractive patterns, or fretting or openwork motifs. Geometric or floral piercing was sometimes accompanied by flat chasing. Asymmetrical blades were provided for the host who needed servers in both hands to carve up a very large fish, and there were even single fish servers, dating around 1810, comprising a fish slice with a long bolster shank and a smaller handle and blade directly above it.

Out of this curious implement developed the numerous kinds of double-bladed servers joined at the centre and fitted with twin handles, like an outsize pair of scissors. Servers have been produced in silver, Sheffield plate, electroplate and polished or japanned hardwoods. Items such as sardines, asparagus and sugar lumps that required greater dexterity in handling were handled by TONGS.

SEWING BIRDS

Now that embroidery is becoming a fashionable pastime once more there could be a real need for these gadgets of the eighteenth and nineteenth centuries. They were constructed of wrought iron or brass and clamped to the table, with a device often shaped like a bird's beak to hold the material taut while it was being embroidered. Others had grips in the form of human hands, animal paws and claws and eventually they were produced in many unusual shapes, from human figures to butterflies and mythological creatures, but they were still known generically as birds. They may be found in ivory, hardwood or electroplate, though iron and brass were the commonest materials and some of the more elaborate examples incorporated small pincushions or workboxes.

SEWING MACHINES

This boon to the home dressmaker had its humble origins in the 1750s when Charles Weisenthal invented a double-pointed needle with the eye in the centre. This was adapted in 1790 by Thomas Saint of Greenhill Rents, London, for a machine that was capable of quilting, stitching and sewing. Saint's invention never got beyond the drawing board, however, though many of the features he devised were later utilised by Isaac Singer (the perpendicular action) and Elias Howe (the eye-pierced needle and pressing surfaces). The first practical sewing machine was invented by a French tailor, Barthelemy Thimmonier in 1829 and the success of his early wooden machines roused the ire of the Paris mob who destroyed them lest their livelihood as handworkers be damaged. Thimmonier persevered with his invention and in

Right: The first Singer sewing machine, made in 1851. *Left:* The Singer 'Turtle Back' machine, the first specifically designed for home sewing, 1856. *Below:* The 1859 'Letter A' machine (All Singers)

1845 all-metal machines were produced by the Magnin company to Thimmonier's design, but once again the Paris mob intervened and the project was totally swept away in the rioting that accompanied the downfall of the July Monarchy.

Elias Howe invented the lock-stitch sewing machine in 1846 and subsequently produced large machines which revolutionized the American and British tailoring industry. Isaac

Merritt Singer of Boston concentrated on the domestic market and produced his first household sewing machine in 1851 – the first great labour-saving device of modern times. Since then there have been countless models and numerous technical refinements, from the lock-stitch and the high arm to the self-setting needle, tension releaser and reverse feed.

Although Singer dominated the world market, there were many other manufacturers whose machines, if anything, are now more desirable. These include Willcox and Gibbs, Jones, Frister and Rossman, Necchi, Wheeler and Wilson and Grover and Baker. Particularly sought after are the tiny machines, designed for children or as portable models.

SEXTANTS ETC.

Navigation was largely a matter of guesswork until 1731 when John Hadley invented an instrument known as the octant, since its principal feature was a graduated arc of an eighth of a circle. Though octants continued to be widely used till the end of the eighteenth century, more accurate measurements of angular distance could be effected with an arc of a sixth of a circle, hence the sextant which came into use in 1757. Prior to 1771 the calibration of quadrants, sextants and octants was fairly coarse, but Jesse Ramsden's dividing machine thereafter made finer and more accurate calibration possible. There are many technical features on sextants, single- or double-frame types with mirrors, shades and lenses, and vernier scales in precious metals as well as brass. The earlier examples were frequently decorated with nautical motifs en-

A sextant by H. Hughes & Son (Christies, South Kensington)

graved on the brass parts and a few bore embossed masks and tiny bas-reliefs showing maritime symbolism and trophies of war. Most sextants produced after 1900 are quite plain and devoid of ornament, but the early bubble sextants used by aerial navigators during and just after the First World War are of great interest to collectors of AERONAUTICA.

SHAVING MUGS

Oddly enough, these vessels belonged to a century (1830–1930) when men sported heavy beards, side-whiskers and moustaches, but they reflect a pre-occupation with good grooming – just like the sets of cut-throat razors inscribed with the days of the week.

These mugs were the direct descendants of the barber's bowls and cups which were produced from the fifteenth century onwards in pottery, porcelain, brass and even silver. The barber's cups of the eighteenth and early nineteenth centuries were usually decorated

An elephant shaving mug c.1900 (David Cripps)

with transfer-printed scenes of tavern life, or more demure floral patterns and heraldic motifs. Although shaving mugs may be found in a wide variety of shapes and styles, their common factor is the separate compartment for the soap, either in front or at the side. The earliest mugs were of pottery, often with relief ornament, but by the 1850s elegant mugs in silver or Sheffield plate were being produced in England. The Americans specialized in unusual designs, one of these – the Utility of Boston – having up to four compartments for soap, razor and brush as well as water. Between 1860 and 1940 no fewer than 94 patents were issued in the United States alone for shaving mugs of different types. Up to about 1930 it was the custom for men to be shaved at their local barber shop which kept racks containing personalized mugs for each customer. These mugs may be found with relatively plain black and gold labels covered with a thick transparent glaze, or with fancy floral patterns or even inset photographs of wives and sweethearts. Birds, animals, scenery and heraldry were other popular subjects, while a rather later fashion (around 1900)

favoured symbolism alluding to the owner's profession, sports or hobbies. Less popular are the mugs with a purely numeral design, kept by barber shops where the turnover of custom was great (as in garrison towns).

There were also many novelty shapes ranging from the plentiful fishes and dolphins to the rare monkeys, elephants, dogs and hippopotami. Quite a few mugs may be found with transfer prints of holiday resorts and tourist landmarks, decorated with gold or pink lustre. Patriotism was expressed in the mugs at the turn of the century, portraying generals and heroes of the Boer War or the Spanish-American War. The First World War which forced many men to shave themselves for the first time, led to the decline of the barbershop visit as a daily ritual but it survived for a further decade in the United States, and the individual shaving mug became a thing of the past.

SHIP MODELS

One tends to think immediately of ships in bottles, the folk art practised by sailors from the early nineteenth century up to the time of the First World War, but there are many other varieties that are just as collectable. In recent years there has been quite a revival of interest in this craft and the kinds of ships imprisoned in glass have consequently diversified. As it is difficult to date such models the value tends to depend upon the skill and craftsmanship involved, the most desirable models being of full-rigged sailing ships. Models with intricately painted or modelled background scenery also rate a handsome premium.

When ship-building became more of an exact science with the advent of steam, it became customary for the builders to prepare preliminary scale models. These range from the half models of hulls, mounted on painted wooden panels, to the fully three-dimensional models in glass cases. Builders' half models were once fairly plentiful at no great cost but they have long since been snapped up and are quite elusive. The working scale models of

A clockwork tinplate model of a liner named Provence, c.1910 (Christies, South Kensington)

naval architects, however, are exceedingly expensive; they were costly to produce initially and their value has been greatly enhanced by their antique status. The same remarks apply to almost any ship model that is well made, bearing in mind the number of hours of loving workmanship which have gone into its construction.

SHOE HORNS

Devices for easing the feet in and out of boots and shoes have probably been in existence for centuries, the earliest examples being fashioned from strips of cow-horn. From the eighteenth century date shoe horns carved from hardwoods, and metal horns date from the second half of the nineteenth century. The more serviceable brass or steel horns were often decorated with the names, addresses and trademarks of shoemakers and were an early form of advertising giveaway. More elegant shoe horns at the turn of the century were diestruck in classical or floral motifs and silver-plated. They were often produced with button-hooks in matching sets. As footwear became lower at the ankle the design of horns was modified and even the name altered to shoe lift. These were made of ebony, ivory, BAKELITE, xylonite or other early PLASTICS, the more decorative examples having inlaid brass or silver ornament on the handle. Patent shoe lifts even had button-hooks or GLOVE STRETCHERS combined.

SKIRT LIFTERS

The vagaries of fashion at the turn of the century gave rise to these gadgets designed to enable the well-dressed woman to cope with the problems of the S-line. This fashion demanded that skirts be worn long, trailing the ground majestically, but since it also involved the moulding of the female form into an elongated S by means of tightly laced corsets of an inordinate length, thrusting out the bosom in front and the bustle behind, it was impossible to stoop and gather up the hem of the skirt while traversing dusty or muddy streets.

The answer to the problem was the skirt lifter, a device with a curved, hooked or pincer-shaped end attached to a long stick. The simpler varieties had a plain hook and handle, but the more elegant varieties had the business end modelled in the form of a human hand or bird's talons and the handles were silver-mounted. Patent devices had a spring-loaded catch which held the hem firmly without risk of tearing. The lifters in the form of a hand, in carved hardwood, ivory or cast silver, are sometimes confused with head scratchers – themselves a relic of an earlier and even more preposterous fashion for very elaborate coiffures which were kept intact for months on end – disturbed only by the headlice and other vermin that resided therein.

SLOT MACHINES

Only the other day I passed a village post office in the north of Scotland and saw a cast iron vending machine embedded in the wall, allegedly dispensing a slab of a well-known brand of chocolate for a penny – an old, pre-decimal penny at that! Such machines were a common sight on railway station platforms and other public places before the Second World War but most of them fell prey to war-time salvage drives. A few, however, survived and are now among the more treasured of RAIL RELICS, along with the penny-in-the-slot weighing machines, hair-cream dispensers and chewing gum machines of the immediate post-war era.

Actually, devices for dispensing goods or

services by means of a coin date from the sixth century BC when Egyptian temples used holy water dispensers operated by coins. In practice, vending machines have only become widespread since the advent of milled coinage in the late seventeenth century and range from the tobacco dispensers of oldstyle drug stores to the nickelodeons and pennyanos of the late nineteenth century. The modern slot machines were pioneered by Percival Everitt of London in 1883. Everitt's first machines were designed to sell stamped postcards but within a few years his Sweetmeat Automatic Delivery Company was selling an astonishing range of goods and services, from handkerchiefs and perfumes to accident insurance and cough lozenges. The earliest American machines, patented in 1886, sold chewing gum but the vending industry expanded rapidly and by 1901 Americans could obtain anything from a pack of peanuts for a penny to an instant divorce (in Utah) for $2.50! From the collector's viewpoint the more interesting 'slots' are the smaller varieties – ticket and stamp dispensers and those devices fitted to lavatory doors which gave rise to the euphemism 'to spend a penny'.

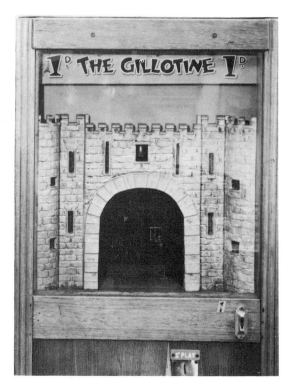

A coin-in-the-slot amusement machine (Christies, South Kensington)

SNUFF BOTTLES

Snuff boxes have been widely collected for centuries, but not so much attention has been given to their Oriental counterpart, the snuff bottle. Snuff bottles were the Chinese solution to the problem of keeping snuff dry in compact form. The earliest examples were miniature vases with a tightly fitting stopper. Later tiny bottles were specifically produced for the purpose and the shape of the lip improved to give a tighter fit. These bottles were made with tiny spoons or scoops attached by chains to the stopper so that a small quantity of snuff could be extracted. The bottles were made of porcelain or glass, often delicately enamelled or painted on the inner surface. Other bottles in opaque or coloured glass are relatively modern and still fairly reasonable in price. At the other extreme, however, are the very

A red glass snuff bottle (Lyle Publications)

expensive bottles carved from Imperial jade, agate, tourmaline, aquamarine, beryl, amethyst and other semi-precious stones. Even the flaws in these stones were ingeniously turned to advantage and made the focal point of the intricately carved relief. Stoppers and spoons were fashioned in silver or gold and iron and brass were also used for rims and mounts, sometimes inlaid with precious metals. Less common are the bottles made from ivory or horn, the crest of the Malayan Helmeted Hornbill being used for the latter.

SOAP BOXES, DISHES ETC.

The problem of keeping bars of soap reasonably dry has occupied the mind of many an inventor, as witness the numerous varieties of patent soap dish produced over the past two centuries. Most of them operated on the principle of draining away surplus moisture by grooved channels or holes and dishes and boxes may be found with detachable liners of porcelain, pottery or glass. Soap boxes made entirely of glass were fashionable in the late nineteenth century and may be found with enamelled ornament on the lid, or press-moulded decoration in plain or coloured glass. Ceramic boxes and dishes, of course, run the entire gamut of decorative treatments found in pottery and porcelain and these dishes were often produced *en suite* with CHAMBER POTS and other articles for the bedroom washstand.

Among the more interesting varieties are the small travelling cases of various metals – a relic of the times when hotels did not provide guests with soap. These boxes may be found in brass, copper, steel, japanned metal, nickel-plate, electroplate or even silver (occasionally with gilt inner surfaces), and they were often diestruck with floral or scenic patterns. More elaborate fixtures include the bathroom tidies evolved in the 1890s with separate compartments for soaps and sponges, toothbrushes and face cloths.

SOUVENIRS

Strictly speaking this term ought only to apply to those trifles and bibelots which are actually inscribed in French 'Souvenir de . . .' followed by the name of the place for which they serve as a remembrance, but its meaning has now been widened to include any tourist memento. The most desirable, of course, are those which bear this inscription and range from PICTURE POSTCARDS of the 1890s and early 1900s to small painted wooden boxes of all kinds and mugs and RACK PLATES. Counterparts in other languages include the German 'Gruss Aus' (greetings from . . .) and the Italian 'Memento di'. English examples dating from the late eighteenth century were usually inscribed 'A Trifle from . . .' and are now much in demand by collectors who specialize in the products of one town or locality. Trifles in the form of inkwells, trinket boxes, snuff boxes, mugs and small dishes, embellished with ornamental inscriptions from copperplate transfers, were the forerunners of the more colourful Goss crested china and the pottery souvenirs of the late nineteenth century with their scenic motifs.

A selection of souvenirs: *From top left:* A Victorian transfer printed wooden scent bottle case, a copper lighthouse money box, *c.*1860, a Goss porcelain of Shakespeare's cottage, a Jacob & Co. Coronation coach biscuit box, and a Victorian plate commemorating Gladstone (All Lyle Publications)

SOVEREIGN CASES

If ever the British Government should emulate the Isle of Man and re-introduce a one-pound coin in the size of the gold sovereign there could be a revival in the demand for these cases. Indeed, the necessity for such cases would be even greater in view of the fact that the modern pound pieces do not have the distinctive advantage of gold in being a much heavier metal than others in current use. Sovereigns replaced the slightly larger guineas in 1816 and being about the size of a shilling – a silver coin a twentieth of its value – there was a very real problem that the two might be confused, especially in the poor lighting of nineteenth-century towns. Although the earliest sovereigns featured St George and the Dragon (as do the modern gold coins) many of them had a coat of arms like the device on the shilling and this even encouraged dishonest individuals to pass off gilded shillings as sovereigns.

From left: a gilt metal double sovereign case, a Victorian case and a single gilt case. (Lyle Publications)

The simplest form of sovereign case was merely a purse designed to house a certain number of sovereigns and half sovereigns, but the more elaborate versions, in silver or electro-plate, had spring-loaded platforms which facilitated the dispensing of the coins one at a time when the case was opened. Others incorporated ingenious devices for weighing the coins to check that they were genuine. Late nineteenth-century cases had additional compartments for postage stamps, matches, sealing wax and needles and were often fitted with a silver or gold ring for suspension from a watch chain or chatelaine.

SPECTACLES AND CASES

These aids to vision have been around for almost 700 hundred years in one form or another. The principles of optics were enunciated by Roger Bacon in 1266 and within two decades spectacles with lenses of rock crystal were being produced in Italy, a contemporary account of this new invention being given by Sandro di Popozo in his *Treatise on Family Conduct*, written in 1289. Silver-framed spectacles valued at two shillings were listed in the inventory of Walter de Stapledon, Bishop of Exeter, in 1326 and a fresco portraying Cardinal Ugone in a Treviso church, painted in 1352, shows him wearing a kind of pince-nez.

At first spectacles were confined to the very small class of society which could read, but the extension of education to the ordinary people in the sixteenth century and the greater use of printed books created a demand for spec-

Five pairs of dark glasses, worthy of Elton John! (Christies, South Kensington)

tacles. By 1600 lenses were usually ground from glass and most towns in Europe boasted its optician. The earliest spectacles were held in place by cords looped round the ears and it was not until 1727 that so-called temple spectacles, with rigid side-pieces and curved ends to rest on the ears were invented by

Edward Scarlett of London. The monocle also dates from this period, the best examples being produced in England where the grinding of lenses had developed into an exact science. Bifocals date from 1760, when Benjamin Franklin had a pair made for him, and sunglasses date from the mid-nineteenth century, the earliest examples having primitive lenses of blue glass. Later types had smoked glass or tinted celluloid sandwiched between thin sheets of plain glass.

Apart from the technical features of the lenses, of great interest to opticians and optometrists, antique spectacles possess considerable charm in the styling of frames and side-pieces and the use of such materials as gold, silver, brass, steel, mother of pearl and

'Full-size spectacles which will conveniently fold into the smallest of cases for the handbag or pocket, and yet conform to the most exacting optical requirements' (Army & Navy Stores Ltd)

tortoiseshell. Similarly, the cases were often made of matching materials. The nineteenth century in particular witnessed many kinds of patent device for securing spectacles firmly on the bridge of the nose. Cases containing engraved advertisements of spectacle makers are also worth looking for.

SPORTS EQUIPMENT

Here is a vast field for the sportsman who is also a collector, since most of the popular sports have a history spanning several centuries and have evolved subtly over that period. Golf, whose Scottish origins are lost in the mists of antiquity, has yielded an enormous range of collectables, from the all-wooden clubs and leather balls stuffed with feathers to the modern rubber-cored gutta percha balls (patented in 1898), and steel-shafted clubs patented in 1910. Tennis rackets have varied considerably in size and shape within the past century alone, and prior to the establishment of the Lawn Tennis Association in 1874 the variety must have been infinite. Rounders and their descendants, baseball and cricket, used

bats and balls of shapes and materials that differed radically from those that became standardized in the 1870s. Footballs, polo sticks, croquet mallets and stands, badminton and squash rackets and shuttlecocks, bowls, archery equipment and sabres, foils, epees and singlesticks used in fencing have all been subject to variation in the past century alone. Among the indoor sports the greatest scope lies in darts and billiards, both of which have undergone many stages in their development in the same period. Since billiards was being played in Elizabethan times there should be plenty of scope in cues, balls and scorers, though I do not imagine that many Tudor or Jacobean billiard tables have survived.

SPURS AND STIRRUPS

It is the smaller pieces of tack that provide the greatest variety and interest to the collector of equestrian antiques. Spurs, derived from the same Anglo-Saxon word to kick which gives us the modern word 'spurn', were originally a single tiny spike fixed to the horseman's heel

but by the late thirteenth century the rowel spur was coming into use. In this type, from which all later forms of spur are descended, the pricks that goad the horse are produced from a spiked wheel. Early spurs had enormous shanks to enable the rider to strike at his

The Mohawk Pelham and Curb, for riding and driving, and a Peacock stirrup iron (Army & Navy Stores Ltd)

charger's flanks below the bards or horse armour. From the fifteenth century till the 1670s these long-shanked spurs became highly decorative with gold and silver inlays on the steel sides. Gilded spurs were regarded as the badge of knighthood and in those rare cases of ceremonial degradation they were hacked from the knight's heels by the scullion's chopper. The finest spurs were those produced in Germany, France, Italy and Spain in the sixteenth and seventeenth centuries, and they have their more modern counterpart in the extravagantly barbed spurs affected by Mexican caballeros.

Similar forms of decoration, both inlaying and gilding, may be found on stirrup irons, which also vary considerably in shape and breadth. The selection of the right bit to suit a horse's mouth is a complex business and there has always been a wide variety to choose from. An old catalogue before me lists the Ninth Lancers Polo bit and curb, the Mohawk Pelham, the Stanley Pelham, Swale's Patent Three in One bit, the Weymouth bit and bridoon, the Turn Ring race bridoon, the Egg Butt race bridoon, the Centaur Mouth and the Cheltenham Gag among many others in hand-forged steel or nickelplate.

STAMP BOXES AND CASES

It is not always possible to be precise about the introduction of an object, but with stamp boxes and cases we know that they made their appearance shortly after the advent of the world's first adhesive postage stamps in May 1840. Up to 1854 in Britain, and in some countries for many years thereafter, postage stamps were issued without perforations and had to be cut apart by means of scissors or a penknife. The inconvenience of having to cut off a stamp every time one was needed was lessened by having a stock of stamps all ready cut and these were stored in small boxes designed for the purpose.

The earliest and simplest boxes were small rectangular wooden cases with a tight-fitting but detachable lid. Square or oblong boxes were produced for this purpose in Tunbridge ware and circular tartan-covered boxes were a speciality of Mauchline ware. These boxes are particularly desirable if they happen to have an actual example of a Penny Red stamp inset in the lid. Later boxes were made with one, two or three compartments to hold stamps of different denominations and generally they have a sloping or slightly curved base

A silver stamp case

to each compartment to facilitate the removal of the stamps. They may be found in hard-wood, ivory, ceramic materials or cast brass.

Silver stamp boxes with tiny glass windows containing specimens of stamps date from the 1860s and remained fashionable up to about 1914, even though stamps were now perforated and latterly were produced in handy booklet form. Again, they may be found with up to three apertures and though silver was the favourite medium they were also produced in gold and semi-precious stones such as malachite and agate. There are also tiny silver stamp cases, in the form of an envelope with a ring for mounting on fob or chatelaine. Stamp boxes were also incorporated in other articles, such as BLOTTERS, INKSTANDS, SOVEREIGN CASES and WRITING SETS.

STEINS

A collection of pewter steins (William Doyle Galleries, Inc., New York)

Probably the most popular form of SOUVENIR of a visit to Germany is the beer stein with its elaborate relief decoration, high-domed lid and handle with thumb-piece in silver or more likely in pewter. The tall straight sides of these tankards lend themselves admirably to scenic motifs, the better examples being hand-painted in low relief and the more commercial examples in transfer prints. The German stein or beer mug has a very long and honourable history, stretching back to the Middle Ages when the production of *steingut* or *steinzeug* (stoneware) began in the Rhineland about the year 1300. The earliest mugs and jugs were known as tigerware on account of the mottled surface of the stoneware resembling the hide of a tiger.

Later tankards paralleled the development of the bellarmine, those bulbous vessels bearing the relief portrait of a bearded cleric and said to be none other than the infamous Cardinal Bellarmino himself. Steins of the sixteenth and seventeenth centuries were frequently decorated with relief portraits, animal masks and latterly scenic motifs, and this developed out of simple incised ornament into the extravagant confections of the eighteenth and nineteenth centuries with deeper relief baroque and rococo decoration showing the strong influence of France and Italy. Important centres of production were Cologne, Siegburg, Raeren and Westerwald but steins were much imitated by the potteries of Flanders, north-eastern France and England. The somewhat drab colour of the stoneware was enhanced by the use of richly coloured glazes, of which a deep cobalt blue was predominant, to give sharp contrast to the relief ornament.

In the late nineteenth and twentieth centuries the production of steins became more commercialized, the leading manufacturers in this field, Villeroy and Boch, producing countless patterns including numerous steins of a commemorative nature. Highly prized by collectors of MILITARIA are the steins bearing patriotic motifs from the Prussian wars of 1864, 1866 and 1870 against Denmark, Austria and France respectively and the vast range of military steins produced during both world wars.

STEVENGRAPHS

Thomas Stevens (1828–1888) hit upon the woven silk picture as a means of relieving unemployment in the Coventry silk-weaving industry, at a time when the market was flooded by cheap silks from the Continent. The result was the Stevengraph, woven on

Jacquard looms, and sold for a few pence at country fairs and exhibitions, notably the York Industrial Exhibition of 1879. Stevengraphs were approximately the size of postcards and, suitably mounted and framed, made excellent wall ornaments. Stevens ranged over the entire spectrum of late Victorian life in search of subjects. All the celebrities of the last quarter of the nineteenth century were immortalized in silk – actresses and politicians, generals and war heroes, jockeys and cricketers, royalty both British and foreign, and anyone else who happened to catch the limelight for a time.

Sports, such as cricket, regattas and foxhunting, were popular subjects, as were pictures of transport old and new. A favourite theme was the contrast between the modern expresses and the primitive locomotives of the 1820s and these Stevengraphs are much sought after by collectors of RAIL RELICS.

Stevens also produced BOOK MARKERS woven in silk, as well as the usual run of RIBBONS and BADGES. Several other companies emulated him, notably W. H. Grant and Cash of Coventry and several attempts have been made to revive them in recent years. These latter-day Stevengraphs are usually woven in

A Stevengraph of Leda and the Swan

nylon and can readily be distinguished from the originals. The production of Stevengraphs declined after the First World War and the Blitz on Coventry in 1940 destroyed the Stevens factory.

STOCK AND SHARE CERTIFICATES

Now that banknotes and other forms of paper money are well established as collectables, notaphilists are exploring other forms of security printing and have discovered that old stocks, bonds and shares, long considered worthless by virtue of default or bankruptcy, may have a value after all. Generally speaking, it was the more questionable shares which had the most attractively engraved certificates. Whatever the shortcomings of a goldmine or railroad in actuality, on paper considerable care and skill were lavished in making them as inviting as possible to the would-be investor. Many of these old certificates, replete with finely engraved vignettes of mine-workings, locomotives and grandiose public works, have lain neglected in stockbrokers' and lawyers'

A Russian stock certificate (Stanley Gibbons)

basements and attics but are now being resurrected for sale to collectors.

Other certificates pertain to the public utilities in Tsarist Russia, or in the former Baltic states which were absorbed by the Soviet Union in 1940. Since there is always the faint hope that some day the Soviet government may honour the obligations of past regimes to their stockholders, these beautifully engraved documents may have an intrinsic as well as aesthetic value.

A 1905 New York, New Haven and Hartford Railroad Company registered debenture (Stanley Gibbons)

STOVES

Up to about 1930 the coal-burning stove was to be found in most homes and as an important focal point of the domestic scene much care and decoration was invested in them. The countries of Northern Europe, with their rigorous winter, produced the most lavish stoves, often taking up a large part of one wall in the room. Though few collectors would be able to give them houseroom, their hafnerware tiles are eminently collectable in their own right. They can be recognized by their relief decoration covered with thick glazes of various colours.

From left: A Carbotron marathon stove, for heating or laundry, a Solesse stove for anthracite, coke or coalite, and a Courtier stove for coal (Army & Navy Stores Ltd)

A beautifully elaborate home sunshine range offered by Sears, Roebuck & Co. for $20 in 1894 (Sears, Roebuck)

In more temperate climates the cast iron stove provided adequate domestic heating and was produced in an incredible range of shapes and sizes, from diminutive portable stoves mounted on wheels to the large and highly ornate wall models complete with oven and cooking hob. Not so long ago these old stoves could be picked up from scrap-merchants' yards for little more than their scrap value, but now there are specialist dealers snapping them up and restoring them to their pristine glory, picking out the lavish decoration in different colours and reselling them as unusual ornaments at hundreds of pounds.

STRING BOXES

The year 1937 was an important landmark in the history of stationery, because it was then that adhesive tape was marketed for the first time. The Second World War accelerated its application and by 1950 it had all but driven old-fashioned string and tape out of home and office and relegated the string box or twine holder to the scrap-heap. Fortunately many charming examples of these boxes have survived and provide us with yet another example of antiques created from obsolescence.

The commonest variety is a small box of polished hardwood, about five inches square, with a drum inside and an aperture in the lid through which the string passed. Less common are the cylindrical or completely globular boxes in polished whitewood decorated with black transfer prints of scenery – one of the stock lines found in Mauchline ware. Then there are the metal varieties ranging from the painted tole and TINWARE boxes to the cast iron circular string holders, either mounted on ornamental feet or fitted with a ring for suspension. The two hemispheres were hinged on one side so that a ball of string could be inserted. There are many novelty shapes, from cottages and beehives to drums and cones, in copper, brass or japanned iron. There was a brief vogue in the 1920s for cretonne-covered string boxes in stout card and, being rather ephemeral, this type is now quite elusive.

STUD BOXES

The introduction of the stiff collar of gutta percha, which superseded the stock and cravat in the early nineteenth century, also witnessed the arrival of the collar stud. Nothing was more annoying than to mislay either back or front studs and for this reason small boxes were soon being manufactured for this specific purpose. They were circular, oval or square, produced in wood, leather, shagreen, ivory, porcelain or various metals, and usually had the word 'Studs' or its equivalent in other languages incised or inlaid in the lid. As the nineteenth century wore on, stud boxes became more highly decorative and were regarded as an object of vertu, the more expensive examples being delicately enamelled and gilded or set with precious stones. At the other

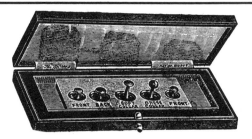

A box of gold studs offered in the 1939–40 Army & Navy catalogue.

end of the scale, however, there are plenty of examples with embossed or pokerwork decoration and also the souvenir boxes embellished with scenery and landmarks of the tourist haunts at the turn of the century. Later stud boxes tended to be much plainer and considerable use was made of BAKELITE, Erinoid, Ivorine and other early forms of PLASTIC.

STUFFED ANIMALS AND BIRDS

Although the skins of animals have been preserved since time immemorial taxidermy as a science dates only from the early seventeenth century. The earliest surviving examples tend to look like overblown soft toys since little heed was paid to anatomy, but by the 1850s a more realistic approach was being pioneered by Jules Verraux in Paris and Henry Ward in New York. Ward had a virtual world monopoly at one time, but gradually his techniques spread to Britain and Europe and there was even something of a craze for 'do-it-yourself' taxidermy – though it never quite attained the status of one of those social accomplishments cherished by Victorian young ladies.

There were two distinct schools of thought and both seem to have won equal acceptability, judging by the number of domed cases and glass cabinets which have survived. The one preferred animals and birds stuffed in a realistic manner and set against a background reproducing their natural habitat. The other struck an anthropomorphic stance and preferred animals and birds arranged in humanoid poses. The best example of this genre is

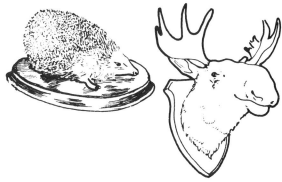

A Victorian stuffed hedgehog and a stuffed moose head (Lyle Publications)

Potter's Museum in Brighton, Sussex, with its bizarre little tableaux of the rats' wedding, the guinea pigs' cricket match and the gentlemen's club full of squirrels in nineteenth-century businessmen's attire. If anything, the latter style of taxidermy is probably the more desirable, shedding an interesting light on Victorian attitudes towards our feathered and furry friends.

SURGICAL INSTRUMENTS

The modern surgical scissors, saws, forceps and scalpels, forged out of single pieces of stainless steel with a minimum of crevices and joints wherein germs might lurk, are a far cry from the beautiful but highly insanitary instruments used in the operating theatre until a century ago. Early scalpels, for example, were constructed like penknives, with the blade folding into the elegantly chased handle. The handles of saws were decorated with inlaid work, and often had embossed animal masks securing the tang end of the blade. The blade was held in a richly chased metal frame – beautiful to look at, but what a paradise for microbes. It seems to have been the custom to decorate surgical instruments as ornately as possible, perhaps to demonstrate the elevated social status of the surgeon.

Even the more functional instruments of the early nineteenth century had elegant handles of hardwood or ivory, decorated with a fine pattern of criss-cross lines which no doubt gave the surgeon a better grip, but must have defied all attempts at sterilization. The discoveries of Lister and Semmelweis, however, revolutionized surgical practice and these fine old instruments were banished overnight.

Though the instruments of the late nineteenth century lacked the beauty of their predecessors they made up for this in their variety. The advent of anaesthesia as well as antiseptic surgery greatly extended the scope of operations and led the way for exploratory surgery which, in turn, produced a whole host of specialized instruments. The bronchoscope, cystoscope, laryngoscope, opthalmoscope and sigmoidoscope, which made much more accurate diagnosis feasible, also led to even more specialized surgical instruments, and as techniques in surgery have continually improved over the past eighty years the improvements and modifications in operating instruments have been many and diverse.

TAPE MEASURES

Now that metrication is upon us, the time has come to look out for examples of tape measures expressed in inches, feet, yards, poles and perches and all those other outmoded units which evolved gradually over the past thousand years and more, but which have now given way to the more prosaic metre, its multiples and subdivisions.

Tape measures range in size from the giant furlong and chain measures in heavy leather or wooden cases with brass winders, used by surveyors of the past, to the tiny pocket measures used by seamstresses. The latter include the more collectable varieties, with novelty cases shaped like drums and windmills, beehives and beer barrels. They may be found in tin-

The patent 'Constantia' measuring tape in a bakelite case (Army & Navy Stores Ltd)

plate, japanned steel, brass, copper or silver, decorated with chasing, inlays or enamels, while, at the other extreme, are those elusive measures with imitation tortoiseshell cases, in erinoid or celluloid and dating around the turn of the century.

TELEPHONES

'Mr Watson, come here, I want to see you' hardly ranks as a masterpiece of rhetoric, yet these words are now among the most famous in the English language, being the first ever spoken over the telephone. In fact, the speaker, Alexander Graham Bell, probably said something quite different, since he had just accidentally spilled some acid over his trousers, but doubtless this mishap was forgotten in the excitement when it was realized that Watson heard his master's voice on a reed receiver in an adjoining room. The date was March 10, 1876, and the telephone had found its voice. This was no overnight discovery and there were many experiments on both sides of the Atlantic leading up to this invention. Physicists like Sir Charles Wheatstone in England and Philip Reis in Germany had produced primitive talking machines, but it was Bell, the speech therapist, who overcame the problems of producing recognizable sounds of the human voice.

A French telephone in 3 brass columns on a mahogany base, and a mahogany table telephone with dial and separate handset by Société Industrielle des Téléphones (Christies, South Kensington)

Having perfected his 'gallows' telephone, Bell established the company which still bears his name and soon telephone exchanges were installed in many American cities. The telephone spread to Britain in 1878, though it did not become a nationalized undertaking under the Post Office till 1912. With the rapid development of the telephone network went numerous improvements in the instruments. The 'gallows' of 1876 was swiftly followed by the 'butterstamp' of 1877, and then, in succession, there were Thomas Edison's rival 'chalk' receiver of 1879, the Swedish 'cradle' telephone, combining transmitter and receiver (1895), the highly ornate Stanley telephone of the 1890s used for internal communication, the first wall telephones and pay telephones in the early 1900s, the 'candlestick' phone introduced during the First World War, the first dialling telephones in 1920 and the BAKELITE handset telephone introduced in 1929 and still going strong in many instances. Each of these important landmarks in telephonic development produced numerous sub-types and minor variants, so that the entire subject is a vast one.

TELESCOPES

It was a Dutch spectacle-maker, Hans Lippershay, who opened the way for the science of astronomy in 1608 by inventing the refractor telescope, using convex lenses to magnify distant objects. Galileo worked out the optical theory behind Lippershay's discovery and came up with an improved version the following year, using a concave lens in order to get the image the right way up. The Dutch persevered with the Lippershay refractor and produced some quite large telescopes, up to 150 feet in length, but the simple lenses used suffered from colour fringing and it was not until John Dollond of London invented the achromatic telescope in the mid eighteenth century that the modern telescope was really born.

Meanwhile, James Gregory solved the problem of colour fringing by inventing the reflecting telescope, using mirrors to reflect the light rays and this was greatly improved on by Isaac Newton, while Cassegrain in France produced another version with a modified optical system. The Gregorian, Newtonian and Cassegrain telescopes have since formed the basis for most of the modern powerful instruments used in the world's astronomical observatories.

From the collector's standpoint, however, the greatest interest lies in the smaller refracting telescopes from the late seventeenth century onwards. Examples prior to about

A 6 in (15 cm) brass Gregorian reflecting telescope by W. & S. Jones of Holborn, *c.*1800 (Christies, South Kensington)

1750 are of the greatest rarity, but thereafter there are still many different models available. They may be found with ponderous brass cases, or quite light, portable varieties with leather or shagreen covered card tubes, or with vellum reinforced by brass mounts. The larger models of the early nineteenth century, fitted with a tripod or stand, had cases of mahogany and were often extremely decorative, with unusual technical features. All-metal table or floor telescopes from 1840 onwards may be encountered with a polished brass finish or a black oxydised body. Among the more recent varieties the greatest interest centres on the pocket telescopes used by soldiers and seamen.

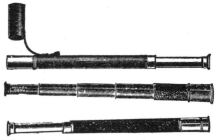

An Officer of the Watch Naval telescope and two Ross telescopes 'particularly suitable for tourists' (Army & Navy Stores Ltd)

THERMOMETERS

The art of measuring temperature had its tentative beginnings in the thermoscope invented by Galileo but it was extremely unreliable and it was the Florentine glassmakers about 1650 who produced the first thermometers on modern lines, using alcohol hermetically sealed in a bulb with a fine tube attached. Gabriel Fahrenheit, a Baltic German living in Holland, invented the mercury thermometer in 1714 and devised a scale divided into 212 parts between the coldest object he could find – freezing brine – and the hottest – boiling water. Though fairly rough and ready it is surprising that the Fahrenheit scale has survived until now. The French scientist Reaumur divided the scale into 80 parts and the Swedish astronomer Anders Celsius divided it into 100 and so gets the credit for having stumbled upon the centigrade system.

Pyrometers, which are capable of measuring intense heat, were evolved during the course of the nineteenth century, using bulbs of porcelain, gold and even platinum and fluids or gases ranging from olive oil to

A combined pocket thermometer, compass and barometer (Christies, South Kensington)

iodine! Early pyrometers are understandably rare but industrial and clinical thermometers of the past hundred years are fairly plentiful and come in a wide range of sizes, types and scales. Since 1900 most of the developments have been in the quality of the glass used, and the styling of the tube and lenses.

THIMBLES AND THIMBLE-CASES

Small, domed caps for protecting the finger-tip while sewing date back to Roman times when cast bronze was used. In the Middle Ages thimbles were made of leather and are consequently extremely rare, but later examples in hardwoods or ivory have survived. By the fifteenth century European thimbles made of silver or even gold were not uncommon and were often highly ornate. Simpler thimbles in brass or iron began to appear in the seventeenth century and were followed by steel thimbles with a brass rim or lining. Silver remained a popular material throughout, but since thimbles were exempt from hallmarking because of their small size it is difficult to date them prior to 1870 when hallmarking became compulsory for such small objects. Thimbles with irregular indentations on their domes probably date back before the mid-eighteenth century when the nose machine was introduced.

Aside from the materials, which also include mother of pearl, bone, horn, tortoiseshell, pottery and porcelain, thimbles may be found with scenic or pictorial motifs either chased or embossed on their sides, or delineated in enamels. There are thimbles that commemorate important events such as a royal wedding, a coronation or a jubilee; others strike a patriotic note in times of crisis such as the American Civil War or the First World War, and many express sentiments of affection and were clearly given as LOVE TOKENS.

Seven silver thimbles engraved with the names of the Lost Boys from *Peter Pan* (Lyle Publications)

Apart from the thimbles themselves, the tiny boxes and cases in which they were stored are of considerable interest, being found in all kinds of metals and wood, ivory, tortoiseshell, leather and shagreen, with inlays of mother of pearl or precious metals and enamels. There are many novelty types, mainly produced in the late nineteenth century, ranging from barrels and lighthouses, castles and cottages to animal and human figures. Thimble cases were a speciality of the manufacturers of Tunbridge and Mauchline wares, in wood mosaic or scenic transfer prints respectively.

TICKETS

The origins of this word are curious and show some of the unusual quirks that occur in the development of language. It is, in fact, a corruption of the French word *etiquette* which itself originally meant a sticker, from the verb *estiquier* to attach. How etiquette came to mean the forms required by good breeding for social deportment is a mystery to me. Perhaps the French had a colloquial expression like our 'Just the ticket' to mean the correct or desirable thing.

From being a small document or certificate attached to something, the ticket developed into the familiar piece of paper or pasteboard which now denotes the pre-payment of fees and charges for all manner of services, transportation or admission to places of entertainment. The most popular tickets are those which have been issued in connection with railways over the past 150 years but bus and coach tickets, airline and shipping tickets also have their devotees. They range from the small

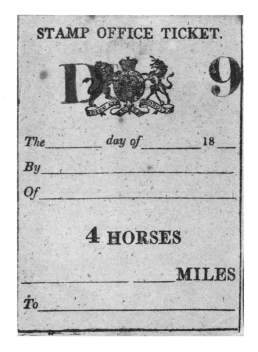

STAMP OFFICE TICKET.

The _____ day of _____ 18 ___

By _____

Of _____

4 HORSES

_____ MILES

To _____

A 19th-century stagecoach ticket (Author's collection)

QUEEN OF THE SOUTH

Amateur Christy Minstrels.

GRAND OPENING

ENTERTAINMENT

IN THE

MAXWELLTOWN HALL,

ON

Wednesday, 6th April, 1892.

FRONT SEATS, 1s.

DOORS OPEN AT 7.30; COMMENCE AT 8 P.M.

A marvellously designed ticket (Author's collection)

pasteboard tickets of the Edmonson type, used extensively in ticket machines since the 1880s, to the large and often ornate European and American tickets, some of which even incorporate maps of road and rail routes.

Tickets of admission are only now becoming popular with collectors of theatricalia and MOTION PICTURE SOUVENIRS, particularly those which were prepared in connection with a first night or premiere or as mementoes of special performances. Tickets for admission to museums, tourist attractions, buildings of public interest and stately homes are often decorated with pictorial motifs, the European tickets being especially ornate. Then there are the tickets of admission to world's fairs and international exhibitions, from the Great Exhibition of 1851 to Osaka '70 and these are desirable for their importance as social documents as well as aesthetic considerations.

TIE-PINS AND SCARF-PINS

Sometimes known as stick-pins, these may be regarded as the male counterpart of HATPINS – though intended for quite a different purpose of course. They made their debut at the beginning of the nineteenth century when cravats replaced stocks as neckwear and died out in the 1920s when neck-ties became much narrower, though they have enjoyed sporadic revivals ever since.

The pins themselves may be found in steel, either plain or blued, enamelled or plated, in gold, silver, or plated alloys, with straight shanks, spiral shafts or in brooch form. The chief interest, however, lies in the decorative treatment of the head, every kind of precious

A selection of tie and scarf pins (Army & Navy Stores Ltd)

and semi-precious stone, from diamonds and rubies to onyx, jasper and amethyst, being used. There are also numerous varieties of pin with tiny figural motifs – the male equivalent of the good-luck talisman on charm bracelets. Among the more desirable types are those in which the head unscrews to serve as a stud, and trick pins with tiny compartments which conceal portraits or locks of hair.

TIMETABLES

On the road between Lauder and Coldstream in the Scottish Borders is a curious wall plaque in the form of a clock face, whereon is inscribed the times of the stagecoaches that

ran to and from Edinburgh in the late eighteenth century. Though these services have long since vanished this stone timetable remains as a permanent reminder.

More ephemeral, but more practicable from the collector's viewpoint, are the printed time-tables for coach and carrier services which date from the 1780s and the shipping time-tables of the early 1800s, often taking the form of small broadsheets replete with woodcut engravings of coaches and ships. The earliest railway timetables appeared in 1839 when Mr Bradshaw of Manchester published his modest booklet at a shilling. Early Bradshaws are of immense interest to the collector of RAIL RELICS and some of them have been reprinted in recent years. The working tables used by the employees of the railways are of immense interest, giving much greater detail concerning routes, gradients, points and crossings, as well as a host of information about the working of the trains.

Many of the old shipping companies, particularly those operating coastal services, pro-

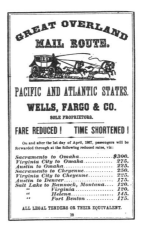

A Wells Fargo timetable of 1867 (Wells Fargo)

duced attractive timetables which combined tourist guides and maps. Modern timetables may appear more functional, but they should not be ignored since they contain information which will be of vital interest to the transport historians of the future.

TINS AND TINWARE

This form of PACKAGING has captured the imagination of collectors in recent years and many people are rediscovering the delights and old-world charm of the printed tinware of the past. Tins came into prominence in the 1870s when improved machinery for canning was invented, more or less at the same time as techniques for printing on tin were devised. This coincided with the rise of branded goods in every section of the consumer market and the manufacturers of products that acquired household names were not slow in appreciating the value of attractively designed and printed tins for their wares. The most desirable tins are the early examples with their surfaces decorated by transfer printing. By the 1880s, however, multicolour offset lithography was replacing transfer-printing and this permitted much more complex and detailed pictorial designs. Around the turn of the century there was a vogue for handsome embossed and gilded tinware and during this period the first tins with lids reproducing famous paintings, in simulated gilt frames, were produced. Improved techniques of manu-

A Jacob's biscuit tin and a Cherry Blossom polish tin of the 30's (Army & Navy Stores Ltd)

facture in the early 1900s encouraged a craze for tins in novelty shapes – anything from books to fishing-baskets, from rustic cottages to stage-coaches were produced in tin as containers for confectionery. In the interwar years there were even tins incorporating a mechanical device so that they doubled as containers as well as toys. In this class belong the tinware windmills, perambulators, aircraft and shooting galleries.

There have also been tins designed to commemorate important events. The most popular are those containing tobacco, chocolate and confectionery given as troop comforts in various campaigns from the Boer War onwards, and the tins given to children to celebrate coronations and jubilees.

TIPSTAVES

This subject is generally associated with MILITARIA, though seldom produced for military use. Rods and wands of wood or metal were at one time borne in ceremonial procession by law officers and municipal officials and symbolized their authority – the more modest counterpart of the civic mace. Their shafts were often richly enamelled with civic or national heraldic emblems, and the tops surmounted by a crown in gilt metal. At one time a wide variety of civic dignitaries had their own tipstaff, ranging from the Inspectors of the Poor to the Night Watch and Town Constables, forerunners of the modern police. the carrying of tipstaves gradually declined in the second half of the nineteenth century, the later examples being less decorative.

TOASTING FORKS AND RACKS

The toasting fork is a charming relic of the times when muffins were toasted at tea-time in front of an open hearth. When not in use, the toasting fork hung from a hook by the fireside and was generally designed to be an attractive ornament. A long shaft of polished hardwood or japanned beech was fitted with a brass tang and ring at one end, and a heart- or U-shaped metal end with two or three sharp-

An electro-plate toast crisper and the Toast-with-Ease (Army & Navy Stores Ltd)

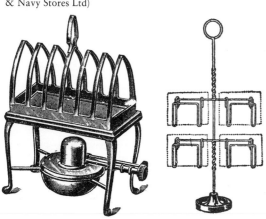

pointed prongs. The metalwork was frequently decorated with pierced or openwork ornament and the prongs either spiral or slightly tapered. Brass was commonly used, but wrought iron was also popular, while silver and Sheffield plate were fashionable in the early 1800s and even gold toasting forks are not unknown. Sir Edward Thomason, the Birmingham medallist and silversmith, invented several unusual types of sliding or telescopic toasting fork and even one in which the prongs collapsed as the shaft was telescoped and the whole contrivance housed neatly within the casing shaped like the body of a snake. Later toasting forks were of an all-wire construction in nickel- or chrome-plate. An interesting device dating from the early years of this century was the Toast-with-Ease, a vertical rod mounted on a stand and having horizontal wire racks capable of toasting four slices of bread in front of the fire simultaneously.

Toast racks, the traditional standby for wedding presents, were originally known as toast trays and were first produced in silver or Sheffield plate about 1780. The earliest racks were constructed entirely of wire, at first with a rounded section and from 1800 with an oval or oblong section, as many as nine bars being mounted on a base of slightly curved metal plate with paw, scroll, ball or bracket feet. As the nineteenth century progressed toast racks became more elaborate, with cast finials and embossed ornament and there were even racks which included horizontal rings to hold eggcups.

TODDY LADLES

The accession of King George III in 1760 coincided with a craze for hot toddy – a beverage consisting of rum mixed with hot water, sugar, lemon juice and grated nutmeg – and Georgian cabinetmakers had a steady line in puncheries, the eighteenth-century equivalent of the COCKTAIL cabinet. This contained the punchbowl or menteith, the squat little cups or glasses and the toddy ladles and lifters which have become collectable in their own right.

Toddy ladles may be recognized by their long handles and deep bowls, either ovoid or circular. The handles of turned wood gave the ladles buoyancy, allowing them to float upright in the punchbowl and prevent the ladler from scalding his fingers. The bowls were made of silver, Sheffield plate and latterly electroplate and the handles often intricately carved. Less commonly ivory was used for the handles.

As an alternative to the ladle, the toddy lifter seems to have been a peculiarly English gadget, consisting of a glass vessel with a long knopped neck and having a hole in the flat base of the bowl. The stem was held between the first and second fingers and plunged into the punchbowl until the vessel was filled. Then the thumb was placed over the mouth of the vessel to create a vacuum and prevent the hot liquid escaping until the lifter was positioned over the toddy glass. The majority of toddy lifters look like tiny decanters, though their Scottish counterparts were generally club-shaped.

TOILET SETS

These relics of the days before wash basins with running hot and cold water replaced the old-fashioned wash-stand are becoming quite elusive, especially those sets comprising up to a dozen separate items. The basic items included a large shallow wash-bowl and ewer, smaller bowls, SOAP DISHES, CHAMBER POTS (often in matched pairs) and slop-pail, and they may be found in an infinite variety of styles in pottery and porcelain and white or coloured enamelled metal. Even though the individual items may have got scattered over the years, with a bit of determination and patience the persistent collector can often assemble sets again.

Two toilet sets, one in enamel and the other in chintz china (Army & Navy Stores Ltd)

A dressing case in pigskin with all the necessities for the perfectly groomed gentleman (Army & Navy Stores Ltd)

Toilet sets of an entirely different kind come under the general heading of fancy goods and consist of leather or wooden cases containing all the equipment required for impeccable grooming: hair brushes and combs, mirrors, hat and clothes brushes, nail polishers, cuticle knife, nail file, nail pusher, button hook, shoe lift, toothbrush, shaving brush, shaving soap tube, soap jar, scent bottles and atomisers, razors. Similar articles are also described under the heading of DRESSING TABLE SETS and VANITY CASES.

TONGS

The dictionary defines this as a grasping device consisting of two pieces joined at one end by a pivot or hinged like a pair of scissors and, indeed, it covers a wide range of objects from the large coal tongs to the tiny stamp tongs or tweezers used by philatelists. In between come numerous implements designed for specific purposes and commonly found in silver, silver-gilt, Sheffield plate, electroplate, nickel plate, stainless steel, blued steel, brass or bronze. Coal tongs were originally of the spring bow type, with spade or claw ends. Even larger tongs were intended for handling logs and often had shanks cast in the form of animals' or birds' legs. Later and smaller coal tongs were fashioned like large scissors with serrated grips. Tongs of polished or painted wood were used for handling vegetables and also used in the laundry for handling washing, to prevent scalding or chafing the hands.

Lazy tongs were instruments with concertina joints which permitted their extension to several feet. They were intended for the bedridden who could not reach out very far and may be found in electroplate, polished steel or ALUMINIUM with anything up to ten sets of joints. Fear of nicotine staining induced many cigarette smokers, particularly women, in the 1920s to use cigarette tongs, with a relatively large circular bow spring and a slide which could be adjusted to the diameter of any kind of cigarette. These tongs were usually made of silver and were often elegantly decorated with enamels or gold inlays.

Most of the tongs which the collector will come across, however, had to do with the serving of food. The only variety which survives to any extent today is the sugar tongs for handling lump or cube sugar and ranging from the plain type with rounded or spade ends to the ornate kinds with spiral shanks and bird claw ends. Asparagus tongs were in use from the 1750s till the beginning of this century and had wide rectangular blades pierced all over in geometrical or floral patterns, with flat chasing on the bow-spring and serrations on the inner sides of the blades. Similar but much larger tongs were used during the same period for serving fish. Plainer implements, usually

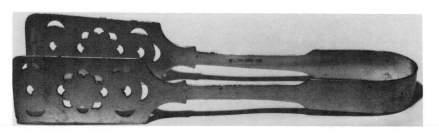

A pair of asparagus tongs

Silver cigarette tongs, and a Lazy Tongs (Army & Navy Stores Ltd)

made of polished steel, were used for handling steak. Somewhat larger than sugar tongs were those intended for handling ice cubes. There were even special sardine tongs, like miniature fish servers and often decorated with tiny relief or die-stamped fishes.

TOOTHPICKS, HOLDERS AND CASES

The delicate removal of particles of food lodged between the teeth has never been considered quite the done thing in polite English society – which may account for the high incidence of dental caries in Britain. Europeans and 'other lesser breeds without the law' quite cheerfully attack their molars with pointed instruments almost as soon as they have downed knife and fork. For this reason the more collectable tooth-picks have tended to be mainly Continental in origin and include some very handsome implements in gold and silver, with intricately engraved shanks and mounted with precious stones. It must be admitted, however, that no matter how beautiful these picks may seem, they are not exactly

hygienic and they have been rendered obsolete in recent years by the more functional quill toothpicks or antiseptic and sterilized wooden ones hermetically sealed in tiny paper packs.

Such a delicate instrument as a tooth-pick required careful treatment and naturally was provided with a case. The commonest variety consists of a tapered tube into which the toothpick can be screwed, so that the handle of the pick also serves as the cap to the case. These cases were made in precious metals, hardwoods, ivory or bone and I have even seen some modern examples from the Far East in various plastic substances. The outer surface of the case and the cap or handle were frequantly jewelled or carved with figural motifs.

TRADE CARDS

In their original form these cards were produced as ADVERTISEMENTS for shopkeepers and merchants, tradesmen and craftsmen of all kinds and were given away to customers, both real and prospective. They were in existence by the late sixteenth century but understandably early examples are of the greatest rarity. Specimens from the eighteenth and nineteenth centuries, however, are reasonably plentiful and range from the simple visiting card with a copperplate engraving of the tradesman's name and address, to the highly ornate pictorial cards featuring samples of his wares or a view of his shop. From the 1870s onwards trade cards may also be found in the guise of POSTCARDS and it was from the more ornamental trade variety that they evolved.

The front and reverse of a Cow and Gate trade card of the 30's (Author's collection)

A colour lithograph, late 19th century, and beautifully printed of course (Author's collection)

One form of trade card which developed in the 1880s was the CIGARETTE CARD, originally no more than a stiffener in a paper pack but soon regarded as an object worthy of collection and study. The same principle was applied to other consumer goods at the turn of the century, notably the food extracts manu-factured by the Liebig Company whose beautiful chromolithographed cards were published in several different languages. Trade cards of this kind, with matching albums, have been produced in connection with breakfast foods and confectionery, tea and petrol right down to the present day.

TRADE TOKENS

At various times many governments have been unwilling or unable to provide their populace with base metal small change and the deficit has been made good by innkeepers and shopkeepers whose token coins, though strictly unofficial and sometimes illegal, have been accepted as currency within a certain locality. Token halfpence and farthings were widely used in Britain from the seventeenth century onwards to make up for a lack of low-value copper coins, the Stuart and early Hanoverian kings considering it beneath their dignity to strike anything other than silver and gold. The number of varieties of tokens issued by traders and private banks up to 1816 (when the practice was suppressed) runs into many thousands. The eighteenth- and early nineteenth-century tokens were often extremely well designed and because people were actually collecting them by that time, many of them were produced with the numismatist in mind,

A selection of trade tokens from the author's collection.

with attractive vignettes of scenery and land-marks or extolling the virtues of a company's products.

Tokens of this type have been used in many other countries. Numerous tokens were produced in Canada in the nineteenth century, ranging from the copper sous and halfpence of the provincial banks to the brass 'Made Beaver' tokens of the Hudson's Bay Company. Penny-sized tokens were also produced in the United States during the Civil War and often had patriotic motifs as well as traders' advertisements. The same practice was adopted by several European countries during the First World War when there was a grave shortage of coinage. Tradesmen and local chambers of commerce in Germany even used tokens made of such unlikely materials as wood or porcelain.

TRAPS

Since man is the greatest predator in the world, it follows that the traps with which he preys on birds, animals, reptiles, fishes, insects – even his own kind – form a very large group of artefacts with a history that dates back thousands of years. The cruel and vicious man-traps of the eighteenth and nineteenth centuries reflect the brutality of the game laws then in force and were a sad misuse of the blacksmith's craft. Just as deadly in their own way, however, were the host of small traps designed to snare and kill all manner of birds and animals. A catalogue for 'country gentle-

The 'Shave' rubber-jaw humane real Dorset rabbit trap (Army & Navy Stores Ltd)

men' before me as I write lists the following distinctive traps: badger, beetle, bird, fish, fly, lion, mole, mouse, otter, pigeon, rabbit, rat, slug, sparrow, squirrel, vermin and wasp, and the gadgets themselves were just as varied in size and shape as the creatures they had in mind. Many of them were quite weird and bizarre in their complex arrangement of springs and wires; others – especially the insect traps – are often quite handsome and innocuous in appearance, with their fragile glass globes to lure unsuspecting flies and wasps. Often the names given to these traps by their manufacturers had an evocative ring: the Nipper, the Holdfast, the Breakback, the Delusion and the Demon, or even the sinister Capito whose speciality was the drowning of mice. For the more tender-hearted there were the Humane Toothless and the Rubber-Jaw and the Catch-alive, but as their purpose was to trap rats, mice and other small vermin the point of keeping them alive escapes me.

TRAYS

I have already discussed ASHTRAYS, but there are many other kinds and virtually every category may be found in a wide variety of materials and decorative treatments. It is quite astonishing the number of trays that have been produced over the years for some specific purpose. Casting my eye over the mail order catalogues and hardware brochures of the past hundred years alone I find that there have been trays for butchers and butlers, children and invalids, armchairs, beds and motor cars, all with distinctive styles and attachments.

There are special trays for cheese, hors d'oeuvre, pins, sweets, starch and soap, trays for the kitchen, cafe and library, for tea-table and dining-room.

The most interesting are those in inlaid, pierced and chased brass, the products of Benares and Moradabad, and the beautifully lacquered and inlaid trays of Japan and China, many of which have found their way to Europe and America over the past century. CRUMB TRAYS are the poor relations of all those trays and salvers in silver, electroplate, and Sheffield plate which have brought a touch of elegance to drawing-room and dining-room and are still a favourite medium for presentation pieces. Wooden trays range from turned and polished hardwoods to chip-carved, pokerwork and painted trays with motifs aimed at the tourist. Tin trays bearing advertising matter have been used by breweries, tobacco manufacturers and soft drinks companies since the late nineteenth century as giveaways and range from the artistically

A finely engraved brass Moradabad tray on a carved stand (Army & Navy Stores Ltd)

pretentious, with reproductions of Old Masters, to the frankly commercial with raucous slogans extolling the merits of this or that beer or cigarettes.

TREEN

This old English word has been given a new lease of life, largely due to the indefatigable efforts of Edward Pinto whose vast collection of wooden bygones has now been acquired by the Birmingham Museum. It is a neat little term that covers an enormous field of collectables and conveniently describes any small wooden artefact but usually confined to the more utilitarian objects rather than the decorative articles such as Tunbridge and Mauchline ware or FERNWARE. Among the turned wooden articles are cups and goblets, bowls, trenchers and platters, spoons and spirtles, in oak, elm, sycamore, yew, beech and other traditional woods, as well as the more exotic lignum vitae, ebony and mahogany which were used increasingly from the eighteenth century onwards. Implements and tools are another large category, ranging from mallets, pegs and pins to clothes' stompers and wash-dollies, dibbers, rakes and shovels and even mechanical items such as hand-looms and spinning-wheels.

A collection of treen (Phillips)

TRIVETS

Like IRON STANDS, these examples of wrought or cast iron and brasswork come in a tremendous variety of styles which reflect their importance in an age before cooking stoves and ranges were commonplace. Strictly speaking the trivet has only two legs which stand on the hearth and two angled hooks or claws which fit over the bar at the front of the grate, but the term is also used loosely to include hearth stands. The latter were not hooked to the grate and had four feet or a tripod arrangement enabling them to stand on their own. As their decorative treatment was the same as trivets the difference in construction and purpose is largely academic.

They were wrought or cast with an openwork pattern and this gave free range to the skills and imagination of blacksmiths and brassfounders, with the result that some highly ornate patterns were evolved. Apart from the stylized motifs there were many figural patterns and even commemorative designs, though these are rare. Much sought after nowadays are the copper or bronze trivets of

A George II trivet in brass (Christies, South Kensington)

the turn of the century with tulip and lily motifs in the spirit of Art Nouveau, though I see from the mail order catalogue of one well-known company that such trivets were still available as late as 1940.

TSUBA

Occasionally one used to come across, in the bric-à-brac trays of junk dealers, large circular or roughly square plates of iron with an elliptical slit in the centre and intriguing patterns of repoussage, piercing, chasing and inlays of other metals. Now these objects are instantly recognized as tsuba, or Japanese sword guards, and they have all graduated to the specialist shops of dealers in Orientalia and MILITARIA.

The central slot accommodated the *nakago* or tang of the sword-blade, and sometimes smaller holes at the sides were pierced for the blades of the small knives carried *en suite* with the sword. Because they were produced by swordsmiths, tsuba were invariably forged in iron, but despite the unprepossessing nature

of this metal, the Japanese craftsmen imbued it with great artistry. This was achieved by the skilled use of various solutions to pickle the iron and produce striking patinas. Later inlays of bronze, silver and even gold were used extensively and hammering and chasing applied to produce low reliefs of landscapes and figures, flowers, animals and insects.

The most ornate tsuba belong to the nineteeth century, when gliding and lacquering were at the height of fashion. In more recent years, however, there has been a return to the more austere patterns favoured by the Samurai of the seventeenth century.

TYPEWRITERS

From left: A Mignon No. 7 typewriter in leather case; a Royal Barlock typewriter; an Imperial model D typewriter (Christies, South Kensington)

There is almost as much controversy over the invention of the typewriter, as over the origins of the wheel, with half a dozen countries claiming it as their own. As long ago as the 1720s Henry Mill, an Englishman, took out a patent for a writing machine but his plan was clumsy and impractical. The Italian Pellegrino Turri actually produced a typewriter almost a century later and though the machine itself has not survived several letters written on it have been preserved, showing that it had 23 letters in capitals and four punctuation marks. Patents were taken out in France by Progrin in 1833 and in the United States between 1829 and 1843 by Burt and Thurber respectively, but the first practical patent was that taken out in 1868 by Latham Sholes and Carlos Glidden of Milwaukee. It took them five years to perfect and market their model, and in the interim Malling Hansen of Denmark produced his Skrivekugle or writing ball – an enormous machine weighing 80 kilos. There were many later versions of the Hansen machine, reduced in size and complexity, up to the time of the First World War.

Sholes and Glidden sold their patents to E. Remington and Sons in 1878 and this company dominated the world market in standard keyboard machines for many years. Their competitors were forced to adopt various unusual mechanisms, now classified as type-bar, type-cylinder and wheel machines, often with highly unorthodox arrangements of keys, and it was not until the expiry of the original patents in the early 1900s that typewriters of the keyboard variety became universal. The half century from 1874 to 1924 yields an amazing range of models, from the tiny Blickensderfer and Columbia portables to the giant Maskelyne pedal-operated machines and the Hansen flatbeds.

U

UMBRELLAS AND PARASOLS

The derivations of these words, from the Latin meaning 'little shade' and the French for 'sun shield', give a good indication of their original purpose, and it is as a sunshade that they are principally used in the more torrid climes to this day. Umbrellas as an emblem of authority seem to have been employed in India and China for centuries before they made their debut in Europe. Waterproof umbrellas as protection against rain date from the early seventeenth century when they figured in an inventory of goods belonging to Anne of Austria, Queen of France.

Umbrellas of the seventeenth century are virtually unknown and those of the eighteenth century are very scarce. For many years they were regarded as a female prerogative and though manufacturers did their best to encourage a wider use by marketing plain models, it continued to be regarded as the height of effeminacy for a men to be seen holding, let alone using such a contrivance. Jonas Hanway, the London philanthropist, was the first Englishman to make a deliberate habit of using an umbrella in inclement weather, doggedly ignoring jeers and insults for almost forty

A parasol with black lace mount and ivory handle, c.1860 (Christies, South Kensington)

years (1750–90) before umbrellas ceased to be regarded as a decadent French custom.

Thereafter the scope of both umbrellas and parasols widened considerably and many ingenious folding and telescopic varieties were produced for the use of both sexes. The nineteenth century witnessed the finest flowering of the umbrella art, and great attention was paid to the decoration of the handles, following contemporary styles in CANES, WALKING STICKS and WHIPS. Oriental parasols with silk shades decorated in Chinese, Thai, Japanese and Javanese patterns, became all the rage in the 1870s and miniature versions were even incorporated in fashionable interior decoration at the turn of the century.

Three children's umbrellas (Army & Navy Stores Ltd)

UMBRELLA STANDS

The tremendous increase in the popularity of umbrellas in the early nineteenth century gave rise to an article of furniture which once featured in almost every household but is sadly now seldom met with except in junk yards, second-hand shops and jumble sales. There seem to have been almost as many varieties of stand as there were of umbrellas and they remained in fashion till the Second World War. The simplest kind consisted of four or more uprights with a rail at the top and a tray at the foot to catch the drips of water. This may be found in turned wood, copper, wrought iron, brass or even chromium plate. Another type had a single central upright of cast or wrought metal with a heavy and rather ornate base containing depressions on which ferrules of the umbrellas stood. Near the top of the column was an arrangement of rings or spring-loaded clips which held the handles of the umbrellas secure.

The commonest varieties were those comprising tall cylinders or vases with heavy bases, into which the umbrellas were placed. Appropriate to the Oriental parasols of the 1880s was the Chinese export porcelain stand with its lavish ornament of dragons and phoenixes in blue and white underglaze decoration, or the lacquered papier-mâché stands, inlaid with mother of pearl and gilt with *Chinoiserie* ornament. The latter were

Two umbrella stands, in wrought iron and Chinese style (Army & Navy Stores Ltd)

fitted with a lining of tinplate or brass to prevent sopping wet umbrellas from damaging the delicate lacquer. Among the more unusual stands were those fashioned out of brass shell cases, for which there was a certain vogue in the aftermath of the First World War, and those made from the giant feet of elephants and hippopotami, in which the bazaars of India and East Africa did a brisk trade in the bad old days when wildlife conservation was unheard of.

UNIFORMS

Three cards from *Military Uniforms of the British Empire Overseas,* a series of 50 issued by John Player & Sons in 1938 (Ian Fleming)

The standardization of the dress worn by soldiers was only gradually effected during the first half of the eighteenth century. Prior to that, the colour and facings of tunics and breeches were largely a matter for the colonel

of the regiment, but the Duke of Marlborough laid down uniform patterns and thereafter the red coat became the recognized garb of the British soldier. The same remarks apply to the soldiers of European armies and the troops under the command of George Washington in the American Revolutionary War. Consequently early examples of military uniform are scarce. The nineteenth century, by contrast, affords numerous examples of uniform and much of this type of material is still available, though at a price. The colour and pageantry of military uniforms reached their zenith in the late nineteenth century, to be followed by a period in which muted shades of khaki, field-grey and horizon blue – designed to make the infantryman less conspicious in the field – were used in the colonial campaigns of the 1890s and the conflicts that culminated in the First World War.

Since then there has been a return to handsome dress uniforms for ceremonial purposes, with, at the same time, the evolution of more functional outfits for field service ranging from battledress and overseas dress of the Second World War to the combat suits and jungle green of the present day. Over the past 150 years uniform has been enlivened by the judicious use of cloth badges and insignia worn on the sleeve or breast of tunics, by epaulettes and shoulder boards, by collar badges of brass and white metal, by silk lanyards and aiguillettes of coloured silk, by gold and silver lace, piping, chevrons and other badges of rank. During the same period medal ribbons have evolved a distinctive heraldry of their own.

Naval uniform was rather later in developing and has tended to be more conservative. Distinctive uniform for airmen first appeared during the First World War. Since the air corps of many countries were little more than a branch of the army, tunics and trousers of entirely different designs and colours did not become widespread till the 1940s, though the RAF, Luftwaffe and Regia Aeronautica (in Britain, Germany and Italy) had their own uniforms before the war. Uniform accessories, such as BADGES, BELTS AND BELT-BUCKLES and HELMETS AND HEADGEAR, are discussed separately.

UNION CASES

Slim cases designed to hold two daguerreotypes came into fashion during the American Civil War and came to be known as union cases since they frequently bore patriotic motifs on their covers and propaganda for the Union cause. Doubtless they were devised so that Federal troops might be able to carry pictures of their loved ones when they went off to war. They were made of wood, leather or proto-plastic materials and were heavily embossed, carved or moulded with relief scenery, landmarks, sentimental or genre subjects as well as political and military themes. They were hinged on one side and usually had a clasp or lock on the other. The more expensive cases were made of tortoiseshell, mother of pearl or carved ivory and sometimes had enamelled motifs inset.

Many of these cases have survived and are worth a handsome premium if they still contain their original daguerreotypes. Unfortunately many of them were later converted for use as CIGARETTE CASES, so their value depends entirely on their workmanship and the interest of their pictorial ornament.

UTILITY

To its original meaning merely of something useful was added a new connotation in 1942 when the British government launched its Utility Scheme. Rather unfairly it came to be regarded as the British equivalent of the German *ersatz* – a substitute for something no

An Ogden's cigarette card of 1938, from a set entitled *Air-Raid Precautions*. Utility must have been the key word for equipping the refuge room (Ian Fleming)

longer available because of the war. Utility clothing – still recognised by its CC coding on labels – was introduced in 1941 but it was to combat the shortage of furniture that the full scheme was launched in 1942, the first items becoming available in January 1943. The Utility Advisory Council included some of the finest designers of the 1930s and its efforts, though much derided at the time, turned out to be a blessing in disguise since they purged British taste of its pre-war fussiness and paved the way for the streamlined functionalism of post-war domestic and industrial design.

Utility furniture in a limited range of shapes and styles was soon followed by all manner of objects, from RADIOS to LAMPSHADES, from kitchenware to furnishing fabrics. All this came to an abrupt end when furniture rationing ended in 1948, and Utility clothing was abolished by the Conservative government in 1952. Utility had become synonymous with austerity and seemed out of keeping with the dawn of a new Elizabethan era. With the passage of time, however, its sterling worth is now being appreciated and the simple pieces of furniture of the Forties are being retrieved from attics, toolsheds and junkyards, stripped of their paintwork and restored to their original matt-wax finish.

VANITY CASES

What the etui was to the eighteenth century the vanity case or beauty box was to the early twentieth century. Now that a more liberal application of cosmetics is coming back into fashion there may well be a revival of these compendia of beauty preparations, eyebrow pencils, manicure instruments, scissors, tweezers, rouge pots and powder puffs. The most attractive sets had everything in matching colours and materials, tortoiseshell, nacre, mother of pearl, pastel shades of enamelling, lapis lazuli or malachite being fashionable. Lower down the scale came the erinoid and ivoride and other PLASTIC substitutes for the more traditional but expensive materials.

The cases themselves varied enormously in quality, from engine-turned silver covered with transparent enamels to quilted cloth, lacqured woodpulp and BAKELITE. In between came the leather cases in pigskin, calf, Morocco or Persian goatskin, dyed or embossed and sometimes with ivory cameos

A vanity case in morocco leather, with 4 bottles, 4 cream pots, a powder jar and 2 manicure bottles, a mirror in the lid and a drawer fitted underneath (Army & Navy Stores Ltd)

mounted on the lid. Many cases were plushlined and had a tight-fitting, spring-loaded lid, rather like a jewel case, but zip fasteners introduced in the early 1930s rapidly took over. The most elaborate beauty boxes resembled tiny suitcases, fitted with silver or chromium-topped bottles and jars, with a mirror mounted inside the lid and compartments for sundry other articles, and sometimes with a shallow drawer underneath.

VERRE EGLOMISÉ

Strictly speaking this term should only be applied to glass pictures in which gold or silver foil on the reverse has been engraved or pricked and then covered with a coat of black paint and varnished over. It was a variant of a traditional Italian skill, known as *fondi d'oro*, developed by the French painter, art connoisseur and picture-framer, Jean Baptiste Glomy, who had a lucrative business in Paris during the reign of Louis XVI. Though originally used merely to decorate the borders of picture frames and mirrors it later developed into an artistic medium in its own right and entire pictures were composed in this fashion.

The term has become debased of late and is now used quite loosely by antique dealers to

A Dutch verre eglomisé picture, by Zeuner, 18th century (Pilkington Glass Museum)

describe any underglass painting. Not so long ago these pictures, the product mainly of enthusiastic amateurs in the nineteenth century, were of little account but now their primitive charm and artless naïveté are being re-appraised and real money is being paid for narrative and genre subjects which were hitherto neglected.

VESTA BOXES

The more decorative and, at times, more whimsical, counterpart of the MATCHBOXES commonly used in the last century, these little cases rivalled the snuffboxes and vinaigrettes of an earlier generation in their ingenuity and craftsmanship. Many of them, in fact, resemble snuffboxes but can always be distinguished by the serrated strikers used to ignite the vestas or wax matches. They were made in silver, usually gold-plated on the inner surface to prevent a chemical reaction with the sulphur in the match-heads, ivory, hardwoods, papier-mâché, porcelain, mother of pearl, bois durci, vulcanite and tortoiseshell. Later boxes had the lid set in the end or on one side, rather than on top as in the snuffbox type. The thirty years preceding the First World War saw many novelty vesta boxes in unusual shapes. The commoner varieties include hearts, shields, peardrops and kidney-shaped boxes; the more desirable kinds resemble musical instruments, animals, human figures, horseshoes, champagne bottles, flasks, boots, books and sentry boxes. The metal boxes were often chased or embossed with pictorial motifs, while those with personal inscriptions and dates are highly prized. The most desirable vesta boxes are those which incorporate

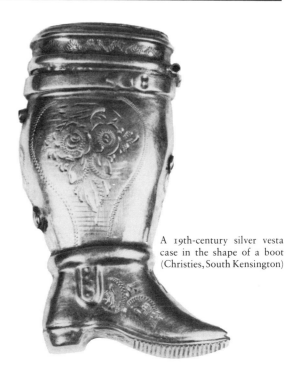

A 19th-century silver vesta case in the shape of a boot (Christies, South Kensington)

small penknives, TOOTHPICKS, PROPELLING PENCILS and even tiny tapersticks and SOVEREIGN CASES. They came to an end during the First World War when matches were increasingly sold in card or wooden boxes.

VISITING CARDS

Sometimes known by their French name, *cartes de visite*, these small pasteboard cards were originally the size of playing cards and a few of the latter have survived in which it is evident that originally it was the custom to write one's name and address on the back of a playing card and present it to one's host or hostess. Significantly the first of the specially printed visiting cards were of the same dimensions as playing cards and did not shrink to their present size until the late nineteenth century.

Many people preferred to purchase plain pieces of card and to write the details in their

A multiple expanding carte-de-visite frame, *c.*1900 (Christies, South Kensington)

own fair hand. Since the Victorians excelled in calligraphy and took a delight in their draughtsmanship, many of the hand-drawn cards of the nineteenth century are exquisitely designed and decorated with drawings in pen and ink and even watercolours. This artistic trend encouraged the pioneer photographers to market visiting cards bearing the individual's portrait, with a space at the foot for a personal message to be added. The reverse of these photographic cards was beautifully engraved with the photographer's own details and thus they may be regarded as

yet another form of TRADE CARD. At the beginning of this century visiting cards became much plainer and simple copperplate engraving became *de rigueur* but I have noted a tendency worldwide over the past twenty years for cards to become much more elaborate again, using letterpress, die-stamping and thermography in place of the more discreet engraving. These latterday cards may not accord with the strict principles of etiquette, but they make attractive and interesting examples of graphic design in miniature.

WAFFLE IRONS

Crisp cakes of pancake batter smothered in syrup have long been a breakfast delicacy in America, whither they were brought from Holland, Denmark and the Rhineland by immigrants in the early nineteenth century. They were traditionally cooked in cast iron utensils consisting of two hinged plates joined to a long handle. The plates were invariably decorated with relief patterns or openwork designs, producing a highly orna-mental effect on the waffles themselves. The most desirably examples bear dates and sets of initials, evidence that they were used as betrothal or wedding mementoes. Even the more utilitarian waffle bakers of the present century are worth looking for, including the early electric bakers with chromium-plated surface and BAKELITE handles, introduced to Europe from America in the 1920s.

WALKING STICKS

Nowadays only the halt and the lame use a walking stick but up to thirty years ago they were commonly used by everyone and an enormous variety was available. Though sticks dating back to medieval times are known, they only became really fashionable towards the end of the seventeenth century, as the wearing of swords declined. Early walking sticks were of stout construction and intended for self-defence as much as an aid to walking. The most desirable types have sword-blades concealed within the stick, and there are numerous varieties that incorporate a firearm. Eighteenth-century sticks with single shot pistols are now expensive, but nineteenth-century sticks housing a small shotgun are reasonably plentiful. Others housed a primitive form of air gun known as an air cane, much favoured by poachers.

The sticks carried by gentlemen in the eighteenth and early nineteenth centuries were usually longer than the modern average and were of polished hardwood, ebony or kingwood, up to six feet in length, with gold or silver tops and ferrules. Later sticks had porcelain knobs or handles, lavishly decorated in polychrome glazes. Others had knobs decorated in Staffordshire enamels. In the first

A crowded selection of walking sticks (David Cripps)

half of the nineteenth century elaborately carved heads came into fashion and gave way about 1850 to the simple gold or silver knob, with decoration confined to a heraldic crest or regimental badge. At the turn of the century there was a revival of porcelain handles, mainly of European origin, and also purely ornamental canes and sticks in coloured and opaque glass. There were also many canes and sticks in the period up to about 1930 decorated with novelty tops in human, bird or animal form. Tortoiseshell, ivory, semi-precious stones and early forms of PLASTIC may also be found decorating the handles of these sticks. Apart from firearms and sword blades, walking sticks may be found with a wide variety of attachments, from watches and compasses to fishing lines, telescopes and spirit flasks – all of which greatly enhance the value.

WATCH PAPERS

Small discs of paper or linen were fitted inside the backs of watches, mainly to keep the works free from dust which might otherwise enter through the keyhole. By the middle of the eighteenth century, if not earlier, they were being used by watchmakers as a form of ADVERTISEMENT, exquisitely engraved with the name and address of the manufacturer and a range of the goods and services provided. Some watch papers had spaces for the insertion of details about repairs carried out on that particular watch. The most interesting examples, however, have tiny engraving of scenery and quasi-symbolic pictures, allegories of time and portraits of Old Father Time with his scythe and hour-glass. Motifs depicting clocks, watches and sundials were not uncommon. Since they bear the advertisements of local watch makers, these papers are of considerable interest to collectors of objects relating to a specific area and they testify to the very high level of artistic attainment in the provinces, often far removed from London and the other major centres of population. The use of watch papers gradually declined in the second half of the nineteenth century, especially after the introduction of the self-winding watch. American watch papers were often produced in silk or cotton with surprisingly well-printed designs, including examples of a sentimental or patriotic theme.

WATER FILTERS AND SOFTENERS

The Scottish town of Paisley takes the credit for having had the first filtered water supply anywhere in the world, as long ago as 1804, a modest 6,700 gallons being available daily. Elsewhere filtration of water, often of a highly doubtful quality, was left to the individual and gave rise to a considerable industry producing water filters. They were still being marketed in Britain up to 1940 and in many parts of Europe and North America they are in use to this day, not to mention the less civilized parts of the world.

Filters were generally tall cylinders with a capacity from one to five gallons and were constructed of earthenware, stoneware, glass or enamelled iron. The pottery filters were often decorated with slipware in contrasting colours or with relief ornament. Glass filters were invariably much smaller in capacity and were designed to sit on the kitchen bench or table. Those produced in the second half of the nineteenth century were often extremely decorative, with coloured, opaque, etched or engraved glass bowls and cylinders. The impure water was poured into the upper

A stoneware filter and a glass table water filter (Army & Navy Stores Ltd)

cylinder and allowed to filter through a carbonised infusorial block into the jug or bowl underneath.

Similar devices, mainly in pottery or enamelled iron, were used as water softeners, the principal internal difference being the compartments for the softening agency and the common salt which regenerated it. The more elaborate examples were fitted with handsome brass or chromed taps.

WATERING CANS

Like their smaller cousins, the OIL CANS, it is surprising what a variety of watering cans has been produced over the past century and a half alone. The old English firm of Haw which specialized in garden requisites listed many dozens of different types in their catalogues, in burnished copper and brass, in japanned and enamelled iron, in various grades of galvanised steel, in ALUMINIUM and in transfer-printed tinplate or *tôle peinte*. There were even elegant miniature cans with long curved spouts, in silver plate or chromium plate, intended for watering house plants and table decorations and they were highly recommended as wedding presents. There were cans of various capacities designated ladies', propagating, garden, greenhouse and nursery. The more specialized cans include the orchid can, with an extra long curved and tapering spout, shelf cans with squat drum-shaped

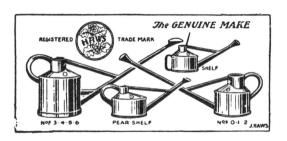

A selection of Haw's 'improved watering cans' (Army & Navy Stores Ltd)

containers, and weed-killer cans with a graduated side for measuring solutions accurately.

The most attractive are the old-fashioned copper cans with joints and roses of brass – all capable of taking an attractive polish – and the painted cans with their transfer-printed scenery and floral patterns, fashionable in the early years of this century.

WAX PORTRAITS

Beeswax has been used for the modelling of figures and bas reliefs for thousands of years. The ancient Egyptians used wax figures of their deities in funeral rites and the Romans raised the art of portrait modelling to a very high level in their *effigies* or *imagines*, the wax masks of ancestors which were carefully preserved by patrician families and paraded on ceremonial occasions. This tradition was carried on in the Middle Ages, wax portraits of royalty, the aristocracy and the ecclesiastical hierarchy being preserved in state collections in many European countries.

The modelling of portraits in wax became secularized during the Italian Renaissance and coincided with the development of the cast bronze portrait medal which was, in fact, produced by the *cire perdue* process from a wax original. There was a considerable vogue in the eighteenth and nineteenth centuries for wax profiles which could be tinted most

A wax relief of Samuel Wilberforce (son of William), mid 19th century (King & Chasemore)

realistically to reproduce the colours of the flesh. Flaxman sculpted wax portraits of many of the celebrities of his day, but numerous lesser artists, many of them unknown, also produced wax portraits for countless sitters. The portraits, usually in profile, were mounted in wooden frames and often glazed. Like their two-dimensional counterparts, silhouettes and portrait miniatures, they were ousted in the 1850s by the development of PHOTOGRAPHY. Quite a number of them have survived and can often be picked up at no great cost, making attractive if unusual wall ornaments.

WAYWISERS

Here is a class of object of immense interest to surveyors, geographers and postal historians – the latter being concerned with the charging of letters according to the mileage carried rather than the weight as in the modern system pioneered by Sir Rowland Hill in 1839–40. The waywiser was a primitive but reasonably effective instrument for computing distances and usually consisted of a large wooden wheel whose hub was connected to a drive mechanism which, in turn, registered the number of revolutions and hence the distance covered on a dial mounted above the fork. The waywiser was trundled along the road by a pole, often fitted with a turned wooden steering bar. Variations include the different diameters of the wheels, from two to four feet being average, the quality of construction and materials used, and the measuring dials, recording distances in yards, poles, chains, furlongs, miles and their European counterparts. The wheels may be found with brass or iron reinforcements and the dials were often beautifully engraved after the fashion of contemporary clock faces. Rare variants consist of two wheels joined at the axle, with the dial mounted above.

An early 19th-century Post Office waywiser (Christies, South Kensington)

WHIPS AND CROPS

Bearing in mind that flagellation is traditionally regarded as *le vice anglais* I have my suspicions about those who find this subject so fascinating, but I am assured by those who collect such things that there is an astonishing range of whips and crops, ranging from the ceremonial fly whisks of Africa and Asia to the fearsome sjamboks, without which no self-respecting Afrikaaner household is allegedly complete. There are rhino whips and

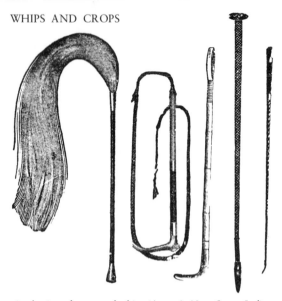

A selection of crops and whips (Army & Navy Stores Ltd)

bulls' pizzles and the enormous cow whips used by old-time cattle drovers, but the varieties with more aesthetic qualities include the elegant riding crops and hunting whips used in Europe over the past four centuries. The finest examples in recent times are described as bone and kangaroo plaited, with castle, plain or beaded collars in silver or silver-gilt. Handles are of stitched leather, bone, ivory or hardwood, occasionally with thong keepers attached. For the sportsman there were polo and cutting whips with overend buttons, steel lining and hogskin covers. Though generally more functional in appearance than CANES and WALKING STICKS, whips may be found with beautifully carved, inlaid or decorated handles.

WHISTLES

Instruments for emitting a shrill blast or a mellow warble seem to have been in existence since the beginning of time. There are copious references in classical literature to pipes of reed or wood but only the more durable forms, in terracotta and bronze, have survived. Nearer the present day there is a vast range of whistles produced for a wide variety of purposes. The highly decorative BOSUN'S PIPES have already been mentioned, but there are many kinds of whistle used by soldiers, police, firemen and others; many of them bear regimental or brigade insignia and are of great interest to collectors of MILITARIA. Among the more popular RAIL RELICS are the whistles decorated with railway emblems used by guards and stationmasters.

Then there are all the different kinds of whistles used in the countryside. Foremost in this group are the silent dog whistles invented by Professor Galton who pioneered research into the wavelengths of sounds audible to dogs and other animals. There are signal whistles fitted with a horn to amplify the sound; these were used at one time to start the beaters on the grouse moor. Other whistles used by hunters imitate the sounds made by various kinds of birds and usually

The Acme 'Silent' whistle, and the 'Thunderer' (Very Loud) (Army & Navy Stores Ltd)

have the name of the bird stamped on them. The Acme Company produced special whistles, such as the Siren or pocket foghorn, the police special or Metropolitan and the famous Thunderer with its characteristic drum containing the pea which gave it a trilling sound. There were combination whistles with a Thunderer at one end and a long-cylindered whistle at the other. A handy gadget used by hunters was the folding whistle extractor, a device for extracting jammed cartridges from rifles and shotguns, with a whistle mounted on a swivel.

Whistles may be found in silver or silver-plate, nickel-plated steel, stainless steel, copper, brass or tinplate. Horn, ivory, bone and hardwood have also been used and various PLASTICS, such as the black Acmeoid devised by the Acme Company. Whistles may also be encountered incorporated in other objects such as children's cutlery and toothbrushes, pens and pencils. Penny whistles include the tiny circular tinplate whistles, often in novelty shapes, which were held in the mouth and emitted different sounds when the whistler blew or sucked.

WINDOW DISPLAY PIECES

The use of eye-catching display pieces in shop windows to attract the attention of passers-by developed in the early nineteenth century, a logical extension of the traditional shop signs and three-dimensional doorway figures favoured by tobacconists. As the trend towards branded goods developed, window display pieces grew and by 1850 they were well-established. Since then they have consisted of two main categories. The first is the two-dimensional display card, often cut to shape, with a representation of human figures or the goods advertised. This kind of display piece was the direct descendant of the dummy board figures used by ale-houses and taverns since the seventeenth century, and is widely used down to the present time. The other category was a self-standing, three-dimensional object, ranging from genre figure groups with a humorous twist, or sculptural personifications of the firm's trademark. I recently saw a beautiful pottery figure with polychrome glaze reproducing 'Bubbles' by Millias which was originally commissioned by the makers of Pear's Soap. These statuettes were produced in pottery and porcelain, chalkware, spelter and bronze. Miniature tailor's dummies were used to model clothing and corsetry. Relicas of products were either greatly enlarged (where the genuine article was tiny) or reduced in size, such as the model houses used by realtors and estate agents. The most desirable display pieces are those incorporating lighting and clockwork or electric mechanism so that they could be animated.

A Thirsk shop window of c.1908, with an impressive display of Walter Willson's flour, and a display piece haystack (Beamish, North of England Open Air Museum)

WINE FUNNELS AND STANDS

Owing to the production methods used, wines invariably threw a heavy sediment and this meant that the contents of a wine bottle had to be carefully poured into a decanter before it was drinkable. The wine was carefully strained through a special funnel lined with muslin. Though silver wine funnels are known to have existed in the mid seventeenth century they are exceedingly rare. The fashion for serving wines in shouldered decanters of clear glass developed in the 1760s led to the widespread use of funnels and strainers and from then until about 1830, when techniques eliminating sediment were adopted, the wine funnel was an indispensible adjunct of the butler's pantry.

The funnels of this period were deep, ogee or urn-shaped, with detachable strainers or silver. Often funnels will be found with matching sets of strainers of various gauges of mesh, together with a ring on which could be mounted the muslin. The rim and sides of these funnels were decorated according to the contemporary styles, from the baroque and rococo of the 1760s, through the gadrooning and reeding motifs of the classical and neo-Egyptian styles at the turn of the century, to the chased and pierced basketwork of 1810 and the elegant scrollwork of the 1820s. The

An electro-plate wine funnel
(Army & Navy Stores Ltd)

tapering spout ran vertically below the bowl of the funnel, then curved at right angles and terminated abruptly; this enabled the flow of the wine to be directed in a fine trickle against the side of the decanter. Wine funnels may also be found combined with orange strainers and when not in use they were placed, spout uppermost on special domed saucers, in silver, Sheffield plate or electro-plate.

Later wine funnels have wider rims and sloping sides, with a straight spout below. These were used for pouring spirits straight into a decanter and for transferring port, sherry and madeira to decanters when the problem of sedimentation had been largely resolved. There was a rash of highly ornamented funnels, with diestruck designs at the turn of the century, but since then more restrained ornament has been employed.

WITCH BALLS

A very small percentage of the glass spheres which go by this name may actually have been produced in the eighteenth century and hung in the homes and workshops of glass-blowers to ward off the evil eye; but the vast majority were probably produced as end of day ware or friggers – in other words merely as objects for using up the molten metal at the end of the day's production and subsequently sold by the glass-workers for a few pennies – one of the perquisites of their trade. They may be found in many kinds of coloured or opaque glass, from deep cobalt blue and bottle green to rich cranberry, in milk glass and even glass with multicoloured spirals. They were pierced at the top or had a small knob, so that they could be strung up as good luck symbols or simply as decorations.

Not all of the so-called witch balls were produced for ornament. Globes of green, blue or clear glass encased in net were, and still are to some extent, used by trawlermen to give buoyancy to their nets and are occasionally found washed up on beaches.

WOODEN MEASURES

One of the more popular kinds of TREEN, these vessels were widely used until recent years and now that metrication has rendered them obsolete they are being snapped up as 'instant antiques'. The smaller ones were produced in turned woodware from a single block of wood, while the larger measures were made by coopers, using tapered or feathered staves set in a circular wooden base and bound by hoops or iron or brass. Because they were often subject to municipal or government control, they were likely to be stamped with their capacity, an official mark and sometimes the date of inspection – features which enhance their interest enormously. They were often produced in sets ranging from a gill to an Imperial bushel, with all the intervening measures of pint, quart, gallon, and peck. Complete sets are decidedly elusive, but odd measures are fairly plentiful.

WRITING SETS

Not so long ago I saw a beautiful little box of oak, with carved decoration on all sides and a sloping lid dating around the middle of the seventeenth century. This was a desk-box or lap-desk, about fourteen inches wide and intended originally to rest on the writer's lap. The red-painted interior had compartments for writing materials and correspondence and evoked the atmosphere of Roundheads and Cavaliers. Such a writing box fetches a three-figure sum today, but there are many different kinds of more modern sets which can still be picked up quite cheaply. The majority of the extant examples belong to the nineteenth century when letter-writing, in the aftermath of the postal reforms of the 1840s, developed enormously. Writing sets of this period came in relatively plain wooden or leather-bound cases, with a drop-front lid that opened to reveal a BLOTTER mounted on the inner side, with tiny shelves and pigeon-holes for envelopes, notepaper, postcards, wafers, sealing wax, paper clips, postage stamps, erasers, ENVELOPE AND STAMP MOISTENERS, penknives, QUILLS or steel PEN-NIBS, scissors, rulers and other equipment. The more elaborate varieties had small drawers concealing pots or bottles of ink in different colours. Carrying handles, corner reinforcements and lock-plates of silver or brass added a decorative touch, and examples with silver plaques bearing family

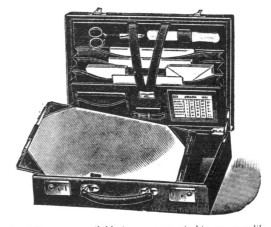

A writing case, available in morocco, pigskin or crocodile, fitted with leather pockets, blotter, address book and calendar (Army & Navy Stores Ltd)

crests or presentation inscriptions are much sought after.

Towards the end of the nineteenth century the more compact and portable compendium came into fashion. Originally highly ornate, with its leather covers elaborately embossed and tooled, or even covered with openwork silver decoration, they became somewhat plainer in design in the 1920s, though even then figural or scenic motifs were fashionable. They were constructed with two or three leaves which folded over when shut, and opened out to reveal blotter, pockets for stationery and recesses for pens, pencils, rulers, scissors and other materials.

YARD OF ALE

These drinking glasses seem to have been an English speciality and were produced from the mid-seventeenth century onwards. They had a bulb at one end and a trumpet mouth at the other, with a narrow stem 36 inches in length. The earliest examples had a deep foot rim but most eighteenth- and nineteenth-century yards have a rounded base. Examples that can be dated before the middle of the last century are very rare but thereafter they became quite common and are probably produced to this day.

They are in the same category as puzzle jugs and joke mugs since the sudden access of air to the bulb forced a jet of wine or beer into the drinker's face, unless he sipped the liquid slowly and tilted the yard very gingerly. Thus the quaffing of a yard of ale was not only a test of one's capacity but also of one's co-ordination. For those who were not quite man enough, there were also half yards and other smaller measures.

YATAGHANS

Halfway between a dagger and a sabre, these long knives were a Turkish weapon much favoured all over the old Ottoman Empire. Because of their relatively small size they were fashionable with ceremonial or court dress and were thus frequently more decorative than lethal. The characteristics of the yataghan include the absence of any cross-guard or hilt (anything in the form of a cross was offensive to the strict Muslim) and the double-curved edge with a straight back. The blades were usually 18 to 25 inches in length, tapering towards the handle. The blades were beauti-fully wrought and damascened and often engraved all over, the pattern being sometimes continued on the handle if the latter was forged in one piece with the blade. More usual, however, is the handle of wood, ivory or silver inlaid with gold. The scabbards were of leather heavily decorated with precious metals and stones. Many of the yataghans produced at the turn of the century were aimed at the tourist trade and are generally of inferior workmanship and materials, with brass mounts instead of silver.

ZARFS

The porcelain cups used in the drinking of Turkish coffee were constructed without handles and in order to prevent the hands from scalding these special holders were devised. In effect, they are not unlike egg-cups in size and shape, with an ogee bowl, slender stem and small raised foot. They were produced in brass or silver, intricately pierced, fretted, chased, inlaid or enamelled. Though traditionally they would have been made by metalsmiths all over the Levant, there was a surprisingly large export of zarfs from France, Switzerland and northern Italy in the nineteenth century. They are produced in Turkey, Afghanistan and the Balkan countries to this day and make ideal tourist mementoes.

ZELLENMOSAIK

This German word meaning literally 'cell-mosaic' is applied to a form of decoration in which semi-precious stones are set in gold cells, much in the same manner as *cloisonné* enamels were used in the Middle Ages. The idea was developed by Heinrich Taddel, a silversmith and manufacturer of objects of vertu in eighteenth-century Dresden. Originally Taddel used a quartzite base on which the zellenmosaik was built up but latterly he perfected a technique using a honeycomb of precious metal without any backing so that the translucent qualities of the hardstones could be more fully appreciated. This technique was expanded by Taddel's successors, such as Johann Christian Neuber and Christian Gottlieb Stiehl who used zellenmosaik to create an almost stained glass window effect to decorate snuffboxes, bonbonnieres, trinket cases and other small boxes. The most desirable examples have a secret compartment in the base containing a leaflet describing the stones of which the mosaic is composed. Zellenmosaik was popular from about 1760 to 1830, though some attempts have been made to revive the art in recent years.

ZINC

Such is the inherent instability of this metal that its pure form was not isolated till the early eighteenth century and then it remained little more than a scientific curiosity until the Napoleonic era when it came to be employed as an ingredient of pewter and brass alloys. Since the bulk of the early zinc deposits were mined in Germany it was in that country that the first attempts were made to use the metal commercially. An alloy containing a small quantity of lead was known as spiauter or spelter and because of its ductile qualities was ideally suited to the casting of small ornaments and figurines. This should not be confused with the alloy known as zinkenite, rather similar in colour, which in fact takes its name from the German mineralogist, J. K. L. Zinken, who found that a compound of lead with antimony sulphide had a brilliant steel-grey lustre.

Zinc or spelter, though gleaming like silver when new, tended to patinate badly and turn

to a dull blue-grey, so attempts were made to disguise the basic alloy. The German physicist Geiss invented a method of giving spelter a bronze coating and this was much used in Germany in the late nineteenth century for statuettes, clock-cases picture and mirror frames, candlesticks and brackets.

A zinc-lined cabin trunk 'suitable' for the tropics (Army & Navy Stores Ltd)

ZODIACAL ITEMS

For thousands of years men have studied the skies and noted the groups of stars now known as constellations. Their movements and their significance to navigation, the seasons and the passage of the year were observed and the supernatural powers with which they were allegedly endowed influenced the astrology – literally the star-lore – of the ancient world. Since the Sumerians and Accadians living in Mesopotamia first named the constellations it is not surprising that the oldest star groups were those visible in the Middle East. To the Babylonians and the Greeks the zodiac was the imaginary path in the heavens, eighteen degrees in width, in which moved the sun, the moon, the planets and the constellations. The zodiac was divided into twelve constellations each taken for astrological purposes to extend 30 degrees of longitude. The word zodiac, from the Greek meaning pertaining to little animals, alludes to the human and animal figures by which the constellations were named. The sun entered each constellation in turn, beginning with Aries the Ram on March 21 (hence the original New Year's Day) and ended with Pisces the Fishes on February 19.

Legends concerning these constellations developed from the sixth century BC and both the astrological symbols and the figural representations of the zodiac were imbued with mystic significance. They have appeared in many art forms and are to be found in all the Mediterranean civilizations, Phoenician, Greek, Judaic and Roman and thus passed into medieval European usage. Attempts to christianize the zodiac in the seventeenth century, by using the names of the Twelve Apostles, were shortlived and the original zodiac survives to this day. The symbolism and figural representations of the zodiac are mostly associated with talismans and good luck charms, and have featured in all kinds of objects from jewelry – pendants, brooches, ear-rings and cuff-links – to RACK PLATES, from CRESTED SPOONS to PATCHWORK. The signs of the zodiac are instantly recognizable and have been widely used to decorate objects aimed at those who are looking for something personalized – and as everyone has been born under one or other of these calendar symbols, the sales of such articles must be astronomical (no pun intended). One could therefore make quite an interesting collection decorated with one's own birth sign. My personal favourite consists of glass paperweights featuring the signs of the zodiac, either engraved or etched on the base. Then there are the paperweights encapsulating sulphides of the zodiac, a speciality of the revived Baccarat factory.

ZWISCHENGOLDGLÄSER

Yet another of those jaw-breaking German terms which trip lightly off the tongue of the collector (after a great deal of practice), this one literally means 'gold sandwich glasses'. It implies the use of a very ancient technique, perfected by the Greeks at the beginning of the Christian era, using sheets of engraved gold leaf imprisoned between two layers of glass. This ancient technique was resurrected by the Bohemian glasshouses in the eighteenth century, the best known exponent of the art being Johann Jacob Mildner of Lower Austria in the 1790s. The technique was practised sporadically in Bohemia, Silesia, Austria and Thuringia until the middle of the nineteenth century and attempts have been made in more recent times to revive it, but good examples are elusive. Zwischengoldgläser is found in goblets and tankards, in gold or silver foil, engraved or pin-pierced in highly intricate patterns, decorated with hunting, biblical, classical and allegorical motifs. As a rule the ornament is confined to narrow bands, cartouches or medallions, the rest of the decoration being provided by enamelling and gilding in the more orthodox fashion.

A zwischengoldglas beaker c.1735 from Bohemia (Pilkington Glass Museum)

ACKNOWLEDGEMENTS

The Publishers would like to thank the following for allowing pictorial material to be included in the book.

Aladdin Industries Inc; American Folk Art Museum, New York; The American Museum in Britain, Bath; Antique Wire Sales Inc., Oklahoma; Army & Navy Stores Ltd; Beamish, North of England Open Air Museum; Christies, South Kensington; Clark, Nelson Ltd; Clifford's Dairies Ltd; Coca-Cola; Colman Foods; David Cripps; Doulton; William Doyle Galleries, Inc, New York; Alfred Dunhill; Ian Fleming; Geller Business Equipment Ltd; Stanley Gibbons; Greater London Council; Hallmark Cards Inc, Kansas City; H.J. Heinz Co. Ltd; Tony Hutchings; Kenwood; King & Chasemore; London Fire Brigade; Lyle Publications; James Mackay; Mary Evans Picture Library; Metropolitan Police; Charles R. Meyer, Southold, New York; National Railway Museum; Parker Brothers, Massachusetts; Phillips; Pilkington Glass Museum; Philip Poole; R.C.A., New York; Routledge & Kegan Paul; Sears, Roebuck & Co., Chicago; Stanley Shoop; Singers; Sotheby & Co.; Adrian Tuke for the drawings; Walt Disney Productions; Wedgwood Museum; Wellcome Trustees; Wells Fargo; Young & Co.

Picture research: Susan Fleming and Wendy Edwards.

SELECT READING LIST

GENERAL

AMAYA, Mario, *Art Nouveau*, London, 1966.
ANGUS, Ian, *Collecting Antiques*, London, 1972.
AYRES, James, *British Folk Art*, London, 1977.
BATTERSBY, Martin, *The World of Art Nouveau*, London, 1968.
  Art Nouveau, London, 1969.
  The Decorative Twenties, London, 1969.
  The Decorative Thirties, London, 1971.
BEDFORD, John, *The Collecting Man*, London, 1968.
  Yesterday's Junk Tomorrow's Antiques, London, 1977.
BENNETT, Ian, *American Antiques*, London, 1975.
BRIDGEMAN, Harriet, *Erotic Antiques*, Galashiels, 1974.
CAMERON, Ian and KINGSLEY-ROWE, Elizabeth (eds), *Collins Encyclopedia of Antiques*, London, 1973.
COYSH, A.W. and KING, J., *The Buying Antiques Reference Book*, Newton Abbott, 1974.
DE HAAN, David, *Antique Household Gadgets and Appliances*, London, 1977.
DORFLES, Gillo, *Kitsch*, London, 1969.
GARNER, Philippe, *The World of Edwardiana*, London, 1974.
HILLIER, Bevis, *Art Deco*, London, 1968.
  The World of Art Deco, London, 1971.
  Austerity Binge, London, 1975.
HUGHES, G. Bernard, *The Country Life Collector's Pocket Book*, London, 1963.
HUGHES, Therle, *Small Antiques for the Collector*, London, 1964.
  Cottage Antiques, London, 1967.
HUME, M., *All the Best Rubbish*, New York, 1975.
KLEIN, Dan, *All Colour Book of Art Deco*, New York, 1974.
KRANZ, Jacqueline L., *American Nautical Art and Antiques*, New York, 1975.
LAMBTON, Lucinda, *Temples of Convenience*, London, 1978.
LATHAM, Jean, *Miniature Antiques*, London, 1972.
LAVER, James, *Victoriana*, London, 1966.
LESIEUTRE, Alain, *The Spirit and Splendour of Art Deco*, London, 1974.
LESSARD, Michel and MARQUIS, Huguette, *Complete Guide to French-Canadian Antiques*, Montreal, 1974.
LICHTEN, Frances, *Decorative Arts of Victoria's Era*, New York, 1950.
LYNES, Russell, *The Taste-Makers*, New York, 1960.
McCLINTON, Katherine M., *Art Deco: A Guide for Collectors*, New York, 1972.
MACDONALD-TAYLOR, Margaret, *A Dictionary of Marks*, London, 1962.
MACKAY, James A., *An Introduction to Small Antiques*, London, 1970.
  Antiques of the Future, London, 1970.
  Dictionary of Turn of the Century Antiques, London, 1974.
  An Encyclopedia of Small Antiques, London, 1975.
  Price Guide to Collectable Antiques, Woodbridge, 1975.
  Railway Antiques, London, 1978.
  Price Guide to More Collectable Antiques, Woodbridge, 1979.
MADSEN, Tschudi, *Sources of Art Nouveau*, London, 1956.
  Art Nouveau, London, 1967.
MARSHALL, Jo, *Kitchenware*, London, 1976.
MEBANE, John, *New Horizons in Collecting*, New York, 1967.

The Coming Collecting Boom, New York, 1968.
Poor Man's Guide to Collecting, New York, 1969.
NORWAK, Mary, *Kitchen Antiques*, London, 1975.
PEARSALL, Ronald, *Collecting Mechanical Antiques*, London, 1973.
PETER, M., *Collecting Victoriana*, London, 1965.
RAMSAY, L.G.C. (ed.), *The Concise Encyclopedia of Antiques* (5 vols), London 1955–60.
  The Complete Encyclopedia of Antiques, London, 1975.
REVI, Albert C. (ed.), *Antiques for Men*, Hanover, Pennsylvania, 1975.
  Antiques for Women, Hanover, P., 1975.
  The Spinning Wheel Complete Book of Antiques, Hanover, Pa., 1975.
RHEIMS, Maurice, *The Age of Art Nouveau*, London, 1967.
SAVAGE, George, *Dictionary of Antiques*, London, 1970.
SCHMUTZLER, Robert, *Art Nouveau*, London, 1964.
SPECK, Gerry E. and SUTHERLAND, Euan, *English Antiques*, London, 1969.
STRONG, Dr Roy, *The Random House Collector's Encyclopedia, Victoriana to Art Deco*, New York, 1974.
TOLLER, Jane, *Regency and Victorian Crafts*, London, 1969.
VAN DE GOHM, Richard, *Collecting Small Antiques and Bygones*, London, 1975.
WHITTINGTON, Peter, *Undiscovered Antiques*, London, 1972.
WILSON, Peter, *Antiques International*, London, 1966.
WINTERSGILL, Donald, *Scottish Antiques*, London, 1977.
WOOD, Violet, *Victoriana: A Collector's Guide*, London, 1968.

CLOCKS, WATCHES AND INSTRUMENTS

ALLIX, Charles, *Carriage Clocks, Their History and Development*, Woodbridge, 1974.
BAILLIE, G.H., *Watches*, London, 1929.
BELL, G.H. and E.F., *Old English Barometers*, London, 1970.
BRUTON, Eric, *Clocks and Watches, 1400–1900*, London, 1967.
  Clocks and Watches, London, 1968.
CAMERER CUSS, T.P., *The Country Life Book of Watches*, London, 1967.
CHAPUIS, Alfred and DROZ, E, *Automata*, London, 1960.
CLARKE, J.E.T., *Musical Boxes*, London, 1961.
CUMHAIL, Philip, *Investing in Clocks and Watches*, London, 1967.
DANIELS, George, *English and American Watches*, New York and London, 1967.
DAUMAS, M. *Scientific Instruments of the 17th and 18th Centuries*, London, 1972.
GOAMAN, Muriel, *English Clocks*, London, 1967.
GOODISON, N., *English Barometers, 1680–1860*, London, 1969.
JOY, Edward T., *The Country Life Book of Clocks*, London, 1967.
LLOYD, H. Alan, *Old Clocks*, London, 1970.
MICHEL, H., *Scientific Instruments in Art and History*, London, 1967.
ROSE, R., *English Dial Clocks*, Woodbridge, 1978.
TOWNSEND, George E., *Encyclopedia of Dollar Watches*, New York, 1974.
WYNTER, Harriet and TURNER, Anthony, *Scientific Instruments*, London, 1975.

GLASSWARE

ARWAS, Victor, *Glass: Art Nouveau to Art Deco*, London, 1977.

BARRINGTON-HAYNES, E., *Glass through the Ages*, London, 1959.

BECK, Doreen, *The Book of Bottle Collecting*, London, 1973.

BEDFORD, John, *Bristol and Other Coloured Glass*, London, 1964.
  Paperweights, London, 1968.

CHARLESTON, R.J., *English Opaque White Glass*, London, 1962.

CLOAK, Evelyn, C., *Glass Paperweights*, Neenah, Wisconsin, 1969.

CROMPTON, Sidney, *English Glass*, London, 1967.

DAVIS, Derek C., *English and Irish Antique Glass*, London, 1965.
  English Bottles and Decanters, London, 1972.

ELVILLE, E.M., *Paperweights and Other Glass Curiosities*, London, 1954.
  Collector's Dictionary of Glass, London, 1961.

FLETCHER, Edward, *Bottle Collecting*, London, 1972.
  International Bottle Collector's Guide, London, 1975.

FLORENCE, Gene, *Collector's Encyclopedia of Depression Glass*, New York, 1974.

GROS-GALLINER, Gabriella, *Glass: A Guide for Collectors*, London, 1970.

GROVER, Ray and Lee, *Art Glass Nouveau*, New York, 1967.

HARTLEY, Julia M., *Old American Glass*, New York, 1975.

HOLLISTER, Paul, *The Encyclopedia of Glass Paperweights*, New York, 1969.

HUGHES, G. Bernard, *English Glass for the Collector*, London, 1967.

LAUNERT, Edmund, *Scent and Scent Bottles*, London, 1974.

McCLINTON, Katherine M., *Lalique for Collectors*, New York, 1975.

MACKAY, James A., *Glass Paperweights*, London, 1973.

MIDDLEMAS, Keith, *Continental Coloured Glass*, London, 1971.

REVI, Albert C., *American Pressed Glass and Figure Bottles*, Hanover, Pennsylvania, 1964.

ROBERTSON, R.A., *Chats on Old Glass*, London, 1969.

STENNETT-WILSON, R., *Modern Glass*, London, 1975.

VAVRA, J.R., *5,000 Years of Glassmaking*, Prague and London, 1954.

WARREN, P., *Irish Glass*, London, 1970.

WEBBER, Norman, *Collecting Glass*, London, 1972.

WEISS, Gustav, *The Book of Glass*, London, 1971.

WILLS, Geoffrey, *English Looking-Glasses*, London, 1965.
  English and Irish Glass, London, 1968.
  Antique Glass, London, 1971.

METALWORK

BURY, Shirley, *Victorian Electroplate*, London, 1971.

CATLEY, Bryan, *Art Deco and Other Figures*, Woodbridge, 1978.

COOPER, Jeremy, *Nineteenth-Century Romantic Bronzes*, London, 1974.

ERAS, Vincent, *Locks and Keys Throughout the Ages*, London, 1957.

FROST, T.W., *Price Guide to Old Sheffield Plate*, Woodbridge, 1971.

HARTFIELD, G., *Horse Brasses*, London, 1965.

HAYWARD, John F., *English Cutlery*, London, 1956.

HUGHES, G. Bernard, *Antique Sheffield Plate*, London, 1970.

LANTZ, Louise K., *Old American Kitchenware*, New York, 1975.

MACKAY, James A., *The Animaliers*, London, 1973.
  Dictionary of Western Sculptors in Bronze, Woodbridge, 1977.

MICHAELIS, Ronald, *British Pewter*, London, 1969.
  Base Metal Candlesticks, Woodbridge, 1978.

PEAL, C.A., *British Pewter and Britannia Metal*, London, 1971.

PERRY, Evan, *Collecting Antique Metalware*, London, 1974.

RAINWATER, Dorothy and Ivan, *American Silverplate*, New York, 1975.

REVI, Albert C., *Collectible Iron, Tin, Copper and Brass*, Hanover, Pennsylvania, 1974.

SAVAGE, George, *A Concise History of Bronzes*, London, 1968.

SMITH, Elmer L., *Tinware Yesterday and Today*, New York, 1974.

WILLS, Geoffrey, *Collecting Copper and Brass*, London, 1962.
  The Book of Copper and Brass, London, 1969.
  Candlesticks, London, 1974.

MILITARIA

ATWOOD, James P., *The Daggers and Edged Weapons of Hitler's Germany*, London, 1965.

AKEHURST, Richard, *The World of Guns*, London, 1973.

ANGOLIA, J., *Swords of Hitler's Third Reich*, London, 1969.

BLAIR, Claude, *Pistols of the World*, London, 1968.

BOZICH, Stan, *German Relics, 1929–1945*, London, 1969.

CARTER, J. Anthony, *Allied Bayonets of World War II*, London, 1969.

EDWARDS, T.J., *Regimental Badges*, London, 1966.

FUNKEN, Liliane and Fred, *Arms and Uniforms* (5 vols.), London, 1973–5.

HARDIN, Albert N., *The American Bayonet, 1776–1964*, New York, 1964.

HYATT, S., *Uniforms and Insignia of the Third Reich*, London, 1962.

KERKSIS, Sydney C., *Plates and Buckles of the American Military, 1795–1874*, New York, 1974.

MARTIN, P., *European Military Uniforms*, London, 1968.

MOLLO, A., *Daggers of the Third German Reich*, London, 1967.

STEPHENS, Frederick J., *A Guide to Nazi Daggers, Swords and Bayonets*, London, 1965.

WILKINSON, Frederick, *Militaria*, London, 1969.
  Battle Dress, London, 1970.
  Collecting Military Antiques, London, 1976.

MODELS, GAMES AND TOYS

ANDERTON, Johana G., *Twentieth-Century Dolls from Bisque to Vinyl*, New York, 1974.

BELL, R.C., *Board and Table Games* (2 vols), London, 1960–69.

BLUM, Peter, *Model Soldiers*, London, 1971.

COLEMAN, D.S., E.A. and E.J., *The Collector's Encyclopedia of Dolls*, New York, 1968.

DAIKEN, Leslie, *Children's Toys Throughout the Ages*, London, 1953.

FRASER, Lady Antonia, *A History of Toys*, London, 1966.

GARRATT, John, *Model Soldiers: A Collector's Guide*, London, 1961.

GOODENOUGH, Simon, *Military Miniatures*, London,

GREENE, V., *English Doll's Houses*, London, 1967.

HARRIS, Henry, *How to Go Collecting Model Soldiers*, London, 1969.

HART, Luella, *Directories of British, French and German Dolls*, New York, 1964–5.

HILLIER, Mary, *A Pageant of Toys*, London, 1965.
  Dolls and Dollmakers, London, 1968.

HUBBARD, Donald, *Ships in Bottles*, London, 1971.
JENDRICK, Barbara W., *Paper Dolls and Paper Toys*, New York, 1975.
LATHAM, Jean, *Dolls' Houses*, London, 1969.
McCLINTOCK, Inez and Marshall, *Toys in America*, New York, 1967.
McKENZIE, Ian, *Collecting Old Toy Soldiers*, London, 1975.
MACKAY, James A., *Nursery Antiques*, London, 1976.
NICOLLIER, J., *Collecting Toy Soldiers*, London, 1967.
ORTMANN, Erwin, *Model Tin Figures*, London, 1974.
RAY, William and Marlys, *The Art of Invention: Patent Models and their Makers*, New York, 1974.
REVI, Albert C. (ed.), *Spinning Wheel's Complete Book of Dolls*, Hanover, Pennsylvania, 1975.
SAYER, Philip and Carola, *Victorian Kinetic Toys*, London, 1977.
SPEAIGHT, George, *A History of the English Toy Theatre*, London, 1969.
WELTENS, Arno, *Mechanical Tin Toys in Colour*, London, 1977.

OBJECTS OF VERTU, JEWELRY AND ACCESSORIES

ARMSTRONG, Nancy, *Jewellery*, London, 1973.
A Collector's History of Fans, London, 1974.
BARSALI, Isa Belli, *European Enamels*, London, 1969.
BEDFORD, John, *Small Boxes of All Kinds*, London,
BRADFORD, Ernle, *English Victorian Jewellery*, London, 1967.
Four Centuries of European Jewellery, London, 1967.
BUCK, A., *Victorian Costume and Costume Accessories*, London, 1961.
COOPER, Diana and BATTERSHILL, Norman, *Victorian Sentimental Jewellery*, London, 1972.
DELIEB, Eric, *Silver Boxes*, London, 1968.
ELLENBOGEN, Eileen, *English Vinaigrettes*, London, 1967.
EPSTEIN, Diana, *Buttons*, London, 1968.
FOSTER, Kate, *Scent Bottles*, London, 1966.
GERE, Charlotte, *Victorian Jewellery Design*, London, 1972.
HICKMAN, Peggy, *Silhouettes*, London, 1968.
HILL, Margaret M. and BUCKNALL, Peter A., *The Evolution of Fashion, 1066–1930*, London, 1973.
HOWELL, Georgina, *In Vogue*, London, 1975.
HUGHES, G. Bernard, *English Snuff-Boxes*, London, 1971.
HUGHES, Graham, *Jewelry*, London, 1966.
The Art of Jewelry, London, 1972.
LAUNERT, Edmond, *Scent and Scent Bottles*, London, 1974.
LEWIS, M.D.S., *Antique Paste Jewellery*, London, 1970.
LUSCOMB, Sally C., *The Collector's Encyclopedia of Buttons*, London, 1967.
PEACOCK, Primrose, *Buttons for Collectors*, London, 1974.
PETER, M. *Collecting Victorian Jewellery*, London, 1970.
RICKETS, Howard, *Objects of Vertu*, London, 1971.
TURNER, Ralph, *Contemporary Jewelry*, London, 1976.
TORRENS, Deborah, *Fashion Illustrated, 1920–1950*, London, 1974.

POTTERY AND PORCELAIN

ALDRIDGE, Eileen, *Porcelain*, London, 1969.
ALEXANDER, Donald E., *Roseville Pottery for Collectors*, New York, 1970.
ANDERSON, Margaret, *Victorian Fairings and their Values*, Galashiels, 1975.
BACCI, Mina, *European Porcelain*, London, 1969.
BARNARD, Julian, *Victorian Ceramic Tiles*, London, 1972.
BEDFORD, John, *Wedgwood Jasper Ware*, London, 1964.
Toby Jugs, London, 1968.
BOGER, Louise A., *Dictionary of World Pottery*, New York, 1971.

BUTTERWORTH, A., *Pottery and Porcelain*, London, 1964.
CHARLESTON, R.J., (ed.), *English Porcelain (1745–1850)*, London, 1965.
World Ceramics, London, 1968.
CLARK, Harold, *The Pictorial Pot Lid Book*, London, 1955.
COOPER, Ronald G., *English Slipware Dishes*, London, 1968.
COYSH, A.W., *Blue and White Transfer Ware*, Newton Abbott, 1970.
CUSHION, John P., *English China Collecting for Amateurs*, London, 1967.
Continental China Collecting for Amateurs, London, 1970.
Pottery and Porcelain, London, 1972.
Animals in Pottery and Porcelain, London, 1974.
CUSHION, John P. and HONEY, W.B., *Handbook of Pottery and Porcelain Marks*, London, 1965.
EVANS, Paul F., *Art Pottery of the United States*, New York, 1974.
FISHER, Stanley, *British Pottery and Porcelain*, London, 1962.
GARNER, F.H., *English Ceramics*, London, 1966.
English Delftware, London, 1972.
GODDEN, Geoffrey A., *Encyclopedia of British Pottery and Porcelain Marks*, London, 1965.
An Illustrated Encyclopedia of British Pottery and Porcelain, London, 1966.
Jewitt's Ceramic Art of Great Britain, London, 1972.
British Porcelain: An Illustrated Guide, London, 1974.
British Pottery: An Illustrated Guide, London, 1974.
HASLAM, Malcolm, *English Art Pottery, 1865–1915*, London, 1975.
HENDERSON, Ian T., *Pictorial Souvenirs of Britain*, London, 1974.
HENZKE, Lucille, *American Art Pottery*, New York, 1970.
HILLIER, Bevis, *Pottery and Porcelain, 1700–1914*, London, 1968.
HUGHES, G. Bernard and Therle, *English Porcelain and Bone China*, London, 1955.
IMBER, Diana, *Collecting Delft*, London, 1968.
JOHN, W.D. and BAKER, Warren, *Old English Lustre Pottery*, London, 1951.
LEWIS, Griselda, *A Collector's History of English Pottery*, London, 1969.
MACKAY, James A. *Commemorative Pottery and Porcelain*, London, 1969.
MANKOWITZ, Wolf and HAGGAR, Reginald, *Concise Encyclopedia of English Pottery and Porcelain*, London, 1957.
MOUNTFORD, Arnold R., *Staffordshire Salt-glazed Stoneware*, London, 1971.
OLIVER, Anthony, *The Victorian Staffordshire Figures, A Guide for Collectors*, London, 1971.
PECK, Herbert, *Book of Rookwood Pottery*, New York, 1968.
PENKALA, Maria, *European Pottery*, London, 1968.
PUGH, P.D. Gordon, *Staffordshire Portrait Figures and Allied Subjects of the Victorian Era*, London, 1971.
RAY, Marcia, *Collectible Ceramics*, Hanover, Pennsylvania, 1975.
RHODES, Daniel, *Porcelain and Stoneware*, London, 1960.
RODGERS, David, *Coronation Souvenirs*, London, 1975.
RUST, Gordon, A., *Collector's Guide to Antique Pottery*, London, 1973.
SAVAGE, George and NEWMAN, Harold, *An Illustrated Dictionary of Ceramics*, London, 1974.
SAVAGE, George, *Pottery Through the Ages*, London, 1958.
Porcelain Through the Ages, London, 1961.
SHINN, Charles and Dorrie, *Victorian Parian China*, London, 1971.
STRATTON, Deborah, *Mugs and Tankards*, London, 1975.
TILLEY, Frank, *Teapots and Tea*, London, 1957.

WAKEFIELD, HUGH, *Victorian Pottery*, London, 1962.

WARD, Roland, *The Price Guide to the Models of W.H. Goss*, London, 1975.

WARE, George, *German and Austrian Porcelain*, London, 1963.

WILLIAMS-WOOD, Cyril, *Staffordshire Pot Lids and their Potters*, London, 1972.

PRINTED EPHEMERA

ANGUS, Ian, *Paper Money*, London, 1974.

BAGNALL, Dorothy, *Collecting Cigarette Cards*, London, 1973.

BARNICOAT, John, *A Concise History of Posters*, London, 1972.

BUDAY, George, *The History of the Christmas Card*, London, 1965.

CARLINE, Richard, *Pictures in the Post*, London, 1959.

COPE, Dawn and Peter, *Illustrations of Postcards from the Nursery*, London, 1978.

CRUISE, A.J., *Matchbox Labels of the World*, London, 1946.

DAVIS, Alec, *Packaging and Print*, London, 1967.

DOUGLAS, James, *Scottish Banknotes*, London, 1975.
  Cheque Collecting, Carlisle, 1977.

DUGGLEBY, Vincent, *English Paper Money*, London, 1975.

GALLO, Max, *The Poster in History*, London, 1974.

GENTLEMAN, David, *Design in Miniature*, London, 1972.

HENDY, Robin, *Collecting Old Bonds and Shares*, London, 1978.

HEWLETT, M.R., *Priced Catalogue of British Pictorial Postcards*, Chippenham, 1973.

HILLIER, Bevis, *Posters*, London, 1968.

HINDLEY, Diana and Geoffrey, *Advertising in Victorian England*, London, 1972.

HOLLAND, Vyvyan, *Hand Coloured Fashion Plates*, London, 1955.

HOLT, Toni and Valmai, *Picture Postcards of the Golden Age*, London, 1971.

HUMBERT, Claude, *Label Design*, London, 1972.

JENDRICK, Barbara W., *Paper Dolls and Paper Toys*, New York, 1975.

KLAMKIN, Miriam, *Picture Postcards*, Newton Abbott, 1973.

LANGLEY-MOORE, Doris, *Fashion through Fashion Plates*, London, 1971.

LEE, Ruth W., *The Valentine and its Origins*, London, 1953.

LEWIS, John, *Printed Ephemera*, London, 1962.
  Collecting Printed Ephemera, London, 1976.

MACKAY, James A., *Banknotes at War*, London, 1976.

MANN, Sylvia, *Collecting English Playing Cards*, London, 1978.

NARBETH, Colin, *Collecting British Banknotes*, London, 1970.

PEARSALL, Ronald, *Victorian Sheet Music Covers*, Newton Abbott, 1972.

RENDELL, Joan, *Matchbox Labels*, Newton Abbott, 1968.

RICKARDS, Maurice, *Posters of the First World War*, London, 1968.
  Posters of the Nineteen-Twenties, London, 1968.
  Posters of the Turn of the Century, London, 1968.
  The Public Notice: an Illustrative History, Newton Abbott, 1973.

SPELLMAN, Doreen and Sidney, *Victorian Music Covers*, London, 1969.

STAFF, Frank, *The Valentine and its Origins*, London, 1969.
  The Picture Postcard and its Origins, London, 1966.

TURNER, Michael and VAISEY, David, *Art for Commerce*, London, 1973.

TWYMAN, Michael, *Printing 1770–1970*, London, 1970.

WOOD, Robert, *Victorian Delights*, London, 1967.

SILVERWARE

BANISTER, Judith, *English Silver*, London, 1969.
  Late Georgian and Regency Silver, London, 1971.
  Collecting Antique Silver, London, 1972.

BRADBURY, Frederick, *Guide to the Marks of Origin on British and Irish Silver*, London, 1968.

CAME, Richard, *Silver*, London, 1972.

CHAFFERS, W., *Handbook to Hallmarks on Gold and Silver Plate*, London, 1971.

DELIEB, Eric, *Investing in Silver*, London, 1967.

DENNIS, Jessie M., *English Silver*, London, 1970.

FINLAY, Ian, *Scottish Gold and Silver Work*, London, 1956.

HUGHES, G. Bernard and Therle, *Three Centuries of English Domestic Silver, 1500–1820*, London, 1968.

KOVEL, R. and T., *A Dictionary of American Silver, Pewter and Silverplate*, New York, 1961.

RAINWATER, Dorothy T., *American Spoons*, New York, 1965.
  Encyclopedia of American Silver Manufacturers, New York, 1975.

TAYLOR, Gerald, *Silver*, London, 1965.

TURNER, Noel D., *American Silver Flatware, 1837–1910*, New York, 1972.

WARDLE, Patricia, *Victorian Silver and Silver-plate*, London, 1963.

WHITWORTH, R.W., *Wine Labels*, London, 1966.

TEXTILES

GODDEN, Geoffrey A., *An Illustrated Guide to Stevengraphs*, London, 1970.

KENDRICK, A.F., *English Needlework*, London, 1967.

KING, D., *Samplers*, London, 1960.

MORRIS, B., *History of English Embroidery*, London, 1954.
  Victorian Embroidery, London, 1962.

SPRAKE, Austin, *The Price Guide to Stevengraphs*, Woodbridge, 1970.

WOOD, IVORY, LEATHER AND FURNITURE

AGIUS, Pauline, *British Furniture, 1880–1915*, Woodbridge, 1978.

ANDREWS, J., *Price Guide to Antique Furniture*, Woodbridge, 1978.

BEIGBEDER, O., *Ivory*, London, 1965.

BOOTHROYD, A.E., *Fascinating Walking Sticks*, London, 1973.

BUIST, John S., *Mauchline Ware*, Edinburgh, 1974.

DAVIS, Frank, *A Picture History of Furniture*, London, 1958.

DEVOE, Shirley, *English Papier Mâché*, London, 1971.

GLOAG, John, *Victorian Comfort*, London, 1961.

GOODMAN, W.L., *British Planemakers from 1700*, London, 1978.

HAYWARD, Helena, *World Furniture*, London, 1975.

JONES, Barbara, *English Furniture at a Glance*, London, 1954.

PHILP, Peter, *Furniture of the World*, London, 1974.

PINTO, Edward H., *Encyclopaedia and Social History of Treen and other Wooden Bygones*, London, 1969.
  Tunbridge and Scottish Souvenir Woodware, London, 1970.

TOLLER, Jane, *Antique Papier Mâché in Great Britain and America*, London, 1962.

WATERER, J.W., *Leather Craftsmanship*, London, 1968.

WILLS, Geoffrey, *Ivory*, London, 1968.